"*Inner Bonding* is a welcome addition to the material on the Inner Child. It gives us a pragmatic, solution-oriented framework for resolving inner conflict."
  —Stephanie Covington, Ph.D., clinical consultant and author of *Awakening Your Sexuality*

"Margaret Paul offers us a simple and very effective tool for healing our inner upsets and quieting the confusion in our minds. I recommend that you use this valuable tool daily on your path to wholeness."
  —Susan Jeffers, Ph.D., author of *Feel the Fear, Do It Anyway*, and *Dare to Connect*

"A surprisingly powerful process! It teaches us to meet our innermost needs."
  —Gerald G. Jampolsky, M.D., author of *Love Is Letting Go of Fear*

"The system of reparenting discussed in this book will supply you with the most loving, dependable, supportive friend you'll ever have—yourself. What a joy to know you're not alone anymore."
  —Lindsay Wagner, actress and coauthor of *The High Road to Health*

"Inner Bonding is a powerful book for anyone interested in quality relationships. It offers practical tools, not just theory, to help us reach inside and heal those deep problems and addictions that have held us back for so many years."
  —Thomas Crum, author of *The Magic of Conflict*

"A wake-up call to the most exciting miracle of the universe: your life."
  —Peter and Lynda Guber, film producers

INNER BONDING

OTHER BOOKS BY MARGARET PAUL, PH.D.

Free to Love (with Jordan Paul)

Do I Have to Give Up Me to Be Loved by You? (with Jordan Paul)

If You Really Loved Me (with Jordan Paul)

From Conflict to Caring (with Jordan Paul)

Healing Your Aloneness (with Erika J. Chopich)

INNER BONDING

Becoming a Loving Adult to Your Inner Child

MARGARET PAUL, Ph.D.

HarperSanFrancisco
A Division of HarperCollins*Publishers*

For information regarding Inner Bonding Therapy, lectures, and workshops, please contact:

Dr. Margaret Paul	Dr. Erika Chopich
Inner Bonding Therapy	Inner Bonding Therapy
2531 Sawtelle Blvd. #42	P.O. Box 5081
Los Angeles, CA 90064	Santa Fe, NM 87502–5081
(310) 390-5993	(505) 986-8084

Harper San Francisco and the author, in association with the Rainforest Action Network, will facilitate the planting of two trees for every one tree used in the manufacture of this book.

Grateful acknowledgment is given to HarperCollins Publishers for permission to reprint two charts previously published in *Healing Your Aloneness,* by Erika J. Chopich and Margaret Paul, © 1990. The charts appear herein on pages 72–74.

Library of Congress Cataloging-in-Publication Data

Paul, Margaret.
    Inner Bonding: becoming a loving adult to your inner child/
Margaret Paul. — 1st ed.
        p. cm.
    ISBN 0–06–250710–9 (alk. paper)
    1. Inner child.   2. Self-actualization (Psychology)   3. Adulthood—
Psychological aspects.   4. Psychotherapy.   I. Title.
BF698.35.I35P38   1992
158'.1—dc20   91–58163
                                                                                    CIP

To Erika Chopich,
who taught me Inner Bonding.

Contents

Acknowledgments

I wish to thank my friend and editor, Bonnie Hesse, for her brilliance and her willingness to work at breakneck speed to complete this book on time. Working with Bonnie is truly a gift.

I wish to thank all my clients for their own dedication to Inner Bonding, through which I learn so much.

I wish to thank Barbara Friedman for her loving support of my own Inner Bonding process.

I wish to thank my family—my parents, Charlotte and Izzy Brustein; my children, Eric and Lisa; Josh, Sheryl, and Bobby and Jenni; and my Aunt Anne—for their loving support and caring.

I wish to thank my husband, Jordan Paul, for his dedication to his own Inner Bonding process, which, along with my own inner work, has led to our reconciliation.

I wish to thank Dr. Erika Chopich, not only for teaching me Inner Bonding and for her contribution to this book, but for challenging me to become all that I can be.

Verbatim accounts of clients are used with their permission; names and biographical details have been changed to protect their privacy. In most instances the portraits presented are composites. In these cases any resemblance to specific individuals is coincidental.

Introduction

There are many wonderful books on reclaiming and healing the wounded Inner Child, and many people are deeply involved in this profound inner work. However, they find as they move through the healing process that it is not enough to reclaim and heal the Child of the past. The Child of the present needs to be seen, heard, and loved every moment of the day, when around others and when alone.

Taking care of ourselves on an everyday basis is an even greater challenge than healing the Child of the past, because there are so few role models in our culture of truly loving behavior—that is, behavior that is loving to ourselves and others. It is not as if we can reach into our own past or present experience for examples of loving behavior in specific situations with others or when alone with ourselves. We cannot reach into a collective unconscious for this information, because the information isn't there due to a lack of role-modeling in our society. We have to make it up as we go along, through trial and error, staying tuned to the Child within in order to know whether or not our choices are enhancing or diminishing our self-esteem.

I have spent years learning how to take care of myself in specific situations in ways that are loving to myself and others. This is an ongoing process for me, one that I expect will continue my whole life. The suggestions I've come up with are just that—suggestions. There is never one "right" way to handle a given situation; what I am presenting are options that work for my clients and for me. I hope these options will lead you into your own creative thinking regarding new patterns of behavior that truly support and nurture your Inner Child.

Becoming a loving Inner Adult/Parent to our Inner Child is the key to a productive and joyful life, as well as to the ability to establish and sustain intimacy. It is not enough to tell the Child within that we love and cherish him or her, and that he or she did not cause our parents to be abusive. Unless we become the parents to ourselves that we always wanted, every moment of the day, our Inner Child will never believe he or she is really lovable. If the Adult in us does not treat the Child in us lovingly, then telling the Inner Child he or she is lovable is just lip service and will create no real change in our present life.

This book illustrates the psychotherapy of Inner Bonding, a psychotherapy developed by Dr. Erika Chopich and me, and introduced in our book *Healing Your Aloneness: Finding Love and Wholeness Through Your Inner Child*.[1] Since the book's publication, we have received many letters from people wanting to know more about the process of developing a loving Inner Adult. I hope this book helps you along the path toward wholeness and love.

The usefulness of understanding the process of Inner Bonding Therapy is not primarily for therapists. This book is written for all those who have a desire to help themselves and others.

Margaret Paul, Ph.D.
January 1992

Part 1

INNER BONDING THERAPY

CHAPTER 1

Finding the Life We Lost in Living: Understanding Inner Bonding

> It is difficult indeed to struggle against what one has been taught. The child's mind is a helpless one, pliable, absorbing. It makes what it learns a part of its very nature. . . . Yet . . . you must change your minds, you must renew your hearts, and you must do it alone. There are no teachers for you.
>
> *To My Daughters with Love*
> PEARL S. BUCK

You've achieved everything you've ever thought would make you happy, but the gnawing, empty feeling that something is missing is still there. To paraphrase Rabbi Harold Kushner, you've discovered that "all you've ever wanted isn't enough."

You may feel lost, out of touch with yourself and others, in an emotional fog much of the time. You often feel as if you're doing nothing more than going through the motions. You may agonize over feeling insecure, inadequate, unlovable, and alone.

These are deeply painful feelings, pervasive and persistent—so painful, in fact, you may have discovered any number of dysfunctional ways to ignore, deny, cover up, or numb the ache of your emptiness: alcohol, food, work, TV, sex, drugs, all of the above. Then one day something happens, a traumatic experience or an internal shift. You reach a turning point and ask yourself, as Jeremiah Abrams states in *Reclaiming the Inner Child*, "Where is the life we lost in living?"[1]

Certainly you're not alone with these kinds of feelings. Most of us struggle with continuous or periodically recurring emotional pain for significant portions of our lives. This happens either because we don't know another, better way, or because we're unwilling to try, afraid we'll only make matters worse. Unfortunately the pain often has to become intolerable, or a crisis must force the issue, before we take action on our own behalf. Take the case of Tom, for example.

Tom had never been in a therapist's office and he wasn't happy about being there now. He sat stiffly in his dark blue suit, unaware that his fist was clenched and his expression stern. He would never have come at all, but the CEO of his company took him aside last week and told him that his outbursts of temper were undermining employee morale and driving potential customers away. "Get some help," the CEO told him. Frustrated and angry, but seeing no other choice, Tom made an appointment.

After we talked for a while about Tom's stress level and work load, I said, "It sounds like you're not taking very good care of yourself."

"Take care of myself? That's not realistic. I have too much to do!"

"But you fly into unpredictable rages, and you could lose your job because of that. And being so stressed out, you're likely to lose your health as well. Can you really afford not to take care of yourself?"

"I don't think I can," he said softly. "I don't know how."

Tom was telling the truth. He didn't know how; he'd never learned. He had been "at work" since early childhood. His father was an abusive alcoholic, so Tom's earliest memories were of trying to protect his mother and sister from harm. When he realized his father treated them better when he wasn't around, Tom left home and lived on his own. He was fifteen.

Most of us don't grow up in these extreme circumstances; but even in the best possible beginnings, very few of us know what it looks like to take care of ourselves. We haven't seen that kind of behavior anywhere—not in our families, not even on TV. So we follow the patterns we've learned, and we let ourselves down because we don't know what it looks like to be loving to ourselves as well as to those around us. We abuse ourselves, ignore or deny our pain—all because we don't know what else to do. We desperately need to begin to think about these questions: "How do we take care of ourselves? How do we make ourselves happy? How do we bring joy into our lives?"

Take Sandy, for example. Sandy is a divorced mother of two young daughters, a third-grade teacher. Long hours of preparation have paid off—her students love her, their parents praise her, and the principal has commended her in glowing written evaluations. Practically the only one who isn't convinced that she is a competent, worthy, lovable person is Sandy herself. Constantly exhausted, nagged by indecisiveness and depression, she's discounted everything she's accomplished, including others' affirmations. The only reason Sandy entered therapy was for her daughters. She was determined that they wouldn't suffer the way she had.

In therapy sessions Sandy said bluntly that she rejected others' loving support "because I don't deserve it." When asked, "Why do you drive yourself so hard? Why don't you take better care of yourself?" she answered, "Because selves aren't for taking care of."

Where do beliefs like this come from? Why does Sandy believe that she doesn't deserve love? After all, if she did, she'd take care of herself. She loves her daughters and takes great care of them, making sure they eat right, rest enough, and so on. Sandy values her car. If it's not running well, she gets it fixed. Sandy is no different than any of us: *We all take care of whatever we value.*

How, then, can we learn to value ourselves so that we can become loving to ourselves, as well as to others? That's what this book is about. It's about Tom and Sandy and the multitudes of others who have absorbed or assumed the false beliefs and self-defeating attitudes and behaviors they saw in their childhood years. Because that's what they have believed in and unwittingly copied, they have limited the potential for joy and love and fun in their lives. The purpose of this book is to teach all of us, each with our different pasts and present circumstances, another way of being in the world—a freer way of loving and living than the one we have known. That's the promise and the power of Inner Bonding.

Inner Bonding is about giving ourselves, each and every moment, what we never had—or never learned—as children. It is about developing a loving relationship between our Adult and our Inner Child, a relationship that takes care of our Selves when we are around others and when we are alone.

What Is Inner Bonding?

Inner Bonding is a process of connecting our Adult thoughts with our instinctual gut feelings, the feelings of our "Inner Child," so that we can live free of conflict within ourselves. Inner conflict is any kind of upsetting difference between our *thoughts*—what we think we should do or feel—and our *feelings*—our gut-level emotions and attitudes. When the conflict isn't resolved—that is, when we go ahead and take action without regard for our feelings, or take action that is opposed to what we feel, or take no action in response to our feelings—then we've abandoned our feelings or disconnected from them. This disconnection creates the inner turmoil, the unrest we experience as discontentment and unhappiness.

The incredibly good news is that what has been disconnected can be re-connected, and with reconnection comes healing and wholeness. The power of Inner Bonding is the power of love as the force that heals, love from Inner Adult to Inner Child. Others' love can support this process—love from mate to mate, from friend to friend, from therapist to client; but it is only when the Inner Adult loves the Inner Child that true healing and joy occur.

It would be ideal if our thoughts and feelings could be connected at all times. Although we cannot expect this state of perfection, we can learn the Inner Bonding process by practicing it until it becomes internalized, an automatic part of our thinking and feeling processes. To learn the process most effectively, we need to understand more about how we function, both internally and externally.

To begin with, the Adult aspect of our personality is our external aspect, the part of us that is able to take action in the world. Inner Bonding requires our Adult to be in conscious contact or connected with our inner, natural self, the vulnerable, feelings-driven self, referred to as the Inner Child. When our Inner Adult is connected to our Inner Child, that is Inner Bonding. When our rational and emotional aspects are connected in this way, we don't feel internal conflict, because there isn't any. Free of inner conflict, we feel peaceful, open to joy, and open to giving and receiving love.

Knowing how to initiate this connection is part of what we need to learn. This book hopes to teach that in two different ways: (1) by describing the actual dynamics of the process of Inner Bonding; and (2) by demonstrating Inner Bonding in action, providing examples of people in specific situations and relationships, so you can watch and learn from their individual bonding process.

Before we define the integral, working parts of Inner Bonding, let's get an overview of the Inner Bonding process as a whole. This will also give you an idea of the process and the goal—in terms of your own internal state of peacefulness or ease, and in terms of your loving relationships with others.

Inner Bonding in Action, An Overview

On the simplest level, the first step to Inner Bonding is to become aware of your inner discomfort, "dis-ease," or conflict. The second step is to acknowledge that you have a choice, one that only you can make, to ignore your feelings or to heed them: You have to *choose* whether you are going to be closed to your feelings or open to them. The third step is to recognize that, whether closed or open, either choice you make has consequences. This means that if you choose to be closed, you are also choosing the negative consequences of being closed. If you choose to be open, you are choosing the positive consequences resulting from your openness. You can't choose to be closed and realistically expect the consequences of being open.

With just that much as a basis for understanding the process, let's look at Inner Bonding in action with the example of Tom.

The Case of Tom

This was Tom's first experience with therapy. He was resistant to the process and a beginner in terms of examining his own feelings. We already know that he is a high-achieving corporate executive, and that his father was an abusive alcoholic. Now let's add that Tom has a wife and one son. No more personal history or context is needed to show what the consequences would be for each of the choices he can make: to be closed or to be open to the gut-level feelings of his Inner Child.

Tom's internal and external dialogue is shown in diagram form in Figure 1. As you read, you'll be aware that there are many other possible thoughts and feelings Tom could have had. However, what becomes strikingly clear is that once he makes his initial choice to be open or closed, the consequences that follow are unavoidable.

Figure 1. Tom's Inner Conflict

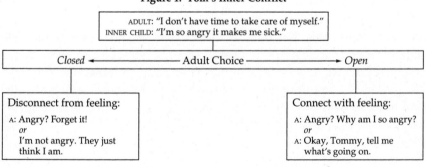

Tom has stated the belief of his Inner Adult, that he has no time to take care of himself. He's also realized that his gut feeling is anger. The thought of his Adult and the feeling of his Inner Child are in conflict. His choice is either to deny that this conflict exists or to acknowledge it. One of his options is to disconnect from the feeling, refusing to take responsibility for learning about it. His other option is to be open to the anger, connect with the feeling, and take responsibility for learning why he feels this way.

Figure 2. Tom's Inner Conflict

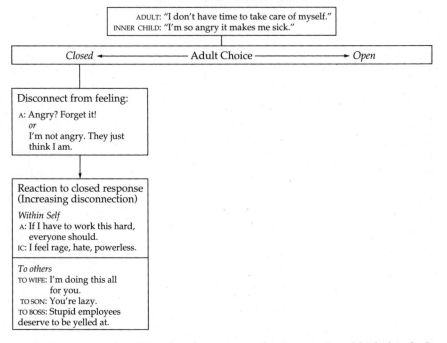

Let's assume that Tom decides to try to be "strong" and hide his feelings, even from himself. He chooses to disconnect from his anger by denying or repressing it. As the discomfort or pain escalates, the pressure builds. The disconnection between his Adult and his Inner Child increases, and he takes out his anger on those around him. Unloving to himself, he is increasingly unloving to others.

Figure 3. Tom's Inner Conflict

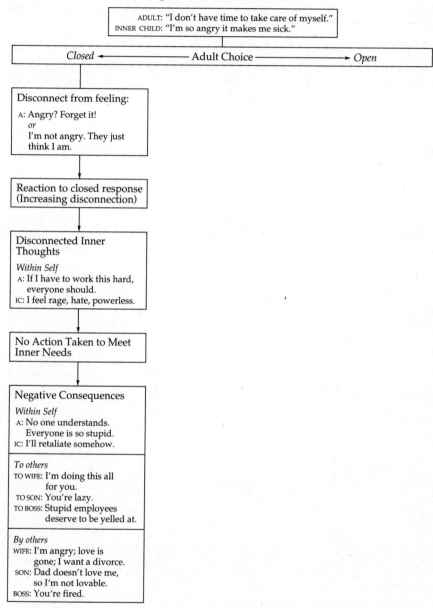

ADULT: "I don't have time to take care of myself."
INNER CHILD: "I'm so angry it makes me sick."

Closed ◀———————— Adult Choice ————————▶ Open

Disconnect from feeling:

A: Angry? Forget it!
   or
   I'm not angry. They just
   think I am.

Reaction to closed response
(Increasing disconnection)

Disconnected Inner
Thoughts

Within Self
A: If I have to work this hard,
   everyone should.
IC: I feel rage, hate, powerless.

No Action Taken to Meet
Inner Needs

Negative Consequences

Within Self
A: No one understands.
   Everyone is so stupid.
IC: I'll retaliate somehow.

To others
TO WIFE: I'm doing this all
         for you.
TO SON: You're lazy.
TO BOSS: Stupid employees
         deserve to be yelled at.

By others
WIFE: I'm angry; love is
      gone; I want a divorce.
SON: Dad doesn't love me,
     so I'm not lovable.
BOSS: You're fired.

As you can see, Tom's choice to disconnect from his feeling and act in increasingly unloving ways is causing others to disconnect from him, a negative consequence of his choice to close to his feelings. The final blow in this scenario is that Tom is alone, separated from love within himself and from those who love him. Eventually the feelings of his Inner Child will find some kind of destructive release—addictions, stress-related illness, and so on.

The picture changes dramatically if Tom chooses to connect with his feelings and to learn from them. Through the Inner Bonding dialogue process (described in detail in chapter 2), he can focus his inner dialogue on the cause of the pain by asking what the Inner Child needs. This enables him to explore the options open to meet the needs of his Inner Child and relieve the cause of his anger, while meeting his Adult needs as well. Then he can know what action to take, based on that internal decision-making process.

Figure 4. Tom's Inner Conflict

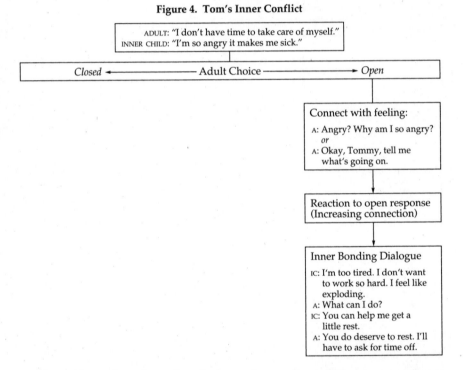

Once Tom takes the action, he experiences the positive consequences almost immediately. Tom feels more powerful, not less. He feels lighter and happier and eager to reestablish connection with those he loves. In this case Tom has not waited too long. His family is affirmed by the reconnection; and his boss has renewed faith in Tom's qualities as a top employee when he sees Tom's anger at others diminish.

Figure 5. Tom's Inner Conflict

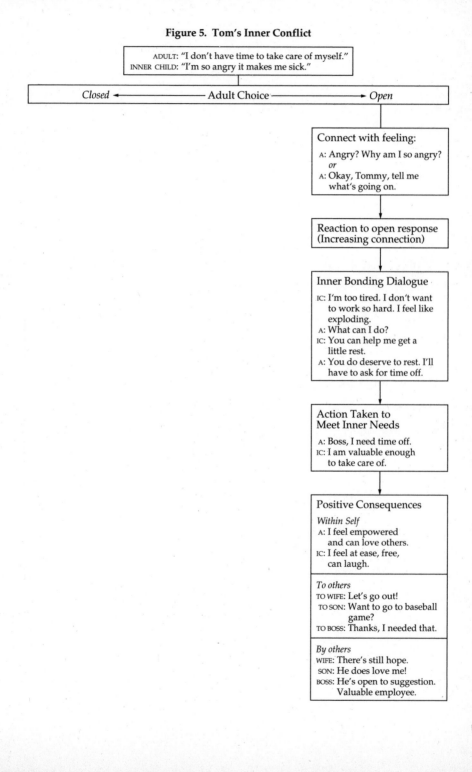

ADULT: "I don't have time to take care of myself."
INNER CHILD: "I'm so angry it makes me sick."

Closed ◄――――――― Adult Choice ―――――――► Open

Connect with feeling:

A: Angry? Why am I so angry?
or
A: Okay, Tommy, tell me
what's going on.

Reaction to open response
(Increasing connection)

Inner Bonding Dialogue

IC: I'm too tired. I don't want
to work so hard. I feel like
exploding.
A: What can I do?
IC: You can help me get a
little rest.
A: You do deserve to rest. I'll
have to ask for time off.

Action Taken to
Meet Inner Needs

A: Boss, I need time off.
IC: I am valuable enough
to take care of.

Positive Consequences

Within Self
A: I feel empowered
and can love others.
IC: I feel at ease, free,
can laugh.

To others
TO WIFE: Let's go out!
TO SON: Want to go to baseball
game?
TO BOSS: Thanks, I needed that.

By others
WIFE: There's still hope.
SON: He does love me!
BOSS: He's open to suggestion.
Valuable employee.

Figure 6. Tom's Inner Conflict

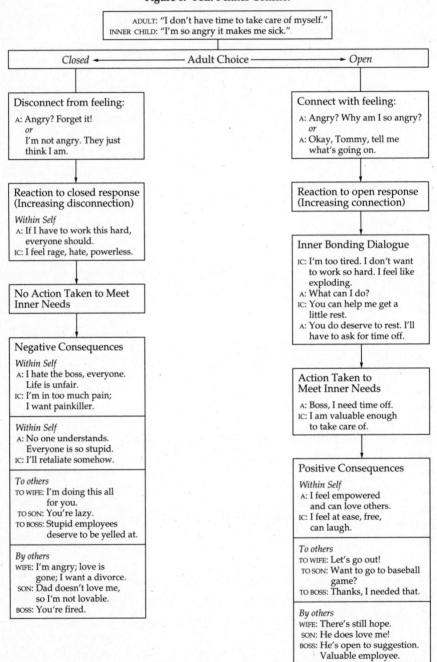

ADULT: "I don't have time to take care of myself."
INNER CHILD: "I'm so angry it makes me sick."

Closed ◄——————— Adult Choice ———————► Open

Disconnect from feeling:

A: Angry? Forget it!
   or
   I'm not angry. They just
   think I am.

Connect with feeling:

A: Angry? Why am I so angry?
   or
A: Okay, Tommy, tell me
   what's going on.

**Reaction to closed response
(Increasing disconnection)**

Within Self
A: If I have to work this hard,
   everyone should.
IC: I feel rage, hate, powerless.

**Reaction to open response
(Increasing connection)**

**No Action Taken to Meet
Inner Needs**

Inner Bonding Dialogue

IC: I'm too tired. I don't want
   to work so hard. I feel like
   exploding.
A: What can I do?
IC: You can help me get a
   little rest.
A: You do deserve to rest. I'll
   have to ask for time off.

Negative Consequences

Within Self
A: I hate the boss, everyone.
   Life is unfair.
IC: I'm in too much pain;
   I want painkiller.

Within Self
A: No one understands.
   Everyone is so stupid.
IC: I'll retaliate somehow.

To others
TO WIFE: I'm doing this all
           for you.
TO SON: You're lazy.
TO BOSS: Stupid employees
           deserve to be yelled at.

By others
WIFE: I'm angry; love is
        gone; I want a divorce.
SON: Dad doesn't love me,
        so I'm not lovable.
BOSS: You're fired.

**Action Taken to
Meet Inner Needs**

A: Boss, I need time off.
IC: I am valuable enough
   to take care of.

Positive Consequences

Within Self
A: I feel empowered
   and can love others.
IC: I feel at ease, free,
   can laugh.

To others
TO WIFE: Let's go out!
TO SON: Want to go to baseball
           game?
TO BOSS: Thanks, I needed that.

By others
WIFE: There's still hope.
SON: He does love me!
BOSS: He's open to suggestion.
        Valuable employee.

When we see the total picture and contrast the positive and negative responses and consequences, some general conclusions are very clear:

1. When you are disconnected from your feelings, you act in disconnected ways to others, creating further disconnection from them and within yourself.

2. When you are disconnected from your inner self, or Inner Child, you can't realistically expect the positive consequences that go with being connected to your feelings.

3. The choice to be open leads to greater inner power and more love of self and others. The choice to be closed leads to isolation and alienation between others and within yourself.

Tom's case is just one specific example, but the dynamics are universal: Closed, unloving choices perpetuate closed, disconnected reactions and negative consequences. Open, loving choices initiate the chain reaction of open, connected, and positive consequences.

Now that you have seen the process overview, let's define some terms and explain some dynamics. Before you go on you will need to know what I mean by the terms Inner Child, Inner Adult, and Loving Behavior.[2]

Who Is Your Inner Child?

The Inner Child is the aspect of our personality that is soft, vulnerable, and feelings-oriented—our "gut" instinct. It is who we are when we were born, our core self, our natural personality, with all its talent, instinct, intuition, and emotion. The Child is our right-brain or creative aspect of being, feeling, and experiencing. It's the part of us that existed before we had experience. It is useful to refer to this aspect of our personality as a Child because it allows us to get a handle on those feelings and senses that existed before our maturing experiences merged or confused our impression of the two aspects of our personality, our Adult and our Inner Child.

To speak of an Inner Child is not to over-romanticize childhood. When we were very young we did many child*ish* things—we talked baby talk, we played in the mud, we slapped our sisters and brothers when we were angry, we pouted or stomped our feet when we didn't get our way.

Our Inner Child, however, is child*like*—our vulnerability, intuitiveness, sense of wonder, imagination, innate wisdom, and ability to feel our feelings have not changed or aged with our growing, adult experience. Thus, while many of us had very unhappy childhoods, that doesn't mean our inner nature is essentially unhappy.

Does Everyone Have an Inner Child?

We all have a vulnerable, intuitive, instinctual inner self. As psychiatrist Carl G. Jung said so well, "child" is only the means to express this psychic fact, the symbol of our preconscious nature:

> The child motif represents not only something that existed in the distant past, but also something that exists now; that is to say, . . . a system functioning in the present whose purpose is to compensate or correct, in a meaningful manner, the inevitable one-sidedness and extravagances of the conscious mind.[3]

It is clear that we all do have an Inner Child. When people ask whether this can really be true, it usually reveals that they are not in touch with that soft and vulnerable part of their nature. When life is fairly easy and there are no major problems at hand, this lack of awareness is not a particular problem. But when there is conflict or a personal crisis and we feel unhappy or distressed, being out of touch or disconnected from our Inner Child can prevent us from restoring our emotional equilibrium.

One of my clients, Laura, was particularly resistant to the Inner Child concept, even though she understood that this was a just a label for her vulnerable, natural inner self. Eventually, however, a time of unusually high stress at work coincided with an emotionally difficult time at home, and she found herself getting more and more stuck. Instead of working faster, she was going slower. Instead of being able to think things through logically and find satisfactory solutions, she found herself getting more anxious and emotional, crying at unpredictable times.

Finally, when this state became unbearable, Laura had the following experience:

> I was driving along one day, and I thought to myself, well, if I'm ever going to get with this "Inner Child" bit I may as well give it a try. So I said to myself, "If you [her Inner Child] are in there, speak up." I was dumbfounded to hear a small voice within me say, "Help!"
>
> In a flash of understanding—and this surprised me even more—I knew what that meant, and I said back to myself, as if to my Child, "You don't have to do this work all alone." And in the amount of time it took me to say those words, my stress level dropped so many degrees I could feel energy pouring back into by body.
>
> I had absolutely no idea how helpless and overwhelmed I had been feeling—like a little girl left to do an adult's work all alone. I was able to still feel myself as a child, watching my father so stressed out and irritable and miserable over all the endless work to be done, with never any time or permission to play. And when he'd kiss me goodnight, after he'd been working all day and I had been playing, he'd say, "But good hard work will make you feel better . . ." He was kind and loving to all of us kids, gentle

and truly adoring. He meant so well and the message was so subtle. All four of us daughters learned it by heart: Play doesn't make you feel good; hard work does. Now we're all workaholics.

Who Is Your Inner Adult?

The Adult is the logical thinking part of us that has collected knowledge through our years of experience in the world. It is our intellect, our left-brain, logical, analytical, conscious mind. It is the part of us that is thought and action, as opposed to feeling and being, which are the realms of the Inner Child. The Adult is concerned with doing rather than being, with acting rather than experiencing.

The Adult is the choicemaker regarding intent and actions. It is always the Adult that chooses our actions, just as it is in a family. A young child cannot take actions on its own behalf—it cannot shop for food and cook the meals; it cannot earn the money to provide food and shelter, it cannot call a friend or therapist when in need of help. The Child within us cannot take these actions. Taking action on behalf of our Inner Child is the job of the Adult—taking care that our gut feelings and our thoughts are connected, synchronized, not in conflict. As we saw in Tom's case, we can choose actions that are open and loving, or actions that are closed and unloving.

When we are born, we have no worldly, adult experience. But from the moment of birth, our Adult begins to develop. When we are two years old, our Adult is two, with two years of experience in the world. By the time we are three or four, we are doing many adult activities—choosing our own clothes, dressing ourselves, asking for help when we need it. The adult aspect is learning how to be an Adult all along from the adults in our environment. The Adult, then, is the aspect of our personality that is learned. One of the things we can learn is to be loving or unloving to our Inner Child.

What Is Loving Behavior?

Loving behavior is behavior that nurtures and supports our own and others' emotional and spiritual growth. An inseparable part of this is taking responsibility for our own pain and joy. Therefore loving yourself means taking responsibility for healing pain—pain from the past and the present, for exploring and resolving self-limiting beliefs, and for discovering and taking action to bring about your joy.

Loving someone else means that you want for them what they want for themselves and that you support them in whatever they feel would bring them joy.

When we are being loving to our Inner Child, we are open to learning about our Child and from our Child. Loving our Child means choosing to learn about ourselves—our past and present pain, fears, and beliefs. Laura opened to learning about her Inner Child simply by saying, "If you're in there, speak up!" She learned from her Inner Child when the self of her feelings cried out, "Help!"

At that point Laura's Inner Adult again had the choice to be loving or unloving. If she had said, "Stop being so weak and feeling sorry for yourself!" the feelings of the Inner Child would not have been honored or validated as real and worthy of notice. The consequence of that choice would most likely have been that Laura continued to stay stuck with her pain, continued her unexplained crying spells and suffering. Instead she made the choice to acknowledge and learn from these feelings by connecting her present pain with ways of dealing with the world she had learned in the past. Through this connection she came to the conclusion, "That was my Child's belief, but it's not accurate. I am not a child having to do all the work alone. I am a grown-up woman with options for other ways. I am not stuck. I am not a child, alone and helpless, who must shoulder an adult's burden."

The reason for learning about your Inner Child and learning Inner Bonding Therapy, the reason for writing a book about all this, is not to explain how Laura, Tom, Sandy, and so many others like them had imperfect childhoods, or even learned incorrect lessons from the best possible parents. The reason was simply put by Laura, when she said, "My stress level dropped so fast I could feel energy pouring back into my body!" These words were the tools that freed up her energy, released her from her increasing unproductiveness and pain, and allowed her to function at her full potential.

That's what Inner Bonding is all about: freeing ourselves from the false beliefs that create fear and shame. These false beliefs function as shackles, tethering us to inaccurate ways of thinking based on what we saw or what we assumed when we were too young to know any better. Free from false beliefs, we no longer feel the need to sacrifice ourselves in order to get the love we need. We can accept and love ourselves, and we are free to love each other.

CHAPTER 2

Taking the Road Less Traveled: The Inner Bonding Process

For love . . . is the blood of life, the power of reunion in the separated.
quoted in Necessary Losses *by Judith Viorst*
PAUL TILLICH

Tom, the corporate executive in chapter 1, believed he didn't have time to listen to his anger. That was not an accurate belief. His inaccurate assumption was based on a faulty notion that taking care of himself would make him less effective, not more.

Sandy, the single mother who came to therapy "for her daughters," felt she didn't deserve love because she wasn't lovable. That wasn't true. Sandy was loved by many people, and they told her so. It is true, however, that Sandy did not believe she was lovable, and so she didn't love herself.

Tom and Sandy are just two of the countless people whose lives have been seriously limited because their actions have been based on their own false beliefs: incorrect conclusions they drew, inaccurate assumptions they made, or lies they were told long ago.

Usually we form these false beliefs when we're very young. A father dies suddenly, and his four-year-old son believes he caused the heart attack because he had misbehaved that day. A depressed mother runs away from home, and grandmother tells the children she went on vacation. Each of the deserted children forms a false belief based on scanty evidence, adult whispers overheard, and fears about their own inadequacies.

The purpose of Inner Bonding Therapy is, quite simply, to clear out these blocks to truth; to question and to resolve, as much as we possibly can, the false, generally shame-based, self-limiting beliefs we have lived by up to now. Doing so allows us to become free and open to experience and to expand our potential for love and joy.

The Inner Bonding process is one of discovering how to connect with and to love our natural self, our Inner Child, and so to create an Inner Bond between our rational and emotional aspects. Part of the process is to face our fear and shame, and to challenge the false beliefs that create these feelings.

When conflict exists and we are disconnected within, it is extremely difficult, if not impossible, to connect in loving ways with the people we care so much about. Alone on the inside, we're also lonely on the outside—not a happy picture. Fortunately it's not too late to reconnect through Inner Bonding, to feel the self-worth we ache for and the love we long to share.

Learning how to reconnect is the first order of business. In the next chapter we'll examine how we became disconnected, why we developed the faulty belief systems that have lead us to the destructive inner disconnection between our Adult and our Inner Child. But first let's examine the process that can heal the break and bring wholeness to our lives.

The Inner Bonding Process

Learning to connect and to bond with your Inner Child means learning to be a loving Adult to your Inner Child in whatever life situation or conflict, external and internal, you are faced with. When we look at Figures 1 through 6, illustrating Tom's inner conflict, we can see that Inner Bonding is the natural, predictable outcome resulting from the intent to learn—a choice that only you, as the Adult, can make.

When there is conflict between the belief or thought of the Inner Adult and the feeling or need of the Inner Child, the Inner Bonding process seeks to discover what action is needed to bring these two together. What can be done to help to heal the feelings and to meet the wants and needs in loving ways? Since the Adult is the one who takes action in the world, and the Child is the one whose feelings are internal, the Adult must take action on the Child's behalf.

This doesn't mean that the Adult indulges the Child's every whim. Truly loving behavior nurtures and supports the emotional and spiritual growth of both parties involved, or in this case, both aspects of yourself. So, for example, if your Inner Child wants to sleep in, making you late for work, it is not loving behavior on the part of your Inner Adult to agree to that. It is loving, however, for your Adult to listen to the reasons your Inner Child wants to sleep in and to take action to get rest, if that is what is really needed.

How Many People Am I?

You are, now and always, just *one* person. This is one of the most critical points to remember in Inner Bonding Therapy. You are absolutely not split or fragmented into separate entities; you are a single self. Yet your personality has many facets, unique attributes, different likes and dislikes.

As this singular person, you have both rational thoughts and emotions or feelings. Although feelings, like thoughts, originate in the brain, we experience emotions physically—usually in the stomach, neck, shoulders, or chest. That is why feelings, instincts, and impulses are most commonly referred to as being at "gut level."

Why Use the Terms "Inner Adult" and "Inner Child"?

Very often your rational mind says one thing—"I have a huge, unpleasant task that's already overdue"—but your gut feeling says another—"I hate being forced to work fast. I feel nauseated." Or your thought may be, "I know I'd feel better in the long run if I lost the twenty pounds my doctor advised"; but your gut feeling says, "I am miserable right now and I need a piece of candy to cheer me up."

These are common conflicts that go on within each of us all the time. Because we don't know anything about the concepts of Inner Adult and Inner Child, we forge ahead. We may or may not deliberate the choices and consequences, but either we eat the candy or we don't.

No one makes loving choices all the time, but some people are more often able to resolve their inner conflicts in ways that lead to good feelings for themselves and positive consequences. Unfortunately a vast majority of people consistently make choices that lead to exactly the opposite.

Probably everyone has a running internal dialogue. Sometimes it's positive ("C'mon, you can do it!"), but often it's negative ("How could you be so stupid?"). However, not many of us are aware how greatly this self-talk affects how we feel about ourselves. To bring about a fundamental consciousness shift in your life, one of the most helpful, constructive steps you can take is to attach labels to your thoughts and feelings. This helps you clarify what's going on internally, as well as give voice to your different, inner aspects. "Adult" and "Inner Child" provide the added dimension of focusing on the relationship between your rational and emotional selves.

It can be tremendously useful to think of your rational thoughts as your Inner Adult, and your feelings and emotions as your Inner Child. This labeling will help you become aware of your conflicts and identify your options. Then you can begin to make choices for yourself that heal your pain and allow you to enjoy fulfilling relationships with others.

How to Begin Inner Bonding

The Inner Bonding process is very similar to trying to understand and help an external child. If a child was upset and you wanted to help, you would ask the child what is wrong. You would listen to the answer. If there was something you could do, you would act to help in some way.

Consider an incident that might occur between any adult and anyone else's child. Let's say a very young boy is crying on a street corner when a woman walks by. Asking the child what he needs shows that the woman recognizes the child and his feelings. Speaking to him creates a connection, and a bond of caring begins to form. After all, only a loving adult is willing to stop and ask what a child needs. The adult cares and the child begins to feel cared for.

As the woman listens and dialogues, that is, continues her questions and hears his answers, the reasons for the child's feelings are revealed. Loving adults don't ask one question, "Are you lost?" and then walk away. They listen and then ask the next logical question, for example, "Do you know where you live?" The concluding question is critical, and in this case it might be, "How can I help you?" The answer will disclose the loving behavior in this situation. But the child can't find his way home alone. The adult must take the action: "I'll call the police and wait here with you until an officer comes." Taking action on behalf of the child completes the bonding process between the adult and the child. The act is the evidence that the adult truly cares. A loving adult wouldn't leave the child alone and helpless on the street corner. This also proves to the child that he is worthy of this caring; otherwise the adult wouldn't have taken action to help.

The principles and process involved when an adult helps an external child are basically the same as those that apply to the relationship between your Inner Adult and your Inner Child—the Inner Adult needs to *ask, listen, and act.* Before any one of us would choose to begin this process, however, we would first have to choose to be loving. Another way to say this is that we must activate our loving Adult by recognizing our Inner Child's feelings.

Understanding Intent:
The Key to Choosing Loving Behavior

Paramount to understanding Inner Bonding Therapy is to understand the concept of *intent*. Intent has many general definitions, but in the context of Inner Bonding Therapy, intent is our deepest, most primary motivation or purpose, what we want most in any given moment.

There are only two possible intents at any one time: the intent to protect or the intent to learn. These logically follow from the polarities we have already observed. At any one given time, we can only be:

loving or unloving

connected or disconnected

willing or unwilling

open or closed

vulnerable or protected

learning or not learning

In terms of our thinking and feeling processes, it is only when we are open and willing to know the truth that we can learn. When we're closed and protected, we discount, deny, or simply refuse to hear new information about ourselves.

When our intent is to protect ourselves emotionally, we are protecting ourselves against perceiving, experiencing, feeling, and being responsible for the pain, fear, grief, sadness, discomfort, or even joy of our Inner Child. In the above example of the child on the street corner, choosing to protect ourselves would mean turning our heads as we walk by the child, ignoring or avoiding the sight so we don't have to take responsibility for helping. In the same way, when we disconnect emotionally and refuse to recognize our own feelings, our Adult abandons our Inner Child. However, when we recognize our feelings and are willing to experience them, we have chosen the intent to love and to learn about ourselves. Then our Adult is connected with our Inner Child.

The intent to learn means the Adult is open and willing to feel all of our Child's feelings, to explore past and present pain, and to take responsibility for healing our pain and bringing ourselves joy. Rather than choosing to be a victim and to believe that others are causing our feelings, we recognize that we are the source of our own fears and beliefs, causing our own pain and resulting behavior. When we learn about these things, we can take the action needed to change the course of events from negative to positive.

All change occurs at the thought level, beginning with
our choice of intent: the intent to protect or the intent
to learn.

The Adult is the choice-maker of intent. In a family it is the adults who
decide whether that family is open or closed, loving or unloving. In our
lives it is our Adult aspect who decides our intent: to protect and avoid,
or to learn and take responsibility. When the Adult chooses the intent to
protect, it is being unloving to the Inner Child. When the Adult chooses
the intent to learn, it is being loving to the Inner Child.

When we are loving with ourselves, we are loving to
others.

When we are unloving to ourselves, we are unloving
to others.

At any given moment we are either protecting or learning, avoiding
or experiencing, closed or open to our inner experience, the feelings of
our Inner Child.[1]

All Our Actions Have Consequences

The charts illustrating Tom's inner conflict gave hypothetical examples
of the consequences that would follow from either one of his two initial
choices: the intent to be closed and unloving, or the intent to be open and
loving.

Now let's take this same kind of flow chart, describing the choices we
can make as we work through our inner conflict and explaining the dynamics at work within each step along the way, so each of us can use the
Inner Bonding process in our own lives.

First, let's look at what happens when we do not choose to connect
with our feelings (see Figure 7). Why should we look first at the consequences of that choice? Because that's the one most of us make, even
though we seldom realize it; and that is what has led us to the dishar-
mony and discontent that we feel right now in our lives.

The Downward Spiral of Disconnection

Figure 7. Inner Conflict

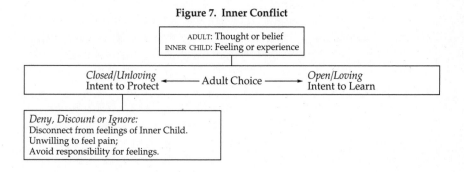

You actively disconnect your thoughts from your feelings by denying their reality ("I don't feel angry. I just appeared that way because . . .") or discounting their degree or significance ("I was only a little irritated for a moment, but then . . ."). Another way to disconnect is to ignore your feelings altogether.

Denying or discounting feelings is an unloving Adult response to your Inner Child. Compare the example of the child on the street corner earlier in this chapter. Adult responses such as, "You're not really lost" or "You're only a little lost" clearly deny the reality of the situation and disconnect from the child's experience. To ignore your feelings would be to turn your head as you passed the child. All three—deny, discount, or ignore—protect the adult from having to take any responsibility to help.

When your Adult responds unlovingly to the feelings of your Inner Child, your rational self is denying the validity and importance of your emotional self. Inner conflict and disconnection can only increase.

Figure 8. Inner Conflict

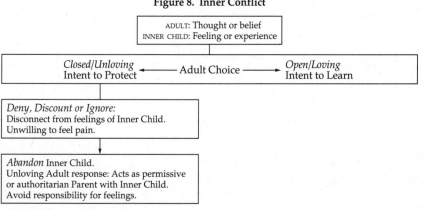

When you choose to disconnect from your feelings, you abandon your Inner Child through being authoritarian (critical, discounting, shaming) or permissive (ignoring, indulging) with your Inner Child. The unmistakable message is that your feelings aren't worthy of loving attention. When you do not pay attention to your feelings, you are acting as if they are not important or they don't exist—*but they do.* By ignoring them you set in motion the chain of actions and responses that increases rather than decreases your pain.

Virtually no one consciously decides to be unloving to themselves. In fact, if we're asked, we probably respond that we are being "mature, correct, and responsible." These words are meaningful, however, only within the context of what happens as a result of what we do. Does our choice lead us to loving or unloving behavior? Do our actions enhance or promote our own spiritual and emotional growth and that of others? Does our self-esteem increase? That's the key.

When you abandon your Inner Child, you don't take action to help yourself. Not taking action is avoiding responsibility.

Figure 9. Inner Conflict

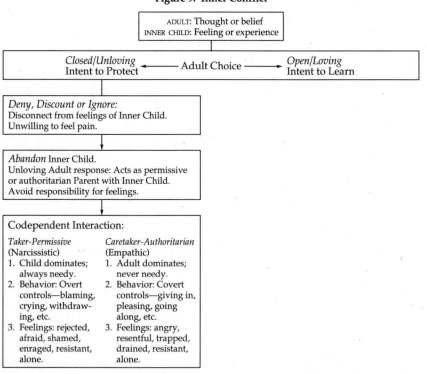

Once your Inner Child has been abandoned, you feel unlovable and unworthy at the deepest gut level. When your own Adult abdicates responsibility for defining you as a valuable person, you are then dependent on someone or something outside yourself for a sense of who you are and what you are worth. Being dependent in this way is the definition of codependence.

Codependent behavior polarizes between the two extremes: (1) The Inner Child is always "taking," attempting to get love and approval in overtly controlling ways; or (2) the Unloving Adult is always being the Caretaker, giving as a covertly controlling way to avoid disapproval or gain approval.

We will discuss codependence in depth later. Regardless of the form of codependence, however, your internal and external interactions will only perpetuate conflict and result in negative consequences.

Figure 10. Inner Conflict

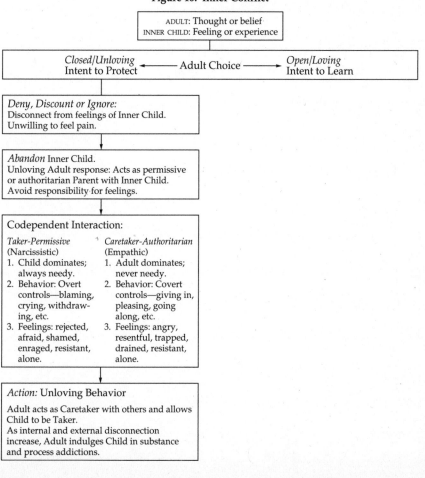

When your intent is unloving, any action you take (relevant to the inner conflict) will only make matters worse for yourself in the long run. Being unloving to yourself through shaming and indulging your Inner Child, or being unloving to others through overt or covert controlling behavior, always creates the very pain we are trying avoid with our protective behavior.

Your unloving behavior causes painful negative consequences for yourself and others. You can count on that every time.

Figure 11. Inner Conflict

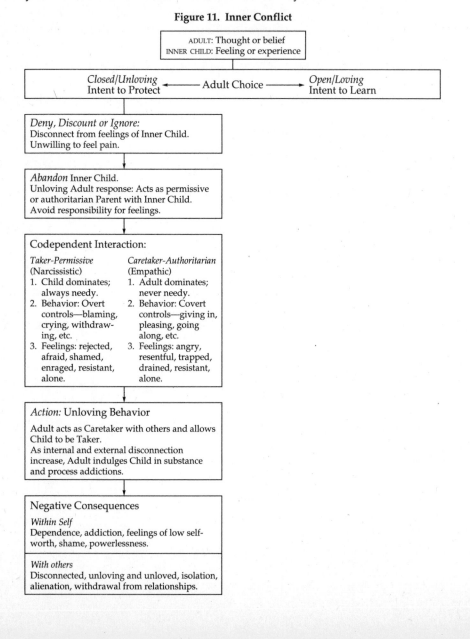

The more disconnected your Adult and Inner Child are, the greater your pain. You cannot endure extreme pain indefinitely. Eventually you will seek relief, no matter what other negative side effects occur as a result. Substance abuse is a prime example.

In addition, the less you value yourself, the less you are able to respond to others in loving ways. Often, their reactions become increasingly unloving. Eventually, unless they are also disconnected and codependent, they will withdraw from the relationship.

The Road Less Traveled:
The Step-by-Step Process to Inner Bonding

Figure 12. Inner Conflict

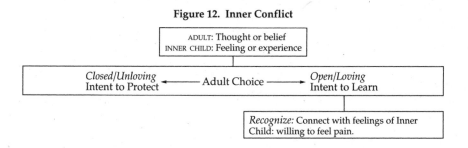

Step 1: Recognize Your Inner Conflict

We cannot help our Child relieve pain, get needs met, or find joy unless we are aware of our feelings. To resolve our inner conflict, then, the first step is to recognize what we feel.

For example, almost everyone has experienced the discomfort of eating too much and then suffering until the food is digested. If you don't recognize that you're full, you won't take the action to stop eating until you physically can't take another bite. Similarly, a great many of us are so out of touch with our feelings that we ignore our own pain and desires, leaving our abandoned Child to endure the pain alone until the agony is so great that the Child finds dysfunctional ways to get relief. Without some kind of help, the Child will continue some method of pain relief until the process (sex, gambling) or the substance (alcohol, food) becomes an addiction or a dependency.

Our feelings are in our bodies. Most of us are aware of bodily sensations, such as hunger, thirst, sexual desire, or sleepiness. Your body gives signals to let you know about these needs. Your body also tells you about feelings of fear, anxiety, depression, excitement, or joy. Perhaps your stomach gets tense or your legs rubbery, or your chest tightens when you are frightened; maybe your skin tingles or your heart flutters when you are excited.

Becoming aware of your body's signals is the first step toward Inner Bonding. Once we are aware of our discomfort or what brings us joy, we can begin to make conscious choices.

Figure 13. Inner Conflict

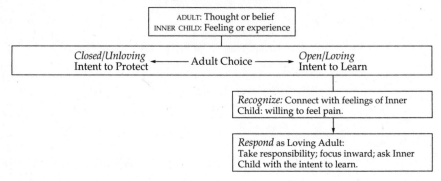

Step 2: Respond as a Loving Adult

Once you have recognized your feelings, your response to them must come from the intent to learn, that is, from a true desire to hear the voice of your Inner Child tell you what is going on within yourself emotionally. This means you show interest, caring, empathy, and compassion.

As you begin to focus inward, you, as the Adult, need to be willing to ask questions to learn about your Inner Child's experience, just as you would with an external child. You might ask, "What is the matter?" or "What do you need?" or simply "What do you feel now?" (Dialogue questions are provided in the next chapter.)

It is not loving to ask what the Child feels and then respond, "No, you don't—or shouldn't—feel that way."

It is loving to ask what the Child is feeling and respond, "Why do you feel that?"

Step 3: Dialogue with Your Inner Child

When you want to understand and find the answers to your pain and your desires, first you must "go down to your gut level," paying attention to the feelings in your body. Allow yourself to feel like a very young

Figure 14. Inner Conflict

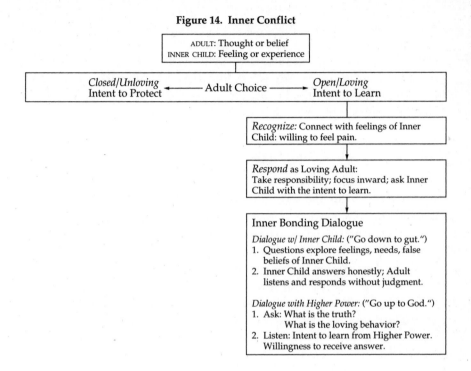

child within. Let the answers float up to your consciousness, and express them as an actual child would.

As the Child is speaking, listen with your Adult mind and try to understand the feelings, and the beliefs behind the feelings. You also need to learn what you, as the Adult, are doing to perpetuate the false beliefs that are causing your pain. Finally you must decide what action to take—that is, what the loving behavior will be in the present situation.[2]

Step 4: Dialogue with Your Higher Power

Once you, as the Adult, have gone inward, dialogued with your Inner Child, and gotten an understanding of the feelings and faulty beliefs causing pain, you may need help in knowing the truth about your beliefs and knowing what action needs to be taken. Where can you go to get this help?

You can, of course, seek help from a therapist or friend. But you can also "go up" to your Higher Power in an attitude of prayerful surrender, opening your mind to receive ideas and truth. (The term *Higher Power* can be God, or Higher Source, or whatever your personal religious or spiritual training leads you to conceive of as the Divine Source of Love and truth.)

My experience is that our Higher Power is always attempting to guide us, and that we can hear that guidance when we ask a question and listen for the answer. There are only two questions we need to ask:

1. What is the truth about this belief that is limiting me or causing me pain?

2. What is the loving behavior in this situation?

The answer may not come immediately. It may come when you least expect it—such as just as you are falling asleep, or through dreams—but it will come. When the answer comes, it may feel as if it is coming *through* you rather than *from* you.

We all like to believe that we can use our Adult intellect or reason to figure out the answers, yet that is not where our personal truth lies. The Adult, being the learned part of us, holds our knowledge; but it does not hold our intuitive or Higher wisdom. We have to reach within to our Child and without to a Higher Source—God, our Higher Power, our Higher Self—to find the whole truth for ourselves.

Step 5: Take Action

All the dialoguing and decision-making in the world won't do any good if we don't take the necessary action, the loving behavior that brings

Figure 15. Inner Conflict

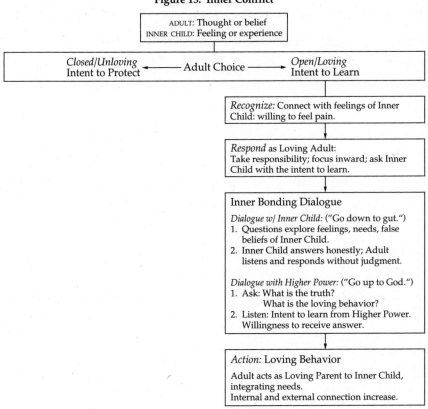

together our Adult thoughts and Child needs. Taking action requires courage and is often very difficult, since it may mean confronting beliefs that you have held all your life. It may also mean taking steps on your own behalf without knowing in advance how others will react. For example, if you decide to stop caretaking, your friends and family are likely to be upset with you and accuse you of being selfish.

Nonetheless, taking action demonstrates the loving intent of your Adult and verifies that your Inner Child is lovable, valuable enough to take care of. Equally important, the action increases your self-worth and initiates the positive consequences.

Some of the action we need to take is inward—talking to our Child and teaching the truth about ourselves and our false beliefs. Some is outward—changing our behavior with people and situations. If the action

Figure 16. Inner Conflict

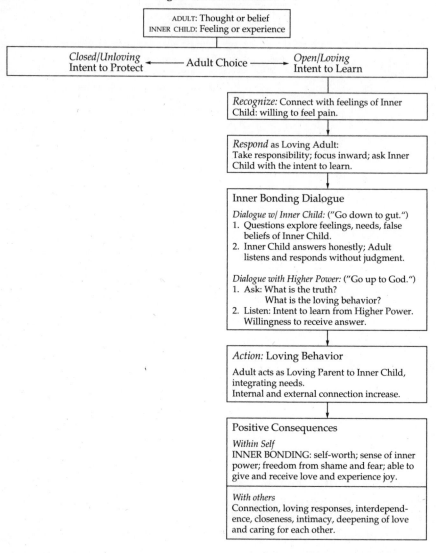

does not bring the desired results, we need to move back into the process and seek further understanding and answers. Eventually, through this process, we will discover the action that relieves our pain or brings us joy.

The Positive Consequences

When you take action to meet your needs, the process of Inner Bonding is complete in that moment and positive consequences will follow.

Figure 17. The Paths Through Inner Conflict

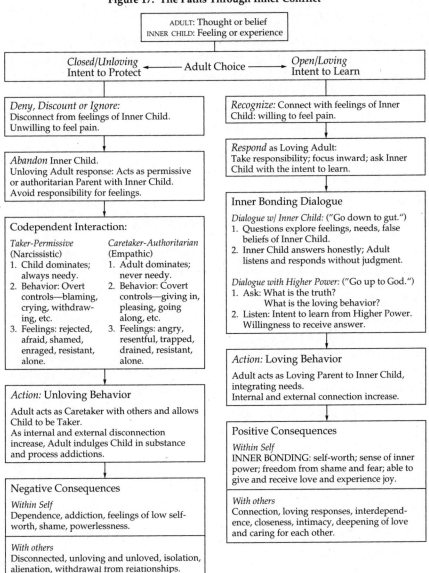

ADULT: Thought or belief
INNER CHILD: Feeling or experience

Closed/Unloving
Intent to Protect ◄——— Adult Choice ———► *Open/Loving*
Intent to Learn

Deny, Discount or Ignore:
Disconnect from feelings of Inner Child.
Unwilling to feel pain.

Recognize: Connect with feelings of Inner
Child: willing to feel pain.

Abandon Inner Child.
Unloving Adult response: Acts as permissive
or authoritarian Parent with Inner Child.
Avoid responsibility for feelings.

Respond as Loving Adult:
Take responsibility; focus inward; ask Inner
Child with the intent to learn.

Codependent Interaction:

Taker-Permissive (Narcissistic)	*Caretaker-Authoritarian* (Empathic)
1. Child dominates; always needy.	1. Adult dominates; never needy.
2. Behavior: Overt controls—blaming, crying, withdrawing, etc.	2. Behavior: Covert controls—giving in, pleasing, going along, etc.
3. Feelings: rejected, afraid, shamed, enraged, resistant, alone.	3. Feelings: angry, resentful, trapped, drained, resistant, alone.

Inner Bonding Dialogue

Dialogue w/ Inner Child: ("Go down to gut.")
1. Questions explore feelings, needs, false
   beliefs of Inner Child.
2. Inner Child answers honestly; Adult
   listens and responds without judgment.

Dialogue with Higher Power: ("Go up to God.")
1. Ask: What is the truth?
        What is the loving behavior?
2. Listen: Intent to learn from Higher Power.
   Willingness to receive answer.

Action: Unloving Behavior

Adult acts as Caretaker with others and allows
Child to be Taker.
As internal and external disconnection
increase, Adult indulges Child in substance
and process addictions.

Action: Loving Behavior

Adult acts as Loving Parent to Inner Child,
integrating needs.
Internal and external connection increase.

Negative Consequences

Within Self
Dependence, addiction, feelings of low self-
worth, shame, powerlessness.

With others
Disconnected, unloving and unloved, isolation,
alienation, withdrawal from relationships.

Positive Consequences

Within Self
INNER BONDING: self-worth; sense of inner
power; freedom from shame and fear; able to
give and receive love and experience joy.

With others
Connection, loving responses, interdepend-
ence, closeness, intimacy, deepening of love
and caring for each other.

The experience of Inner Bonding is different for each individual. Generally, in the absence of inner conflict between your rational and emotional aspects, your Adult feels "together," with a sense of inner power for having taken responsibility and action. Your Inner Child feels free, safe, unguarded, and worthy. When Inner Bonded, your whole being is open-hearted, able to give and receive the love of others.

There are times, in interactions with others who are disconnected within themselves, that positive consequences may not be apparent at that moment. For example, if you ask your employer for a needed break and get yelled at as a result, obviously the verbal abuse won't be pleasant. However, you will still feel positive within yourself for having taken the affirmative action.

To Be Connected or Disconnected? The Choice Is Yours

When you look at the overall picture, you can see clearly that the choice to be open or closed to your Inner Child's feelings creates most of the happiness or unhappiness in your life. It is also clear that if you stay closed and protected, abandoning your Inner Child with either taker or care-taker codependent behaviors, the negative consequences become more and more severe. The only way to reach the positive consequences you hope for is to shift your intent to openness and to connect with and learn about your Inner Child's feelings. When you choose the intent to learn, you can then begin taking the steps to Inner Bonding.

The Five Steps to Inner Bonding

Step 1: Recognize your inner conflict.

Become aware of your feelings.

Step 2: Respond as a Loving Adult.

Ask with the intent to learn.
Focus inward.

Step 3: Dialogue with your Inner Child.

"Go down" to your Inner Child.
Listen to what is needed.

Step 4: Dialogue with your Higher Power.

"Go up" to your Divine Source.
Ask and be open to guidance.

Step 5: Take action.

> Meet the needs of your Inner Child,
> as well as your Adult, by taking action.

Each of these steps is essential in order to complete the Inner Bonding process. However, many people are uncertain how to actually put these steps into practice in their own lives. The next chapter goes more deeply into the Five Steps to Inner Bonding.

CHAPTER 3

Creating the Inner Bond: Using the Five Steps in Your Own Life

It is essential to remember that only the mind can create, and that correction belongs at the thought level.

A Course in Miracles

The Inner Bonding process is so simple and logical, it almost sounds too easy. The concept is simple, but doing it is not easy. It takes time and practice to learn to be aware of your feelings, to explore your feelings and beliefs with an intent to learn, to hear the council of your Higher Power, and to take action. The most difficult part is making the choice to be loving and open, the choice to be in the intent to learn. This is because we've been closed to and afraid of our pain so much of our emotional lives that our protections and defenses have become automatic.

Step 3, dialoguing with your Inner Child, and step 4, dialoguing with your Higher Power, may sound mysterious or vague. This chapter includes many suggestions to help you in your dialoguing.

Step 1. Recognizing Your Inner Conflict: Becoming Aware of Your Feelings

We cannot explore our feelings until we know we are feeling. Many of us have learned to numb our feelings with our substance and process addictions. Until we become willing to pay attention to and feel the feelings of our Inner Child, we cannot begin to learn about them. Feeling your feelings means focusing inward into your body—paying attention to your gut, your neck, your shoulders, your legs—wherever you hold your tension, anxiety, fear, sadness, grief, disappointment. It means not doing the things you normally do to not feel your pain—not taking that drink, not eating that candy bar, not turning on the TV, not working those extra hours, not yelling at your mate or your kids.

Step 1 is the willingness to know that you have an Inner Child who communicates to you through your body. It is the willingness to pay attention when that Child is tugging on your skirt or pant leg, except that the tug is inside you.

Step 2. Responding as a Loving Adult: Moving into the Intent to Learn

Once you've become willing to recognize your feelings and take responsibility for them, the next step is to move into the intent to learn. Remember the earlier example of Laura? When she said, "Okay, Inner Child, if you're in there, speak up!" her inner feelings cried out immediately, "Help!" If there is a secret to Inner Bonding, the clue lies in Laura's example—responding as a loving Adult by moving into the intent to learn.

The Intent to Learn

It is only when one is searching for the truth that one can find the truth. It is only through the intent to learn that a person can begin to dialogue with the Inner Child and examine the false beliefs that create the painful addictive/codependent behaviors that perpetuate the inner disconnection.

There are two conditions necessary for the intent to learn to be present. These conditions are (1) belief in good reasons, and (2) willingness to experience pain.

Belief in Good Reasons

Inner Bonding Therapy, along with other humanistic-existential therapies, states that there are always good, valid, important reasons for feeling and behaving as we do. These reasons are always our fears and the false beliefs that create these fears. These beliefs may have been true when we were children, but they are no longer true now. These include such false beliefs as, "I am powerless," or shame-based beliefs that were never true, such as the belief "I was born bad."

In Inner Bonding Therapy the judgmental concepts of right and wrong, good and bad, are put aside or shelved, since they hinder and are irrelevant to the learning process. That is not to say that right and wrong do not exist—whether or not they exist is not the issue. The issue is that we cannot learn when we fear being wrong. We cannot learn when we are feeling or being shamed. It is often the fear of being judged as wrong and the resulting feelings of shame that block learning. The judgment of wrong carries with it the fear of rejection. Rather than open to learning when offered important information about ourselves, when we fear being wrong we will react as if we've been attacked and become defensive. In order to learn, we must release our concepts of right and wrong, and the only way to do this is to understand that there are always important reasons for feelings and behavior.

I was trying to explain this concept to my daughter one night. She said to me, "But Mom, if a man who was a murderer came to you as a client, wouldn't you judge him as wrong?" I answered, "Killing others is wrong in my personal value system, but how could I help him if I judged him as wrong? My experience tells me that a person who would kill other people has been extremely abused himself and has a set of fears and beliefs that allow him to kill others.

"Just because I help him understand his choices and the reasons for them, and help him heal the pain behind his choices so he can make new choices, it doesn't mean that I condone his behavior. But if I judged him and shamed him, all he would do is become silent and feel even more rageful. My job would be to create a safe, loving, healing space for him to explore his rage and fears and beliefs. And if he were willing to do that, and if he were eventually willing to take full personal responsibility for his choices, he could be healed. There would be no chance of that if I judged him."

Moving beyond looking at behavior in terms of right and wrong is a major step in the healing process. We cannot truly embrace the intent to learn as our primary intent until we are no longer controlled by the fear of other's judgment or self-judgment. Until then, protecting against being seen as wrong and against experiencing the deep pain of shame will be more important to us than learning.

Willingness to Feel Pain

We originally established our protections when we were children in an attempt to protect ourselves from pain that was too overwhelming for our little beings, pain that was too much for us to handle. Most of us suffered pain—from being sexually abused, physically abused, or emotionally abused by being ignored, neglected, ridiculed, put down, yelled at, or called names. And we were alone and trapped with our pain and shame. We were too little to leave, to call a friend for help, or to find ourselves a therapist. For an unfortunate number of us, childhood was hell, and to survive we had to find ways to protect ourselves.

As adults, that pain is still within the Inner Child, and we may still be protecting against it. As long as we choose to protect against it, the work we must do to avoid that pain controls our lives. In order to open to learning, an individual must decide that he or she is willing to feel and learn from the pain. Opening to learning from pain is an essential aspect in healing. Therefore helping an individual explore his or her false beliefs about pain and shame is basic to the healing process.

Once a person opens to learning, he or she can learn to pay attention to the emotional discomfort and pain of the Inner Child. This facilitates understanding that there are good reasons for the discomfort or pain, exploring and challenging the false beliefs that are causing the present unhappiness, discovering what brings joy, and acting to bring it about.

It is through the willingness to experience our pain that we can finally discover the experiences in childhood that created our false beliefs about our badness, wrongness, unlovability, or inadequacy—the beliefs that create our feelings of shame. As the Inner Adult learns to handle the pain of the Inner Child, the door to memory opens and we can finally remember, grieve, and heal the experiences that created our core false beliefs about ourselves.

Step 3. Dialoguing with Your Inner Child

When you have moved into an intent to learn and you want to understand your inner pain or desire, begin by turning your attention inward. Ask a question directly to your Inner Child, saying the words out loud or writing them down, using your non-dominant hand when answering as the Child. Then gently move from thinking to feeling. Pay attention to the feelings in your body and allow yourself to react as if you were a small child. Let the answers to your questions float upward into your consciousness.

Most people find that using a doll, a stuffed animal, or a picture of themselves as a child helps their dialogue process.

This process will virtually always allow your inner feelings to rise from the depths of your gut to your consciousness. The expression of the feelings may appear in different ways. Sometimes it may actually be verbalized, sometimes it comes as instant understanding, too fast for words to be attached. The form of the dialogue isn't important as long as answers that reveal your inner feelings are coming forth. You, as the Inner Child, do have feelings. Therefore if you are not getting answers from within yourself, either you, as the Adult, do not really want to know, or your Inner Child doesn't yet trust your intent.

Consider again the example of the woman and the lost boy on the street corner. If she asks him whether he's cold, he knows how he feels. Unless he is too frightened, he answers yes or no. If she asks how he's feeling, he may respond in many different ways: "I'm cold . . . sad . . . hungry . . . afraid . . . lost" and so on.

When people are asked about their feelings, they will answer—unless they have a good reason not to. When it's our own Inner Child, one of the good reasons for not answering is that our Adult does not want to know or remember. For instance, if we feel shame, we may have buried those feelings so deep that they are hard to find and even harder to uncover. We may need professional help at times.

Another reason for not expressing our inner feelings is that we have refused to recognize them due to a real or imagined fear of the consequences of knowing. The reasons for protecting ourselves from these perceived consequences will be discussed further in chapter 4. For now, it's enough to remember:

> If your Inner Child is silent, your Adult is in the intent
> to protect, not in the intent to learn, or your Child
> does not yet trust your intent.

Beginning to Dialogue with Your Inner Child

Many people are hesitant to dialogue even when they are in the intent to learn; they're simply uncertain how to begin. The French proverb "Begun is half done" is especially true in this case, because your first question will set in motion your own question-and-answer process.

A client named Carl was exploring his Child's sense of shame and fear, and shared this example of an inner dialogue, edited only to make it more concise:

ADULT: I know that you are feeling very upset right now. What is upsetting you?
CHILD: I'm afraid of losing Liz.
ADULT: Why do you think you're going to lose her?
CHILD: I'll never be enough for her.

ADULT: Why do you believe you aren't enough?

CHILD: Because you keep telling me I don't do things right. And you sound just like mom and dad reminding me of everything I didn't get done that day. No matter how much I do, you keep telling me it wasn't enough, I should have done more.

ADULT: I guess I do sound like them when I say that stuff. No wonder you feel bad so much of the time.

CHILD: Yeah, and Liz treats me nice. If she leaves me, then I won't have anyone to treat me nice.

ADULT: So that's why you're afraid to lose her? Because you need someone you can count on to treat you nice?

CHILD: Yes.

As a result of this dialogue, Carl became aware that his Child's fear of abandonment stemmed from being shamed by his parents and that his Adult continued to shame his Inner Child. He then could see what action needed to be taken. In general, Carl needed to value and connect with his inner feelings and to validate his Child's worth, rather than ignoring or shaming himself.

When we dialogue with our Inner Child, the content of the questions we ask will vary with the situation. There are three basic categories of life situations to consider: (1) Inner Bonding for our everyday lives; (2) Inner Bonding in conflict with others or in painful or frightening life events; and (3) Inner Bonding with memories and beliefs. In the following sections, some questions are suggested for each of these categories to help you begin to connect with the feelings of your Child.[1]

Questions for Daily Dialoguing with Your Inner Child

Taking the time to tune into what you really want in everyday situations can not only help establish the habit of Inner Bonding, but can lead you to spend your time in more satisfying ways. When you encounter a minor conflict—for example, your Child wants junk food but your Adult wants healthy food—you can negotiate a resolution that satisfies both.

The following questions can help you learn what you want in any given moment:

"What do you want to do right now?"

"What would you like to eat right now?"

"What color do you feel like wearing?"

"How do you want to spend this day?"

"What kind of music do you want to listen to now?"

"Where would you like to go on vacation?"

"What kind of exercise do you like?"

"Are you happy or unhappy with the work we do?"

"Are you happy or unhappy with our relationships—mate, friends?"

"What kinds of creative things or hobbies would you like to do?"

"What are some of the things you've always wanted to do, but have never done? Have I kept you from doing them?"

Of course, as has already been stated, just getting the information will not help you at all. You then have to take action. That would be like asking a little girl if she wants an ice cream cone, and then responding, "Oh, that's interesting."

We do not ask these questions in order to indulge our Inner Child, automatically giving everything the Child wants, any more than a loving parent would do with a child. But in finding out what our Child wants and what our Adult wants, we can find ways to satisfy both parts of ourselves.

Questions for Dialoguing with Your Inner Child in Conflict with Others or in Painful Life Situations

Much of the pain in our lives occurs as we relate to other people, and our relationships also present our greatest challenge in terms of being loving to ourselves. That is the focus of the second half of this book—learning to be loving to ourselves when in conflict with others.

We are also greatly challenged when painful or frightening life situations occur—the loss of a loved one, a marriage, a job, or difficult financial issues, illness, and so on. Once you've recognized your feelings of distress and moved into the intent to learn, you can begin the dialoguing process with one of the following questions:

"What are you feeling?"

"I know you're angry and I'd like to hear what that's about."

"Are you angry at me? It's okay to yell at me."

"It's truly okay for you to feel this anger, even if it's at me. I won't stop loving you, no matter how angry you feel."

"Are you feeling shamed right now? What has happened that shamed you? How can I help? Am I shaming you?"

"It's okay to cry. You can cry as long as you need to. You are not alone; I'm here for you."

"I know you're feeling anxious (or frightened, hurt, worried, depressed, and so on). Can you tell me more about why you are feeling this way? I will not leave you alone with these feelings."

"How do you feel about _____?" (Name the person you are in conflict with or the difficult life event.)

"Have I let you down in some way with this person or situation?"

"How are you needing me to take care of you right now?"

"What do you want me to do differently with _____?" (Name the person or event.)

"I can tell that your feelings are so big that I cannot handle them alone. Be assured that I will get the help we need."

Throughout the day, whenever you become aware of feeling upset or uneasy—tense, scared, angry, numb, hurt, or sad—you can ask your Inner Child questions. For example:

"What is causing these feelings? Am I thinking things that are upsetting you?"

"How can I help you with these feelings?"

"What do you need from me?"

"Am I letting you down or not taking care of you in some way? How?"

"Have I been ignoring you? Discounting you? Controlling you? Shaming you?"

Remember, if you are in the intent to learn and can't find the answers within, ask for Higher guidance. Reaching out for help from a friend or a therapist may also be necessary.

When you become the Child, it is helpful to turn the bear or doll to face outward and pull it into your stomach. At the same time, allow your consciousness to sink into your body, focusing within, following the in breath, and allowing yourself to feel little. Visualize your Adult sitting in front of you or surrounding you with his or her loving energy. It may help to have a picture of your Adult in front of you when you are speaking as the Child. It is especially important to feel your Adult with you and around you when you are in pain, so as not to feel alone with the pain. When we were small children, we were so often alone with our pain. Now, as a loving Adult, we can take away that aloneness by staying with our Inner Child when we dialogue. We can take the loving and nurturing energy that exists within our heart when we are in a true intent to learn and surround ourselves with it as we allow ourselves to speak or write from our Child within.

After we have spoken or written our feelings from our Child, we can turn the doll or bear around again, looking at it, holding it with love and tenderness, and let our Child know we understand what he or she is feeling and saying to us. We can then ask another question, each time going deeper into understanding our inner feelings.

It's important to take time during the day to affirm your Inner Child, just as a loving parent does:

"I'm here for you. I'm not going away. You are very important to me."

"You are not alone. I am here with you."

"I love you, and your happiness is very important to me."

"You are so smart. Thank you for all this wonderful wisdom."

"Your creativity amazes me."

"It's okay to make mistakes. You are lovable even if you make mistakes. You don't have to do things perfectly for me to love you and stay here with you."

"You don't have to do it 'right.' I will continue to love you no matter what you say, even if you say nothing at all."

Questions for Dialoguing with Memories and Beliefs

Sometimes present conflict situations or painful life events can touch off past painful memories. When this occurs, you can use the questions below to dialogue with your Inner Child.

"Is something happening now that reminds you of something that happened when you were little?"

"Does this person (in the conflict) remind you of mom, dad, a brother or sister, grandparent?"

"Does this situation remind you of a traumatic experience that you had when you were little?"

"I really want to know everything you remember from the past. Your memories are very important to me and I want to help you heal your fears, your shame."

"Do you need me to provide someone to help with this? Do you need to be held while you go through this pain?"

If your child needs to be held and there is no one there to hold you, holding your doll or bear as if it is truly your own Inner Child can, surprisingly, be very comforting. This is a major reason why having a doll or bear to work with is so important.

As feelings of fear and shame come up, you can explore the beliefs behind them:

"What are my beliefs about my adequacy and lovability? Do I believe I am defective, flawed, bad?"

"What are my beliefs about my ability to handle pain, to control others, to be responsible for others, others' responsibility for me, and so on?"

"Where did I get these beliefs? What childhood experiences created these beliefs?"

"What do I gain by acting as if these beliefs are true? What am I afraid of? What would happen if I stopped believing these things about myself?"

Memories can touch off beliefs and beliefs can touch off memories. As you learn about these through the Inner Bonding process, being a loving Adult for the fear and shame of your Inner Child, bringing in the truth can turn present painful conflicts and events into healing experiences. It is the Inner Adult telling the truth and taking loving action that ultimately brings about an inner strength that helps you handle life's difficulties and the personal power necessary to make healthy choices.

Clearing Out Our False Beliefs

To clear out the blocks to truth—our false, self-limiting beliefs—and open the way to love and joy is the real purpose of Inner Bonding, as has been stated earlier.

In the context of Inner Bonding Therapy, problems are not just seen as something to be solved, but as symptoms of a faulty belief system resulting from growing up in a dysfunctional family and a dysfunctional society. This faulty belief system leads to an inner disconnection between the Inner Adult and the Inner Child, resulting in the deep pain of loneliness in the world and aloneness within.

When we attempt to solve a problem without shifting our belief system and creating an inner connection, what often occurs is superficial change that generally does not affect the quality of our lives. The man who stops drinking but does not create an inner connection that heals the old pain and shifts the belief system that caused his drinking is what Alcoholics

Anonymous calls a "dry drunk." He has stopped the outer behavior of drinking, but because on an inner level nothing has changed, nothing actually changes in his life or his relationships. He just learns other ways to fill his emptiness and numb the fear and pain.

We seek help from therapists, friends, clergy, or Twelve-Step programs because we are suffering, and the primary cause of our suffering is the erroneous belief system under which we are operating and which creates the disconnection between the Inner Adult and the Inner Child, which is the real source of pain. The erroneous belief system and resulting inner disconnection causes us to have any number of symptoms: pain, fear, depression, illness, broken relationships, empty relationships, unsatisfying jobs, lost jobs, poverty, substance addictions, relationship addictions, sexual addictions, loneliness. We may even be suicidal.

All these symptoms are the consequences of the inner disconnection that occurs when we do not love and trust our Inner Child. We do not love and trust the Child because of the beliefs we have about our Child— beliefs such as "Deep down, in the core of me, I am bad, unworthy, unimportant, insignificant, unlovable, defective, incompetent, imperfect, inadequate." Virtually all of us, deep inside, have a shame-based belief of this sort that is controlling our life in a very negative way.

We can relieve a symptom in a superficial way, such as taking drugs to control depression; or we can remove the symptom through understanding and challenging the self-limiting belief that is creating the depression. For example, Marilyn, a client of mine, had suffered from severe depressive episodes intermittently for many years and had been hospitalized a number of times as a result of these depressions. She was taking medication to control the symptoms. As we worked together, it became apparent that every time Marilyn went into a depression, it was because she had not listened to her Inner Child. And the reason she did not listen to herself is that she falsely believed that she could not rely on her own inner knowing in personal matters.

As a successful attorney, she had generally listened to her inner knowing in her work; but when it came to her personal life, she believed that others knew what was right or wrong for her better than she did. As she learned to trust her inner knowing regarding herself, her depressions gradually ceased and she was eventually able to withdraw from all medication.

Marilyn was certainly surprised by this outcome, because she had been told that her depressions were primarily physically based. And it is certainly true that when she became afraid, she had physical changes in her body chemistry that created her depressions, and that she had an inherited predisposition toward these particular chemical changes. But it is also true that it was fear that triggered these chemical changes, and that the fear was a consequence of her self-limiting beliefs that she could not trust herself and that others knew better than she what was right or wrong for her. As she learned to trust her inner knowing, her intense anxiety over numerous personal situations subsided to the point where they no longer triggered the chemical reaction that created her depressions.

False, self-limiting beliefs are, simply, those beliefs that create our unhappiness, those blocks that are in the way of our ability to love and be loved and to our joy. It is our own faulty beliefs that create our unhappiness, not outside events or anyone else's behavior.

One of the major false beliefs that we all need to confront—the belief that underlies all codependent behavior—is the belief that our happiness and unhappiness come from outside of ourselves, from how others see us and treat us, from whether or not others love and approve of us, or disapprove of and reject us. Most of us believe that we are victims of other people's behavior, that how we feel is a necessary reaction to how someone else treats us.

As long as we believe this, we have no power to make ourselves happy. We are stuck either feeling alone and looking for someone to make us happy, or trying to change someone so we can be happy. We are stuck being codependent. Until we open to knowing the truth—that how we feel is a consequence of what we believe and how we behave toward ourselves and others—we are stuck feeling powerless and being victims of others' behavior. A major step toward health occurs when we truly begin to take responsibility for our own happiness and unhappiness, joy and pain, through loving connection with our Inner Child.

The Six Major False Beliefs

Most of us have hundreds of self-limiting beliefs that control our lives and cause us pain. I have isolated six major false beliefs that everyone seems to have, and which very often form the basis of our personal and interpersonal difficulties:

1. *There is something wrong with me.* I am unlovable. I am inadequate, basically defective, bad. I am insignificant, unimportant. Therefore, if I let people in on who I am or if I am me, I will not be loved.

2. *I am powerless over how I feel.* Other people or outside events are responsible for making me happy or unhappy. Other people are responsible for my hurt, anger, guilt, or disappointment. I can't

help how I feel. My good feelings come primarily from others' approval and my bad feelings from their disapproval. I do not have the power to make myself happy within myself, or to take care of myself in the world. I have to rely on other people, things, or substances to make me happy or take care of me. I am a victim.

3. *Other people's feelings are more important than mine, and I am responsible for their feelings.* When others feel hurt, disappointed, or upset because of something I've done (with no intent to hurt them), I'm wrong and it's my fault, and I deserve the guilt I feel. Making myself happy (again with no intent to harm others) when others want me to make them happy is selfish and unloving and therefore wrong. To be a loving person, I have to sacrifice what I want for what others want.

4. *I can control what others think of me, feel about me, and how they treat me.* I can "make" them like me or love me or be open to me by being good, nice, or open. Or I can "make" them treat me how I want to be treated by getting angry, righteous, and blaming.

5. *Resisting others' control over me is essential to my integrity.* As soon as someone wants something from me, I have to do the opposite, even if it's something I want to do or give, or I will lose myself to that other person.

6. *I can't handle pain, discomfort, fear, hurt, grief, disconnection from others, boredom, disappointment, shame, or aloneness.* I have to protect myself from these feelings with my anger, caretaking, and withdrawal, with activities such as sex or work, or with substances such as alcohol, drugs, or food.

These beliefs, I have found, are very, very deep in most of us, and challenging their validity is an ongoing process with many layers of self-confrontation. These beliefs create the vast majority of the symptoms listed above, and control much of what we do in our relationships.

Addictions and codependent relationships are direct consequences of the above six beliefs, and there is rarely a child who is not brought up with these self-limiting beliefs. Addiction, whether to a substance, to a thing or activity, or to a person, comes directly from the belief that "I cannot make myself happy. Something outside of me, a person, thing, or substance, has to make me happy." As long as we continue to believe in the self-limiting belief that we are incapable of making ourselves happy, then we are stuck relying on someone or something outside of ourselves, which is what addiction and codependence are all about.

Our overt controlling behavior such as blaming anger or threats, comes from the belief that "I can make others love me, approve of me, see me, hear me." Covert attempts to control through caretaking and niceness come directly from the beliefs that "My feelings are not as important as other people's and I am responsible for other's feelings," and "I can make others love me by being nice."

The purpose of Inner Bonding Therapy is to help us become aware of and challenge the validity of these and other beliefs through connection with our Inner Child. As we remove these blocks to the truth, we stop being victims and assume responsibility for ourselves, which leads to loving and trusting ourselves and others, thus enhancing our self-esteem and creating our joy.

Choice: What Does It Mean?

Understanding the areas in which we have a choice and in which we do not have a choice is essential to the healing process.

> We always have a choice over our own beliefs, intent, and resulting actions and reactions.

> We have no choice over others' beliefs, intent, and resulting actions and reactions.

When we believe we are just reactors, reacting to others' actions, then we believe we are victims, that we have no choice. When we believe we have choice over others' feelings and behavior, we become controlling.

As children, while we had no choice concerning our parents' actions, we chose our own beliefs and reactions. For example, Todd and Matt are brothers. Todd is two years older than Matt. Both Todd and Matt were severely abused as children, physically, emotionally, and sexually. Todd chose, from the time he was a small child, to identify with his parents. He became a bully, taking out on Matt and a younger sister all his rage toward his parents. As an adult, Todd is an angry, controlling man, who puts down therapy as a waste of time and money and drowns his feelings in alcohol.

Matt, on the other hand, chose to survive by shutting down and withdrawing rather than becoming like his parents. Matt entered therapy about a year ago and has shown great courage in remembering the abuse and opening to the rage and pain inside of him. Matt is in a loving relationship with his wife and children, and his friends see him as a warm and caring person.

Two brothers with very similar experiences, each making different choices in how to react to the same circumstances.

In their very wonderful book entitled *The Courage to Heal*, Ellen Bass and Laura Davis explore the healing process for adult women survivors of childhood sexual abuse.[2] Each of the many women who tell their stories made choices regarding how to survive the abuse in their lives and keep their sanity intact. And each of them have made choices in the present to open to the pain of their past and heal so that they can lead full, loving, and joyful lives. They no longer see themselves as victims, but as survivors, and they've learned to value the choices they made for themselves, both as children and as adults. Yet there are many others not in the book who made other choices—who chose to hurt or kill themselves or harm others rather than deal with their past pain.

Marriages and families are prime arenas where people see themselves as victims, believing they are just reacting to their partner or their children rather than making their own choices. The statements below are typical victim statements:

"My husband makes me so angry. He just refuses to communicate with me."

"Of course I drink. It's the only way to handle the tension around the house."

"So I have affairs. So what? It's not my fault my wife doesn't like sex. I have to get my needs met somewhere."

"Yeah, I hit my son last week and I feel bad about it. But I couldn't help it, he makes me so mad."

"I'm lonely all the time. He never pays attention to me. He never has time for me."

"I hate always having to ask my husband for money, but what can I do? He doesn't want me to work."

Each of these people believes that someone else is responsible for his or her feelings and their behavior. Until they understand that it is their own choices, their own *intent* that creates their feelings and behavior, they are stuck being victims.

The Spiritual Aspect of Inner Bonding Therapy: Connecting with Your Higher Power

Psychotherapy generally fails when it does not help individuals to discover the place within or without (depending upon the individual's belief system) where they can go to connect with the spiritual truth. Whether the person believes that their Higher Power exists solely within themselves, solely outside of themselves, or both within and without does not matter. What matters is that they connect to a higher source of knowing, love, and comfort that has nothing to do with another human being.

True healing cannot occur until we learn to know and trust our Higher Self, or true self—who we really are. For it is only then that we will know we are loving and lovable. The Higher Self is the inner source of love, of loving oneself as well as others.

Inner Bonding Therapy states that the Higher Self is reached through the connection between the Inner Adult and the Inner Child. When the Adult connects with the Child through the intent to learn, the head, the heart, and the gut are all open to receiving Higher knowledge. It is this open state that is our place of power, our Higher Self; and it is through this open state that we can connect with God, Goddess, Universal love, Great Spirit, or whatever we call our Higher Power.

The false self, or ego, is who we are when the Adult chooses the intent to protect and disconnects from the Inner Child. The unloving Adult and the unloved abandoned Child are the two faces of the ego.

Inner Bonding Therapy uses the definition of ego described in Eastern philosophy and in such psychological/spiritual texts as *A Course in Miracles*. Here the ego is defined as the constructed personality, the lower self, or the false self. This false self is based on fear and the false beliefs that create the fear, while the Higher Self is the energy of truth and love. The degree of health we have is the degree to which we operate from the truths of the Higher Self, and the degree of illness we exhibit is based on the degree to which we operate from the false beliefs of the ego.

The disconnection from the Higher Self occurs very early in life, when we draw the conclusion (based on our early experiences of being abused: shamed, abandoned, neglected, controlled, physically or sexually violated) that we are unworthy, unlovable, bad, wrong, inadequate, insignificant, defective, unimportant. This is the primary false, shame-based, self-limiting belief of the ego. It is the belief that creates the ego, thus creating the disconnection from the Higher Self and from our Higher Power. This inner and outer disconnection creates an emptiness within, which the ego tries to fill with its various substance and process addictions. When we believe that our true self is bad, unlovable, unworthy, and so on, then we have to create a self that we hope will be acceptable to our parents and to the world. That self we create is the ego.

The Adult is our thought process and takes place in our minds. Our Child is our feeling process and our emotions are felt in the body. The ego is visualized as the space between the two—the Adult and the Inner Child, the rational and the emotional—when they are disconnected. When disconnected, we can say that we are in the ego state. This is the state of being shut down and in fear. It is this state of inner separation, from ourselves and our Higher Power, that creates the emptiness that we try to fill with our addictions. It also creates our inner aloneness, since the parts of us are operating separately and not in the light of truth, but in the darkness of false, shame-based beliefs. It is this ego state that creates our separation from others and our loneliness in the world.

When we are loving and in our Higher Self, this is the connected state. The Adult is open to learning with the Child and the heart is open to give and receive love.

Figure 18.

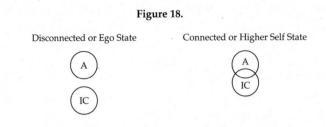

Learning to differentiate between the false beliefs of the ego and the truths of the Higher Self, and learning how to choose the Higher Self rather than the ego is an essential aspect of Inner Bonding Therapy.

Step 4. Dialoguing with Your Higher Power

The next step after exploring the feelings of your Inner Child and false beliefs of your ego is to dialogue with your Higher Power, asking for guidance regarding loving action, and asking for help in carrying out the loving action. Again, you must be in an intent to learn, which opens your heart, in order to hear the voice of your Higher Power. With your heart open and following your breath up and out, you can ask questions or make statements such as:

"What is the truth about this belief that is causing me pain?"

"What actions can I take to confront the validity of this belief?"

"What does my Child need right now to feel loved by me?"

"What is the loving behavior toward my Inner Child in this conflict situation with _____?" (Name a person)

"What is the loving behavior toward my Inner Child in this life situation?"

"Please help me to have the strength and courage to take loving action in my Child's behalf."

It's important to remember that whatever is truly loving toward ourselves is also loving to others. The focus needs to be on what is loving to ourselves, to our own Inner Child, first and foremost. If we focus on what we think is loving to others, we may end up caretaking instead of loving and our Child will get cast aside.

Just as your Child will eventually speak to you if you are consistent in your dialoguing, so will your Higher Power. With practice, you will learn to hear the voice of your Higher Power, though it is generally quite soft. The challenge comes in choosing to listen to the soft voice of your Higher Power rather than the loud voice of your ego. Remembering that your ego's voice is based on disconnection, fear, and false beliefs can help you stay focused on the voice of your Higher Power, the voice of connection, love, and truth. Our ego will constantly try to pull us off track; but if we stay in touch with the feelings of our Child and with what brings us peace and joy, we can learn to stay on track more of the time.

Discovering the loving behavior may be one of the most profoundly creative processes you will ever experience, as well as one of the most satisfying. It is helpful to see this as a creative process, a process in which you are seeking new answers for old problems, or new answers for new problems. Just as an artist needs to be open to the creative forces moving through when facing a blank canvas, so you need to be open to new ideas and possibilities concerning what it means to love yourself. Being in this creative process with your Inner Child and your Higher Power can be one of the most enlivening and exciting experiences in your life.

Step 5. Taking Action: The Key Is within Us

Once you've dialogued with your Inner Child and your Higher Power and decided what the loving behavior would be in a given situation, your Adult must make it happen. Just as you would take action to relieve the pain of your actual child, you as the Adult need to be the one to take action to relieve the pain of your Inner Child. Then, as explained earlier, when your Adult does what is needed to meet the Inner Child's needs in ways that have long-range, positive consequences, your Child feels loved and cared for and your Adult has a sense of inner strength. This is a very powerful combination.

If you had good-enough parenting as a child, you probably have a base level of good feelings about yourself. If you were the child of an abusive alcoholic, as Tom was, or had critical parents like Carl's, who continuously discounted his efforts, you may suffer the very real pain of low self-worth. You have valid, important reasons for your feelings, but reasons are not excuses. With or without good-enough original parenting, the fact is still the same: You are the only one who can affect your internal state.

Nobody else can do for us what we have to do for ourselves. If we're being honest, most of us harbor the hope that someone else will come and do the work of making us feel good or safe or loved. One of the sad but true things about life is that if we didn't get what we wanted and needed from our parents, it is too late as adults to get it from outside of ourselves. As adults, we can get all the love in the world from outside of ourselves and all it does is make us feel good for the moment, as does any addiction. As long as we continue to treat ourselves in unloving ways we will continue to feel unworthy or unlovable, no matter how much outside love we get. We have to give ourselves the love first, before any outside love can even come in in any permanant way. Outside love cannot come into a closed heart, and unless we are open to learning and loving within, our heart is closed and other's love is just a temporary drug.

If we keep looking and waiting for another person, a Perfect Parent or Ideal Mate, to fill up our emptiness, take away our pain, and keep us from feeling alone, we're going to look forever. As a result, we'll always suffer from the notion that we're missing the key to life, and we will be. Without any doubt, the key is within us.

Evaluating the Results of Our Actions

How do you know when you are taking loving action? How can you tell if your Adult is teaching your Inner Child the truth? You know by how you feel about yourself inside.

> When you are being loving to yourself, your shame
> lessens and your self-esteem rises.

This doesn't mean we will always feel joyful and peaceful at the moment of loving action. Often we feel frightened, even terrified, when we confront false beliefs. Nonetheless we will emerge feeling better and better about ourselves. Behavior that is unloving to ourselves and others leads to our feeling angry, anxious, or depressed. Therefore the criteria for knowing whether or not we are being loving is not how we feel about the action itself, but how we feel about ourselves for having done it.

If your home is burning, for example, and you rush in to try to save your family, you will be terrified at the moment and maybe suffer physical pain. But you will feel good about yourself for having courage in the face of fear and trying your best to save the lives of the people you love. In the case of Inner Bonding, the life you're trying to save is your own.

Another example of loving behavior that does not feel good at the moment is giving up an addiction, such as smoking, drinking, or compulsive eating. In fact, you will not feel good physically for quite a while, as you move through the phases of letting go of your addiction and feeling the pain that the addiction has been numbing. But if you truly face yourself and the pain and beliefs that lie under the addiction, you will eventually emerge feeling much better about yourself.

What Does Joy Look Like?

When you take care of yourself and are Inner Bonded, you shift into a higher gear of happiness called joy. But what does joy look like in adult terms? Certainly it does not indicate the feeling gained from the pleasures of childhood, such as skipping hand in hand with your best friend or hitting a home run over the Little League fence.

Adult joy has been described in many different ways: "Everything's right," "a feeling of oneness," "going with the flow." One theme that runs throughout most all of such descriptive phrases is freedom—freedom from fear, from internal struggles, from inner resistance, from the need for emotional protection, from your own or another's attempts at control, freedom to feel and the freedom to value that feeling.

Other variations on this theme include openness, added energy, and feeling centered or balanced.

One certain sign of joy is the ability to laugh spontaneously. Under stress and conflict, you might find a joke funny, or laugh politely when others do, but spontaneous laughter that rises to the surface like bubbles in water only occurs when you feel free. As Sheldon Kopp said, "Laughter is the sound of freedom." It is also the sound of joy.

CHAPTER 4

Who Is Crying in the Night? The Abandoned Inner Child and the Intent to Protect

How stubbornly we refuse to accept responsibility for our own lives.
The Moment Belongs to God
SHELDON KOPP

When we are feeling happy and peaceful inside, we are open to learning. But as soon as we experience any emotional pain or discomfort, we generally revert immediately to the intent to protect. This happens because most of us have the false belief, true in our childhood but no longer true today, that we cannot handle our pain—that we will die, or go crazy, or that the pain or discomfort will be unending, or that we are wrong or weak for having those feelings. So we try to protect ourselves. We ignore, deny, or discount our feelings; and, in so doing, we abandon our Inner Child.

Who Is Crying in the Night?

For many of us, a child crying in the night, unanswered and uncomforted, epitomizes our feelings of being abandoned and alone. A friend of mine, Lynn, asked specifically, "*Who* is crying in the night?"

LYNN: I thought about our discussion last week and the idea of the abandoned child. I thought of the time when my emotional self is most needy and the time that's the hardest is the middle of the night. To see if I understand Inner Bonding Therapy right, I wanted to ask you: Who is crying in the night?

MARGIE: It's your Child feeling abandoned and alone. It's the Child who has fear, sadness, grief, and nobody's there to bond with. When the Child is disconnected from the Adult, the Adult has abdicated his or her job—the job of being the Loving Adult/Parent for the Inner Child. If my Adult comes, I can still cry; but I will not be crying alone, so the feeling is going to be different.

LYNN: Who does the abandoned Child expect to come?

MARGIE: It's different for everybody. Sometimes I visualize someone coming—a spouse or a friend—to take care of my pain. When I was a kid, it was my mom and dad. As a child I had the right to expect that a parent would come. But as an adult my inner little girl immediately starts wondering, "Who's going to come and take care of my pain?" Obviously, when you're an adult, no one is going to come because no one truly can and no one is supposed to. Nobody can fix your feelings for you. Other adults can help you, but they can only do it *with* you—they can't do it *for* you.

So, when I'm crying, I hear my little girl saying, "Oh, I wish someone would come and hold me and take care of me." But the minute I hear that, I know that my Adult is not there. Then I say that I (the Adult) am here now, and I'm going to help you. I'm going to be the one to heal it and do something about it. Then I ask, "What is it you need from me right now?"

Sometimes I have to imagine another adult/parent figure sitting there and allow myself as a Child to tell him or her what I need. Whatever I hear myself say to that person is what I need from my Adult.

LYNN: Who cannot come in the night?

MARGIE: The fantasy will never come—the fantasy bond, the wife, husband, mom, dad, friend—no one can come except your own Adult. If they should try to come to fix you, they are caretaking you and debilitating your own growth. It isn't helpful for them to try to do that.

It is helpful, though, for them to say, "Do you need me to help you be there for yourself? Do you need my help connecting with your Adult right now?"

We don't need to be overwhelmed by the thought that we are our own responsibility. We can use a lot of help to find our own Adult and to find out what it means to be a Loving Adult to our Inner Child. We absolutely cannot do that alone. We can't learn everything about what it means to be a Loving Adult alone, because we don't have enough information.

We may need a friend or a therapist to give us feedback to learn what we need to do to take care of ourselves. We all need help. As we grow, there's more and more we can do alone, but it often helps to get another perspective. We can't live in a vacuum, and we don't want to end up alone. Sharing our love is the greatest joy there is; the point is to learn to fill ourselves up within so we have that love to share.

LYNN: Now that I'm aware of the process, when I can't come up with the answer, I am willing to trust the darkness. I'm willing to let go of all the rational things I know that I've counted on to get me through my life so far, and just step out into the darkness and wait for the answers.

MARGIE: That's the spiritual aspect. That's like letting it go to God, or the Higher Self, or whatever you want to call that.

When I'm upset, there are two places I go: I go down to my Child, and I go up to my Higher Power. My Adult says to my Inner Child, "What do you need?" and I also go up and ask my Higher Power, "What does it look like to take care of myself?" Sometimes the answer will come through my gut and sometimes it will come through my mind. But it's my Higher Self, God-Self, God, whatever the name, that is giving me the information.

The key is that I have to be open. I have to be asking the question in order to get the answer.

LYNN: I'm beginning to get the feeling of what it's like to be there for my Inner Child, but I don't think I even know what it looks like to take care of myself.

MARGIE: That's true for most people, because that's what we didn't see. Also, we've been taught that taking care of ourselves is selfish. Even if our parents were very loving to us, they probably didn't take care of themselves, and now we've copied that.

To get a picture of what it means to take care of yourself, you can read books or watch others, but you do have to be willing to do this, to really take the action. To become willing, some people have to be in such pain that they can't stand it anymore. Also, people have to come to understand that their happiness lies in connecting their Adult with their Child. You see, unless your heart is open, you can't love others or take in love; and an open heart comes from a clear channel between the Adult and the Inner Child.

LYNN: To get connected, then, who can come to the abandoned Child in the night?

MARGIE: The Inner Adult can come. Once that happens, then other people can also be helpful; but others cannot make your Adult be there, nor can they be the Adult for you. If you're asking someone else to parent your Inner Child, you're not activating your own Loving Adult and you will always feel needy, dependent, victimized, or empty.

LYNN: How can I activate my Loving Adult?

MARGIE: You've activated your Adult by the question itself, because then you are in the intent to learn. You can use any words. Some people ask themselves, "What's the loving behavior?" The key for me is to ask, "What do you need from me?" That's how I'm going to find out what will be the loving thing to do. To get the Adult in gear so we can start connecting or bonding with our Inner Child, we have to move into the intent to learn.

LYNN: If I'm crying in the night and my Adult chooses not to show up, what happens?

MARGIE: You feel alone, abandoned, and powerless. Your Adult has chosen the intent to protect and your Child cannot do anything about it.

The Intent to Protect

At any given moment, we are either in the intent to learn or the intent to protect, experiencing or avoiding, open or closed to our inner experience, our Inner Child.

When the Adult chooses the intent to protect against feeling and taking responsibility for the Child's pain and joy, the Adult disconnects from the Inner Child by closing down the heart. The Child—located in our gut, our solar plexus—has no access to the Adult when the heart is closed down. The Child is therefore inwardly unloved and abandoned, just as we were unloved and abandoned by our parents whenever they closed their hearts to us.

The use of the word *protect* needs some additional explanation here, because protection can be both negative and positive. In the context of Inner Bonding, "protect" is used to refer to the unloving Adult who protects against or avoids feeling the Child's pain and taking responsibility for it. The unloving Adult protects by being either permissive or authoritarian with the Child. Also, the Child feels the pain, but protects against it or avoids it with addictive and codependent behavior.

On the other hand, the positive kind of protection occurs when the Adult acts as a loving Adult/Parent protecting the Child from being alone with its pain by being there with a loving, open heart and an intent to learn. The loving Adult/Parent acts to heal the Child's pain and bring about joy. We will discuss the role of the Adult/Parent more in chapter 5. For now we simply need to remember that the loving Adult protects the Inner Child by taking responsibility for the Child, and the unloving Adult protects itself against taking personal responsibility. Note, however, that the unloving use of the word protection is the one I will refer to unless otherwise stated.

We choose the intent to protect because, as mentioned earlier, we incorrectly believe that we can't handle our own pain, or that healing and good feelings come from outside ourselves. Because most of us also believe that our pain and discomfort come from outside ourselves—from someone disappointing us, disconnecting from us, criticizing, blaming, or withdrawing from us, threatening us in some way, or rejecting us—the ways we protect ourselves are both intrapersonal (within our selves) and interpersonal (with others).

The Ways We Protect

The unloved, abandoned Inner Child, feeling so alone within and lonely in the world, numbs out the pain and fills the emptiness with addictive and codependent behavior, which fall into four different categories: (1) All the ways we deaden ourselves and fill ourselves up from the outside; (2) all the ways we overtly attempt to control another person; (3) all the ways we covertly attempt to control another person; (4) all the ways we resist being controlled by another person or by society.

We move into these protections because we believe they will work for us, that is, we believe they will take away our pain, fear, or discomfort. As long as we believe that our protections are working for us, and as long as our intent is to take away our discomfort rather than learn from it, then we will continue to protect.

Addictions to Substances, Things, Activities, and People

To fill the emptiness and numb the pain, the Child becomes addicted to substances—food, sugar, cigarettes, caffeine, drugs, alcohol; to processes, things, and activities—TV, work, reading, sports, exercise, power, gambling, shopping, money, spending, sleep, shoplifting, ruminating, worry, misery, talking, meditation, talking on the telephone, drama, danger, glamor, religion; and to people—relationships, sex, romance, love, approval. The Child, without a loving Adult to define his or her worth, becomes 'dependent on others' love and approval for a sense of worth. An unloved Inner Child is always codependent, because the Inner Adult has abdicated the job of defining self-worth.

The original parental abandonment and the resulting inner abandonment and intense need for outside approval leads to deep fears of being rejected, abandoned, controlled, and engulfed by others. These fears lead to controlling and resistant behavior, which in turn lead to dysfunctional marriages and dysfunctional families, and on and on in a vicious circle.

Overt Control

We have all learned many ways to attempt to make other people do things our way, most commonly by attempting to instill them with guilt or fear. We use blaming anger, accusations, tantrums, threats, lies, violence, irritation, silent withdrawal of love. We use disapproval, shaming, taunting, criticism, interrogation, blame, teaching and lectures, explanations, righteousness, telling our feelings, pouting, tears. We use both loud and quiet ways to make others feel wrong and untrusting of themselves. When we can either frighten them or undermine their trust in themselves, we have little difficulty in imposing our will on them. We use both verbal and nonverbal ways of letting others know they are wrong or that we disapprove of them.

It's not primarily the words we use that convey the intent to control, but rather the tone of voice or "the look." When the voice has a hard edge in it, or when the mouth is pursed, or when the eyes are hard, the disapproval is communicated—regardless of what the person is saying. We cannot hide our intent. It will always be betrayed by the energy we put out.

Inner Bonding Therapy focuses much of its work on understanding and tuning into the energy in a given situation. Much more is communicated through energy than through words. All people react to energy, but most people don't know they are reacting on this level because they are disconnected from their Inner Child—the aspect that experiences another person's energy.

Inner Bonding Therapy helps people trust in the energy that they are experiencing in any given situation, that is, it helps them trust the experience of their Inner Child. When you experience a protective intent from someone, it is likely to be there—even if the other person denies it; therefore you need to respect and trust your experience. The energy of anger or victim energy is very different from the energy of love, and it is important for all of us to know the difference, in ourselves as well as in others.

Covert Control

Covert control occurs when we attempt to make another like us, love us, or approve of us through some form of compliance, caretaking, niceness, or seductiveness. We may act like we agree with someone in an attempt to control their view of us. We may give gifts in the hope of gaining approval. We may go along with what another wants, even if it's not what we want—such as making love when we don't want to, spending time with someone when we would rather do something else, paying for things we don't want to pay for, not buying things we want to buy, or even having a child when it's not what we want—in the hopes of getting the other's love and approval or at least avoiding disapproval and rejection. We may even convince ourselves that we are being loving when we give ourselves up in these ways—but love has no price tag attached.

> When we give in order to get approval or avoid disapproval, we are manipulating.

Our true *intent* is to take or avoid rather than to give. It is only when we offer something for the pure joy of offering it that we are truly giving from a place of love.

Covert control is often difficult to spot. The only sure way to know another's intent is to tune in to that person's energy. Inner Bonding Therapy helps us to trust that when we are feeling pulled at to give something to another person, it is because the other is manipulating us in a covert way.

For example, in a session with Ingrid, she told me that she felt bad about herself because she felt enraged when her husband was being playful, especially when she was feeling down and she knew he was just trying to cheer her up. I asked her to give me an example.

INGRID: Well, sometimes he stands in front of me naked and shakes his hips, waving his penis at me and smiling. For some reason I feel enraged when he does this, but I can't figure it out.

MARGIE: What do you think he wants?

INGRID: I feel like he wants me to touch him.

MARGIE: Does that feel like he is trying to give to you?

INGRID: No . . . it feels like he's a little boy trying to get my attention and wanting me to make him feel good.

MARGIE: So when you're feeling down, instead of being there for you, could he be trying to get you to be there for him?

INGRID: Yes! That's right! I feel so pulled at by him. And I feel like he really doesn't care about me and how I feel. No wonder I feel so angry!

Ingrid's husband was covertly trying to control her; but because she had not been taught to trust her own feelings or her experience of the energy being transmitted to her, she ended up feeling confused and bad about herself and unsure of how to respond. In addition, when Ingrid felt down, she generally made her husband responsible for her feelings and was then angry when he didn't do it "right." In their system she was on the narcissistic side of codependence, using her anger to control him, and he was on the caretaking side, covertly pulling on her for her approval. (Narcissism versus caretaking will be discussed in detail in the sections that follow.)

Praise is another convert way to control, again depending on the intent of the praise. When someone praises in order to get something—get an image of being a giving person or to be seen as a giving person, expecting praise in return—then the praise is a manipulation. When people praise conditionally, that is, they disapprove next time if things don't go their way, then again the praise is a manipulation. The words of true praise (coming from a giving, inwardly connected place within the person) or manipulative praise (coming from a taking, inwardly disconnected place within) may sound exactly alike, but there is a great difference in the energy with which they are delivered. When you are Inner Bonded yourself, then you can trust your own experience of the subtle energy that passes between people.

Niceness, even the act of seeming to give comfort, can be a covert form of control. Patti was struggling with this in one of her sessions:

PATTI: The other day I was feeling pretty down. I had been reading the book on sexual abuse that you suggested I read, and I was becoming aware of some things that had happened to me as a child that I had brushed aside as unimportant. I was crying when I walked into the bedroom. Roger was there and asked me what was wrong. I told him I was upset by what I was remembering, so he came and put his arm around me. But it didn't feel comforting, and I can't figure out why. This has happened so often with him and I don't understand what I'm feeling.

MARGIE: What was his energy like when he put his arm around you? Did he seem to be centered and coming from a loving Adult, or did he feel weak and empty?

PATTI: Oh, definitely weak and empty. He had a sort of sad little-boy look on his face, but at the same time was acting caring.

MARGIE: So what did you experience as the underlying message of his action?

PATTI: Something like, "See what a good boy I am." Or maybe it was, "I don't like it when you feel bad because then you are not there for me."

MARGIE: Sounds like you felt that he was wanting something from you, from his abandoned Child, rather than giving something to you.

PATTI: Yeah, that's the feeling. He was wanting my approval or wanting me to be okay so I could be the way he wants me to be.

MARGIE: So, instead of feeling comforted, how did you feel?

PATTI: I felt drained. I felt pulled at, like I had to respond the way he wanted me to respond or he would feel rejected. He didn't feel solid or reliable to me. I didn't believe he would be there for me if I didn't give him what he wanted. I was afraid that if I said, "That doesn't feel good," he'd get upset with me, that he didn't *really* want to understand what I was feeling. God! It's just like I felt as a kid! My father would hold me and kiss me in inappropriate ways, but if I tried to push him away he would get so hurt that I would feel guilty. That's just what I felt with Roger— that if I pushed him away, he would get hurt or angry instead of wanting to understand, and then I would feel guilty for hurting him. That makes me feel so trapped.

MARGIE: It sounds like you gave yourself up and let him "comfort" you rather than face your fears about his unloving response to you and the guilt that you feel. If so, isn't that a way you are trying to control his reaction to you?

PATTI: Yes, I guess I am. I guess in letting him comfort me, I'm trying to make sure he doesn't get upset with me. It makes me feel lousy, though.

From the above example, it becomes apparent that both Patti and Roger are using covert forms of control. They are caretaking each other, and neither winds up feeling good.

Caretakers often move into overtly controlling methods such as anger when their caretaking does not gain them the love and appreciation they want. It is important to realize that all of us go back and forth between overt and covert means of controlling whenever we disconnect and move into codependence.

All forms of overt and covert control come from the *false beliefs* that we can control how others behave and feel about us, and that others are responsible for our feelings or we are responsible for theirs. The truth is that we can control others only as long as they allow us to; but we truly have no control over how others feel or behave toward us or themselves.

Each of us decides for ourselves, from our Adult, the kind of person we want to be in any given moment. We decide to be accepting, open, kind, gentle, and warm, or we decide to be judgmental, withdrawn, closed, harsh, punitive, and cold, and our feelings come from this decision. No one else has control over this decision. Yet we like to believe that we can make another be loving to us if only we behave the "right" way.

It is certainly true that if we are open and loving, we stand a better chance of receiving love in return, but there is never any guarantee of that. When we are truly loving, we have no expectation of being loved back and we are not dependent on others being loving back—we are defining our own worth and lovability through being loving. Being loving means not trying to control, not protecting ourselves in any way, a difficult position to take. So most of us are very stuck in our controlling behavior, believing that it will work for us, and unaware that it is causing our misery.

Resistance

When the Inner Adult disconnects from the Inner Child, the Child, needing others' approval, is left vulnerable to being controlled by others. The Child, in an attempt to maintain a sense of integrity, may move into resistant behavior, falsely believing that resisting control maintains integrity. We may find ourselves resisting whenever another person wants something from us, resulting in power struggles with lovers, spouses, parents, children, and coworkers. We may resist through denial, defending, procrastination, rebellion, defensiveness, irresponsibility, indifference, withdrawal, rigidity, forgetfulness, or incompetence.

David felt that he truly loved his wife, Barbara. Yet he rarely acted toward her in caring ways, especially when she directly asked for it. David's primary intent was to avoid being controlled by Barbara rather than to care about her. He interpreted her wanting something from him, or even her wanting something *for* him, as her trying to control him. Barbara often saw David as an unhappy person; but when she'd try to offer him some awareness about his choices, he resisted, believing that she was trying to control him, trying to make him into her.

David had a very controlling mother who did try to make him into her. David reported feeling as if his mother were inside him as a young boy, controlling his every thought and action. He decided early that's how women were, and that to survive with any integrity he would have to act as if he were giving in, but inwardly resist. As an adult David is a "nice" guy, seemingly kind and giving. Yet Barbara complains that he doesn't really give anything of himself, that she always feels shut out. She can't even share her own experiences of growth with him without feeling him stiffen in resistance. She is confused because David appears loving, yet she doesn't feel loved or connected to him.

As long as David's *primary intent* is to avoid being controlled, and as long as he *believes* that his wife's primary intent is to control him, then he is stuck by his resistant unloving behavior. Were he to shift his belief about his wife, or were it to become more important to him to be a loving person and be open to learning with his Inner Child and with Barbara than to avoid being controlled by her, then his entire life could shift into aliveness and joy. Until then he is stuck with his unhappiness.

The issue here is not whether or not Barbara is trying to control David. Certainly some of her behavior is controlling, such as offering him suggestions when he has not asked for them. Even if Barbara's primary intent were to control David, his resistant behavior is unloving toward himself and Barbara. Loving behavior would be to move into an intent to learn and examine whether or not her suggestions were valid for him, regardless of her intent, or to explore with her the dynamics between them. To categorically resist perpetuates the unloving behavior between them.

Resisting the intent to learn can create one of the most insidious difficulties in relationships. One partner, Barbara, wants the closeness and connection of learning with David and pulls in various ways to get it—through teaching, blaming, tears, and so on. David believes that opening to learning with Barbara is a capitulation and that he will totally lose himself if he does, so he resists the very thing that can increase his self-esteem to the point where he would not be controlled by another. As long as Barbara pulls on David to be open to learning and David resists, they are stuck in a power struggle.

Consequences of the Intent to Protect

Some people who are disconnected function primarily from their Adult. These are take-charge people who know how to get things done but are generally out of touch with their joy and aliveness and often wonder why life is worth living. Other people function primarily from their Child. These people may be highly creative and charismatic, but have a hard time putting their ideas into form. In addition, because they have no functioning Adult to place appropriate limits, they may harm themselves through their addictions and others with their angry or violent behavior.

All of the above protections, and the beliefs that fuel them, create the arena for the addictive/codependent relationships that are rampant in our society. The basis of all dependence is the emptiness and aloneness within that comes from the disconnection between the Inner Adult and the Inner Child. When two disconnected, dependent people get together, they create a codependent relationship. And since most people have one or more substance or process addictions, their codependent relationships will continue to foster each other's addictions.

Codependence

Codependence exists any time the Inner Adult abdicates responsibility for the Inner Child.

Codependent behavior falls into two distinct categories: (1) narcissistic or "taking" and (2) empathic or "caretaking." We operate from the overtly controlling narcissistic side of codependence when we come from the belief: "You are responsible for my feelings." We operate from the covertly controlling caretaking side of codependence when we come from the belief: "I am responsible for your feelings." Figure 19 illustrates these two aspects of codependence.

The following concepts regarding the nature of codependence were written and developed by Dr. Erika Chopich[1]:

> If we think of ourselves as a diamond, then we can recognize that we have many facets that all come together to create our shining selves. Each facet is a different aspect of our personality. There are two facets in particular that become very important when we look at how we are in relationships and in the world. Those two aspects are narcissism and empathy. It may be helpful to think of narcissism as Self and empathy as Other. *Both aspects of us are very necessary to our personality, but since they are opposites of each other we need to have them in balance.* We can draw that on a continuum. The dot in the center represents a balanced individual. If we look at ourselves honestly, however, we will notice that we generally tend to lean either toward the narcissistic side or the empathy side.

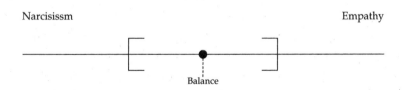

Narcisissm   Empathy

Balance

Figure 19. Core Shame-Based Belief: I Am Bad/Wrong/Defective

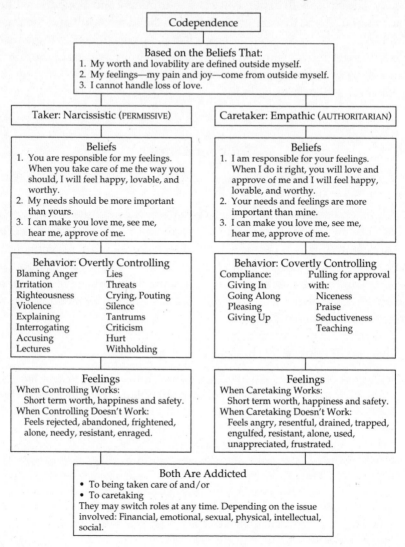

Codependence

Based on the Beliefs That:
1. My worth and lovability are defined outside myself.
2. My feelings—my pain and joy—come from outside myself.
3. I cannot handle loss of love.

Taker: Narcissistic (PERMISSIVE)	Caretaker: Empathic (AUTHORITARIAN)
Beliefs	**Beliefs**
1. You are responsible for my feelings. When you take care of me the way you should, I will feel happy, lovable, and worthy.	1. I am responsible for your feelings. When I do it right, you will love and approve of me and I will feel happy, lovable, and worthy.
2. My needs should be more important than yours.	2. Your needs and feelings are more important than mine.
3. I can make you love me, see me, hear me, approve of me.	3. I can make you love me, see me, hear me, approve of me.

Behavior: Overtly Controlling		Behavior: Covertly Controlling	
Blaming Anger	Lies	Compliance:	Pulling for approval
Irritation	Threats	Giving In	with:
Righteousness	Crying, Pouting	Going Along	Niceness
Violence	Silence	Pleasing	Praise
Explaining	Tantrums	Giving Up	Seductiveness
Interrogating	Criticism		Teaching
Accusing	Hurt		
Lectures	Withholding		

Feelings	Feelings

When Controlling Works:
  Short term worth, happiness and safety.
When Controlling Doesn't Work:
  Feels rejected, abandoned, frightened, alone, needy, resistant, enraged.
	When Caretaking Works:
	  Short term worth, happiness and safety.
	When Caretaking Doesn't Work:
	  Feels angry, resentful, drained, trapped, engulfed, resistant, alone, used, unappreciated, frustrated.

Both Are Addicted
• To being taken care of and/or
• To caretaking
They may switch roles at any time. Depending on the issue involved: Financial, emotional, sexual, physical, intellectual, social.

Most of the clients I see in my office lie in the space between the two brackets. That is, most people who have difficulty in relationships are out of balance to a certain extent. They have either too much narcissism and little empathy or too much empathy and little healthy narcissism.

Too much narcissism makes us self-centered and overtly controlling. We tend to view and define ourselves by how our relationships make us feel. We are pushed to make others responsible for what we feel. If we feel good, it is because the other person has pleased us; if we feel bad or upset it is because of the other person's behavior. When we interact with someone and we are being narcissistic, we tend to focus only on what *we* feel every moment, having no empathy for what the other feels.

For example, I have a client, Ted, a young man in his thirties. He's complained of having poor success in relationships—the women in his life always seemed to leave him. As we explored his interactions with women in more depth, he told me that he has a vigilant awareness of everything that happens when he is with a woman. He "reads into" all of her actions. He anxiously wonders what it means if her hand touches his, or if she looks at him a certain way. He judges and analyzes constantly whether or not she *really* cares. His whole focus is on himself, with little attention to seeing or caring about her.

On a more subtle level, people with too much narcissism rarely hear what is being said to them because they are too busy thinking of what to say next. They are out of touch with the other person and come from a place of wanting to get love rather than being loving. They are on a lifelong search for the right person to take the duties of caring for their own Inner Child.

On the other hand, too much empathy is just as dysfunctional. The people with too much empathy are generally not in touch with what *they* feel because they lack any healthy narcissism. They are too focused on the other person's feelings and ready at a moment's notice to take responsibility for the other person. In other words, they are dedicated to caretaking—taking care of the other's Inner Child and ignoring their own. As a result of this choice, they very quickly lose all sense of self in a relationship.

Janet, a client of mine, feels her husband's feelings to such depth that whenever he is angry at her, her body hurts. So she sets out to please him and get him happy again so he will feel better. In the meantime she is totally unaware of her own pain.

In order to have a healthy relationship, both parties must have both aspects in balance. How do we do this? The answer is in developing a loving relationship between our Adult and Inner Child. If we are balanced within ourselves, if our Inner relationship is healthy and fulfilling, we will be balanced outwardly. In the first of the previous examples, Ted has no functioning loving Adult to validate who he is, so his Inner Child must seek that from women, which is the narcissistic position (Self). In the second example, Janet is out of touch with how badly her Inner Child feels when her husband screams at her. Her Adult is focused only on him (Other). In both cases the lack of balance between empathy and narcissism came from the poor relationship between each person's Adult and Inner Child.

You may be thinking that being a little out of balance is somewhat common, and you are right, it is. What is being examined is the nature of everyday dysfunction and exploring ways to resolve the difficulties. However, let's see what happens when a person's narcissism or empathy is taken to an extreme. If taken far enough, we would see a clinical picture of mental disorder and even psychosis. On the narcissistic side of our continuum, we would see the violent maladies such as antisocial personality disorders, paranoid schizophrenia, and so on, which often lead to physical and sexual abuse, rape, and murder. On the empathy side we would see the opposite, nonviolent end of the spectrum such as catatonia, major depressive disorders, and dissociative disorders. That is not to say that imbalance causes these maladies, but that the imbalance describes them.

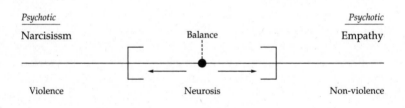

Fortunately, most of us only have to deal with the daily experiences of dysfunctional relationships. Some of us only need look to what our *tendency* toward imbalance is and then we can create better, healing relationships by loving our Inner Child better.

Protections: A Vicious Circle

People come into therapy or seek other forms of help because they are suffering from the consequences of their inner disconnection and resulting protective codependent behavior. As individuals they may be suffering from anxiety, depression, guilt, loneliness, or illness. As couples they may be experiencing fights, distance, and a lack of fun, passion, sexuality, and love. They may be caught in endless power struggles over money, children, time, chores, and sex. Power struggles are an inevitable consequence of the need, dependence on, or addiction to control and the resistance to being controlled.

All protective addictive/codependent behaviors lead to feeling alone, thus reinforcing the addictions and codependent behaviors to fill up the emptiness created by them and by the original inner disconnection from the Self. This pattern leads to low self-esteem, thus reinforcing the original belief in one's unworthiness and unlovability, a vicious circle.

The charts on the following pages, from *Healing Your Aloneness*, sum up the material presented in the preceding two chapters:

Figure 20. Inner Adult Disconnecting from Inner Child

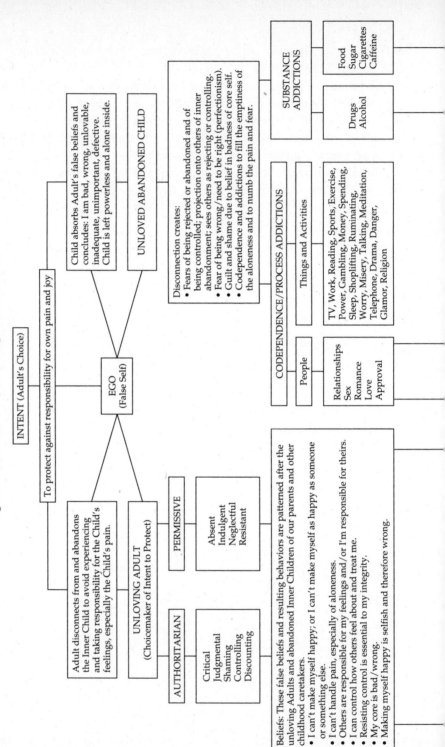

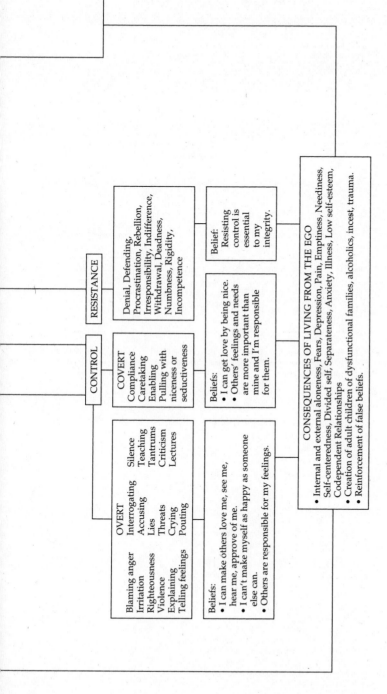

CONTROL

RESISTANCE

OVERT

Blaming anger   Interrogating   Silence
Irritation   Accusing   Teaching
Righteousness   Lies   Tantrums
Violence   Threats   Criticism
Explaining   Crying   Lectures
Telling feelings   Pouting

Beliefs:
• I can make others love me, see me, hear me, approve of me.
• I can't make myself as happy as someone else can.
• Others are responsible for my feelings.

COVERT

Compliance
Caretaking
Enabling
Pulling with niceness or seductiveness

Beliefs:
• I can get love by being nice.
• Others' feelings and needs are more important than mine and I'm responsible for them.

Denial, Defending, Procrastination, Rebellion, Irresponsibility, Indifference, Withdrawal, Deadness, Numbness, Rigidity, Incompetence

Belief: Resisting control is essential to my integrity.

CONSEQUENCES OF LIVING FROM THE EGO
• Internal and external aloneness, Fears, Depression, Pain, Emptiness, Neediness, Self-centeredness, Divided self, Separateness, Anxiety, Illness, Low self-esteem, Codependent Relationships
• Creation of adult children of dysfunctional families, alcoholics, incest, trauma.
• Reinforcement of false beliefs.

Figure 21. Inner Adult Connecting to Inner Child

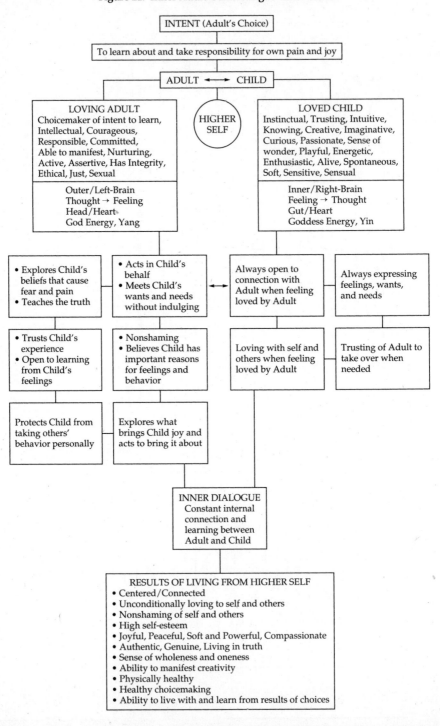

CHAPTER 5

Heading for Home: Parenting, Reparenting, and Staying Bonded

The child survives within us, joined to us for life: perennially the child, fully alive, an inner possibility awaiting our full and conscious acknowledgment.

Reclaiming the Inner Child
JEREMIAH ABRAMS

Baby Mary and Baby Johnny are born into rooms filled with soft, dim lights and soft music, or perhaps they are each born into a pool of warm water. Their mothers are fully alert, having been given no drugs. Their cords are cut only after they stop throbbing and the babies have received all the blood and oxygen. Their mothers, connected and in their own Higher Selves, hold them close at their breasts, looking directly into their eyes, sending Mary and Johnny their deepest love.

After birth the babies stay with their mothers continually, nursing and sleeping and feeling their warmth and love. Mary and Johnny receive a clear message from their mother, their father, and everyone else present: "You are lovable and you are important."

Throughout their infancies the babies' needs for food, warmth, comfort, and love are met. They are held continuously throughout the day, going with Mom or Dad to work or chores or being held by another loving caregiver. At night they sleep next to Mom, nursing whenever they need to, always feeling safe and loved. They are held skin to skin some of the time. Both Mom and Dad spend close, connected time with them. The babies don't cry often, but when they do their cries are heeded and taken seriously. They both receive clear messages: "I am worthy of being loved" and "I have power in getting my own needs met."

When we were small, at any given moment either we felt loved and bonded to our parents, or we felt unloved and disconnected from them. Whatever we experienced then is now reflected within: Either (1) our Inner Child feels loved and bonded to our Inner Adult, which occurs when the Adult is consistently open to learning about the Child's feelings, wants, and needs; or (2) our Child feels unloved, abandoned, and alone inside, which occurs when our Adult chooses to avoid responsibility for our Child's feelings and needs.

As Mary and Johnny become toddlers and want to do things for themselves, their parents no longer rush in to help them with everything. They continue to protect their health and safety as they gradually allow them to do more and more things for themselves, and make more of their own decisions. As a result Mary and Johnny each receive a clear message: "I am adequate and capable."

At the same time, Mary's and Johnny's parents are taking more time for themselves, both individually and together. The toddlers see both of their parents working at satisfying jobs and enjoying interesting hobbies. They see them able to be alone with themselves and able to share their concerns and joys with each other. They see their parents playing, laughing, having fun with each other and with friends. They see them respecting each other and each other's freedom and boundaries. They also see their parents experience sadness and confront their pain. The parents are there for each other and for their children when they, too, need comfort and love. Both of their parents are emotionally available to their own feelings. Through the parents' role-modeling, the children receive a number of clear messages: "I am responsible for my own happiness and I have the right to it." "I am capable of making myself happy and taking care of myself." "I can handle pain." "Men and women are equal in their intellectual and emotional capabilities."

When our Inner Child is feeling consistently loved by our Inner Adult, he or she is a wondrous being—trusting, creative, imaginative, curious, passionate, playful, energetic, enthusiastic, spontaneous, soft, sensitive, sensual, with an incredible sense of wonder and aliveness. Delighted just to be alive, he or she is open and receptive to new ideas and experiences.

Most of us have experienced these feelings only briefly in our lives, perhaps when first falling in love or for a few days after an intense workshop experience. These experiences tend to open the heart for the moment; but the heart closes down again when fears and false beliefs come up and the Adult protects against feeling the pain, rather than opens to learning about the beliefs causing it.

> *As Mary and Johnny become verbal and begin to express their feelings, wants, and needs, they find that their parents take them seriously. When Mary complains about a nursery school teacher, her mother or father actively responds and talks to the teacher, helping remedy the situation. When Johnny is afraid to go to a particular friend's house, his parents investigate and discover some family dysfunction occurring at that house. Because Mary and Johnny experience their parents trusting their experience and feelings, they receive a clear message: "I can trust myself. I can trust my feelings and my experience."*

Because Mary and Johnny are being brought up in an atmosphere of love, caring, compassion, and trust, with adults who role-model loving behavior to themselves and to their children, they maintain a strong connection to their own Higher Selves. They learn to value themselves as a child; they also learn what it means to act as a loving Adult, to themselves and others. As a result of this inner connection, they grow up feeling lovable, adequate, both soft and powerful, able to experience fun and joy, and able to give and receive love.

Obviously this story is an ideal, something none of us experienced. Most of us had to work hard to maintain any sense of inner connection, and many of us completely disconnected from our Higher Selves, moving into the intent to protect as a result of our childhood experiences. A different scenario was true for us. Maybe it went something like this:

> *Dick and Jane are each being born in a hospital delivery room. The lights are bright; the room is cold. The doctor is in a hurry and pulls them out with forceps. Their mothers are semi-drugged or completely drugged. The babies enter the world and immediately feel an absence of love. After being wiped clean they are shuffled off to a nursery, and they don't see their mothers again for at least twelve hours. They are likely to draw a number of conclusions:*

"I'm not important. I'm not lovable. I'm not capable." ("The doctor had to pull me out—I couldn't do it myself.")

If you believe that a newborn infant is too young to draw these conclusions, you have only to speak with people who have been rebirthed and remember their birth. They clearly recall the conclusions they drew. As Stanislav Grof points out in The Holotropic Mind:

People often get in touch with very accurate details about their original birth experiences. Without previous intellectual knowledge of the circumstances of their delivery, people can discover that they were born with a forceps, or in the breech position, or with the umbilical cord wrapped around their neck. They can often recognize the type of anesthesia that was used during the delivery. And not infrequently, they can relive in detail specific events that happened after they were born. In many instances, we had the opportunity to verify the accuracy of such reports.[1]

Dick and Jane are in the hospital for three days, during which time they are brought to their mothers periodically for a bottle. The rest of the time they are in the nursery. Once at home, they are left alone much of the time. Often their cries are unheard or unheeded. Often they are left for seemingly endless periods of time, feeling hungry, frightened, uncomfortable, and alone. Sometimes they cry themselves to sleep. They conclude: "I am powerless to get my needs met." They also conclude: "Adults neglect children because children are not important," which leads to their own Inner Adult neglecting their own Inner Child.

When our Inner Child feels consistently unloved by our Inner Adult, the Child's false beliefs, adopted in childhood when parents were unloving, are reinforced—beliefs that we are bad, wrong, unlovable, unimportant, inadequate, defective in some way. As children we all adopted these shame-based beliefs in varying degrees in response to what we perceived as being unloved by our parents. When our Inner Adult is unloving, we perpetuate these false beliefs that create low self-esteem, and our low self-esteem governs all our behavior when we are with others and when we are alone.

Jane's mother is a cold, distant, angry, and non-nurturing woman. Jane experiences repeated rejection from her mother. Her mother always seems angry and it always seems to be Jane's fault. Jane learns that when she is a very good girl and does everything her mother tells her to do, then her mother doesn't yell so much.

Jane's father is a much warmer and more nurturing person, but his warmth is always tinged with sexual energy. Jane wants her father's love, but is terrified by his sexual energy and by the inappropriate ways he sometimes holds and kisses her. Yet when she pulls away from him, he gets so hurt. So she lets him kiss her on the mouth and hold her too close, even though she doesn't like it.

Jane is a sensitive child and deeply feels her parents' pain. As a result of her mother's anger and underlying pain and her father's hurt, she draws a conclusion: "I am responsible for my parents' feelings." As a result of her success in learning to control their feelings and behavior to a certain extent, she draws another conclusion: "I can control how others feel and how they treat me." In addition, as a result of her parents' lack of any attempt to understand her feelings and needs, and as a result of her mother's blame and her father's hurt, she draws another conclusion: "Other people's feelings and needs are more important than mine. I have to give up what I want to please them. Then they will love me and I will feel worthy." Jane is becoming codependent, learning to depend on caretaking.

Dick's mother is a highly controlling woman who completely centers her life around her children. Empty inside, she tries to fill herself with her children. She is overly affectionate in a very smothering, seductive way. She tries to meet all of Dick's needs before he even has a chance to ask, and expects his love and devotion in return. Dick feels both invaded and taken care of by her. He concludes, "I can't take care of myself," and "Women want to control me."

Dick's father is withdrawn, distant, and alcoholic. He is a weak, pathetic man. Dick concludes, "Men are weak, women are strong. Therefore I am weak and basically helpless. I need a woman to make me happy." Dick is beginning his addiction to relationships.

Neither of Dick's parents are there for him when he is in pain. His father ignores him and his mother distracts him. In addition, he sees his father drown his own pain in alcohol. He concludes: "I can't handle my pain." He disconnects from his own pain and opens the door to substance addictions.

Dick learns early from both his parents that his feelings and perceptions are shameful and not to be trusted. When he says, "Mommy, how come Daddy doesn't love me?" she says, "Don't be ridiculous. Of course he loves you." When Dick says "The

*teacher yelled at me for no good reason," his mother replies, "Well,
you must have done something wrong." When Dick says, "Mommy,
why were you and Daddy fighting?" his mom answers, "We
weren't fighting." So Dick gives up believing that he knows what
he knows and sees what he sees, and starts to rely on others to tell
him how things are.*

Of course, more extreme unloving things could have happened to Dick
and Jane. They could have been physically or overtly sexually abused.
They could have been physically abandoned, rather than emotionally
abandoned by one or both parents. They could have suffered the death of
a parent and been left to deal with it alone.

Predominantly unloving environments, including intentional unloving
behaviors as well as behaviors that we perceive as unloving, create the
false beliefs of the ego and lead to the disconnection from the Higher Self.

Most of us were betrayed in childhood in one way or another. Any
unloving act by a parent who is supposed to love and protect us is a betrayal. Many of us had no safe place to be, no place where we could be
completely ourselves and know that we would be loved. Our physical and
emotional boundaries, our personal integrity, were violated in so many
ways that *many of us lost touch with feeling violated, which allows us to continue to be violated and to violate others as adults.* It is in this unloving environment that we learned how to be an unloving Adult to our Inner Child.

The Importance of Bonding

The most important experience for parents and their newborn babies is
that of bonding—that deep, spiritual experience of connection that takes
away aloneness, reassuring their children that they won't be overwhelmed
and die. Bonding is so important that when the infant cannot bond to a person because there is no person available, the infant will bond to an animal
or even to an object. Without bonding, the infant will die. Extremely abused
infants often dissociate and split off into multiple personalities to avoid
being alone within; or they bond to their experience of a spiritual being,
and it is this bonding that keeps them alive even through unbearable abuse.

Our culture has not understood the importance of bonding. For years
we took newborn infants away from their mothers for the first twenty-four
hours to make sure they were physically healthy, not realizing the importance of those first hours to the bonding experience. Twenty-five years ago,
when I had my first child and they took him away from me "for his own
good," I thought I would die from being away from him. Some primal part
of me knew that I needed to be with him and he needed to be with me. It

felt as if they were ripping my heart out as they took him away. I cried and cried, but there was nothing I could do. Those were the hospital rules and I was powerless against them. Had I listened to my inner knowing, perhaps I could have found another way to have my baby, but I had not yet learned to trust my own instincts and intuition.

Because most of us had inadequate bonding with our parents, resulting from a lack of nurturing or from physical, emotional, sexual, or spiritual abuse, we never learned to bond to ourselves—to the Child within us.[2] Our parents were our role models; how they treated themselves and how they treated us became the model for how we now treat ourselves.

Our task now is to lovingly reparent our Inner Child.

Becoming a Loving Adult/Parent to Your Inner Child

Some of us had parents who deliberately tried to hurt us, probably because they had been badly hurt themselves. Those of us who have suffered from extreme physical, sexual, and emotional abuse have a big challenge trying to create a loving Inner Adult. Most of us had parents who tried hard to love us and did the best they could. Some of our parents who didn't love themselves didn't act in loving ways to us. Other parents acted as lovingly as possible to their children, but they didn't act in loving ways toward themselves, and their behavior toward themselves is the role model we've copied.

Reparenting

For those of us who still suffer from the wounds of childhood, one of our jobs today as a loving Adult is to avoid wasting our precious time blaming others. Blame never feels good inside. It perpetuates the feeling that we are powerless victims and only prolongs our pain. It is always our ego—our unloving Adult or abandoned Child—who blames. When our loving Adult is there, the Adult says, "Okay, this has happened. Now what do we need to do about it?" That's the Adult beginning the process of *reparenting* the Inner Child's pain.

By reparenting our Inner Child, we can release and heal the pain from the past. The loving Inner Adult reparents by learning about, nurturing, and supporting the wants and needs of the Inner Child. When we are open to learning about the old, stored-up pain and shame, we are being loving to ourselves. Our loving Inner Adult has the courage to look within and to know ourselves, and is committed to healing the wounded Inner Child. This healing through reparenting is the way to bring freedom and joy into the present.

What Kind of Parent Have We Been to Our Inner Child?

We may or may not still suffer pain from our childhoods. Still, we must *parent* our Inner Child on an ongoing basis. Depending on our own parents, the other caregivers in our early lives, and our own conclusions based on their examples, we have adopted a mode of parenting ourselves, whether we are aware of it or not. An example of this can be seen if you watch children at play. When one child is playing parent to other children, he or she will mimic the way the parents act and use the words the parents use to scold, comfort, ridicule, or praise.

If, as adults, we have disconnected from our feelings to protect ourselves from pain, then our Inner Adult/Parent has not been loving to our Inner Child. An unloving Adult/Parent's behavior generally falls into two categories: authoritarian and permissive. When the Adult is being authoritarian, it criticizes, judges, shames, controls, and discounts the Inner Child. In terms of a person's behavior, this means that when you feel afraid, you're very likely to tell yourself to stop being cowardly, weak, and so on. When you fail, you're likely to harass yourself for it: "How could I be so stupid! I'm always making a mess of things." Or, when someone is blaming you or pulling on you to take responsibility for their feelings, you tell yourself that your wants and needs aren't important and that if you don't do what the other person wants, you are being selfish, mean, or irresponsible.

When the Adult is being permissive, it is absent, indulgent, and neglectful, and resists meeting the needs of the Inner Child. If your Inner Adult/Parent is permissive and you are afraid, instead of addressing the fear directly, you may indulge your feelings by saying something like, "I feel terrible. I deserve to have another drink." When you fail, your permissive Inner Parenting may be absent or neglectful of your hurt feelings: "I didn't want to finish that project anyway." And then indulgent again: "I think I'll go buy something to cheer up." Or, the indulgent Inner Adult/Parent may allow you to yell at, threaten, or physically violate others to get your needs met.

Accepting the Job of Being Our Own Inner Parent

When people choose to disconnect from their feelings, they give up the job of being their own Inner Parent. Why does this happen?

One reason we don't lovingly parent ourselves is that our Adult doesn't want the job—we want someone else to make us okay. Other reasons are that we don't think we can do it, or we think our happiness lies in somebody doing it for us. We may have a belief system that says, "I can't make myself truly happy or truly give myself self-esteem." We're afraid, then, that we will fail or that we don't know how to be our own Loving Adult/Parent.

When we don't want the job of parenting our Inner Child because we think another person can do it better, it is helpful to visualize having an actual child of our own and deciding to give up that child because we see others around us who can be a better mother or father to our child. But if we gave away the child, would that really be in the child's best interests? Or would the child end up feeling rejected and thrown away? In the case of the Inner Child, the choice is, Do we want to throw ourselves away?

On an internal level, we are our one and only possible parent, regardless of how our parents have treated us. Nobody else can do for us what we have to do for ourselves, yet we stubbornly insist on believing they can. We want to believe there is somebody out there who can give us our worth. We believe that if only they will love us enough, value us enough, then we'll finally have our self-esteem.

We don't want to believe that this is an "inside job," and that we're the only ones who can do it. But if we keep looking around for someone else to take over our Inner Adult/Parent role, we're going to look forever.

We All Need Two Parents

All of us face the job of becoming a loving mother and father to our Inner Child. The loving Adult is both father and mother to the Inner Child, regardless of whether we are a man or a woman. Just because you are a man does not mean you cannot mother the little boy within you, and just because you are a woman does not mean you cannot father your inner little girl. It is the mother part of us that engages in the nurturing inner dialogue with the Child, exploring the false beliefs and asking for the truth and the loving behavior from our Higher Power. It is the father part of us that takes loving action in the world on behalf of the Inner Child. Just as a single parent can nurture, provide for, and protect his or her child, so we each have the capacity to do that for ourselves.

If we do not accept the responsibility of being both the father and mother to our Inner Child, then our Child will seek elsewhere for someone to do it. The woman who refuses to protect herself in the world will seek out a man, a daddy, to do it for her and will establish a codependent relationship with him. The man who refuses to look inward and be responsible for his own feelings will seek out a woman, a mommy, to do it for him, and will likewise become dependent on her.

One of my clients, Madeline, is an attorney with a successful practice. Her mother was physically abusive to her and her father was away in the military most of the time. When he was there, he didn't protect her from her mother's abuse. Madeline always looked for men who would protect her in the world, and that was the root of her codependency. When she didn't have a man, she'd feel alone and unprotected. Madeline's life changed dramatically when she realized that now she could be the father-protector to her own Inner Child's fear.

When we accept the job of reparenting and parenting ourselves, we will eventually feel whole and full inside. Then, instead of looking for a surrogate parent to make us feel complete, we will create relationships based on a desire to share our love and our lives.

Learning to Love Your Inner Child

Once you are willing to assume responsibility for being a loving Adult/Parent, you have the responsibility for loving your Inner Child—even if you don't think the Child is particularly lovable yet. That's not as simplistic as it may sound: If you've always thought of yourself as weak, clumsy, not good-looking or appealing, not talented or smart, then being a loving Adult/Parent means shifting the way you see yourself. Now you will begin to view yourself through the eyes of gentle acceptance, as you would your actual child.

One way to begin is to imagine how you would feel if you were to adopt a little boy, a four-year-old, for example. You've decided on adoption because somewhere within that child is a lovable human being; and if you can be there in a loving way for the child, eventually he will feel and internalize your love and then shift his behavior. But because he was abused and abandoned and is very angry and may be withdrawn, it may be months before this little child will even respond to you.

Now let's say that the child you have decided to adopt is your Inner Child, your own wounded, angry, and withdrawn natural self. Transfer your feelings for the adopted child to your Inner Child. Now what do you do? To start with, as a loving Adult/Parent, you create a loving space or environment for your Inner Child. No criticism, no threats of abandonment, no shaming. Only the loving Adult/Parent words that you would choose to say to any adopted child. The job of the Loving Adult is to validate, accept, and honor the natural Child while healing the wounds of the Child.

My client Lorrie shared the following experience with me. One evening she had been out with friends, and had tripped going up the steps into the movie theater:

> It was so embarrassing! All night I kept making excuses about how clumsy I always am and how ridiculous I must have looked. Then, at home, I still

felt so bad I tried to reparent my feelings. I said, "I'm sorry you felt so ashamed. One fall doesn't mean you always trip. Clumsy people aren't rejected as friends, anyway."

I kept trying to say to myself the things a loving Parent would say. When I began, I didn't have much confidence. But then I started really trying to see myself through loving eyes. After a while my shame subsided and I truly felt comforted.

Finding Your Own Value and Worth

Part of learning to love and value yourself is learning what is uniquely valuable and lovable about who you truly are. We need to learn to value ourselves, not only for our particular talents and personality, but for our essential selves. I believe that our essential beingness is love, that we are a manifestation of God/Love, and our essential worth lies in that fact. It is the Adult/Parent's job to hold up the mirror so the Inner Child can start to see who he or she is and learn to value his or her own being. Remember, a mirror does not selectively show only the negatives, the flaws and limitations. A mirror also shows the positives, the sweetness, kindness, lovingness, as well as the talents and potential. Just as truly loving parents accept and love their actual child *just for being,* regardless of how handsome or winsome the child is, your Adult can accept all that you are and love you just the same.

Our Adult/Parent needs to value who we are essentially, our particular talents and particular form of intelligence. What is valuable about your particular personality, your creativity, your productivity, your way of being in the world?

Melinda was very depressed and suicidal. When she was a child, her father had beaten her while her mother watched. When Melinda began Inner Bonding Therapy, I asked her to speak as her Inner Child and say what it was that her Child needed. "I need to feel special," she answered. But when I asked her Adult, "What is special about this Child?" she answered, "Nothing." Then we began to talk about what might be special. Was she kind? Was she loving? Does she care about people? Is she generous? Does she paint? Does she like to cook? Is she handy at fixing things? We began to talk about valuing those things she inherently is, as well as those things she likes to do or does well. Then we explored why she didn't value her own attributes and why she always saw others' abilities and beingness as being more valuable than her own. Her Adult, being patterned after her parents, was seeing herself through their eyes instead of seeing the truth.

Valuing Your Own Kind of Intelligence

Many of us hinge our self-esteem on whether or not we see ourselves as intelligent. Because our culture places so much importance on the kind of intellect that relates to academic achievement, we base our judgment on how well we did in school. Therefore people with left-brain intelligence— talented in math, science, and logical pursuits— usually feel good about themselves in the world (although not necessarily within), because their minds were well suited for school-related tasks. People with right-brain intellects, who are stronger with creative efforts and intuitive wisdom, often do not feel good about themselves because they were shamed in school or by parents.

There are, without question, many kinds of intelligence, and it is very important for all of us to find our own particular strengths. When you find yourself stubbornly resisting acceptance of yourself with "I'm not as good as . . ." comparisons, that is an important signal to explore in an Inner Bonding dialogue why you feel this way. The Adult's job is to reflect to the Inner Child that his or her form of intelligence is just as important as anyone else's. Still, there is the question, How can you make your Inner Child a believer, both in the Adult's words and in the Child's worth or value?

Taking Action on Your Child's Behalf to Build Self-Worth

It takes more than just discovery of the reasons for feeling inferior. It takes action on the Inner Child's behalf. For instance, if you tell your Child you respect her, but then stay in an interaction where she's being verbally abused and do nothing to protect her, she's never going to believe you. But if someone starts yelling at you and you say, "This is my boundary. I don't allow people to yell at me. I am leaving until you are willing to talk," then your Inner Child begins to believe, "I must really be worth something— my feelings are valid enough reason for my Adult to take action on their behalf."

Once again, the situation can be seen clearly with an actual child. If the child is being abused and the mother watches but does nothing, the child is not going believe the mother when she says, "Oh, I love you so much." But if the mother stands up and says, "You are not going to harm my child. We will have to leave if you do that again," then the child believes the mother's words and believes in the mother's love.

Taking action that respects the Inner Child feelings is the only way to prove the feelings are valuable.

Taking action is the only way to build your self-esteem.

Taking Responsibility for Your Inner Child's Feelings

People often ask what it means to take responsibility for their Inner Child's feelings. If your own daughter came home from school with hurt feelings, who is she supposed to go to for help and comfort? Would you tell her to go away? Or that there's nothing to cry about? What would you like to have heard your parent say when you were hurting? Now you can say those words to your Inner Child.

If you are upset about something and you want to understand it, you can ask your Inner Child what is going on within you. Here's an example of Alice's Inner Bonding dialogue, which occurred in one of our women's groups:

ADULT: What are you upset about?

INNER CHILD: Bill continues to be late for every date.

ADULT: That's really upsetting you. What do you feel when that happens?

INNER CHILD: I feel my time is being violated. I'm not being respected.

ADULT: I really understand that. What would you like me to do to help the situation?

INNER CHILD: Well, I'd like you to tell him that if it happens again, I'm not going to set up any more dates, because it feels too bad. I don't want to be disrespected in this manner.

When Jessica, another member of the group heard this dialogue, she said, "Boy, would I like to say something like that to my boss!" I asked why she thought she couldn't and she said, "I'm just too afraid!" So we had the following dialogue between us. Jessica spoke as her Inner Child, while I spoke as her Adult:

INNER CHILD: I'm too afraid to tell him!

ADULT: That's not your job. You get behind me. It's always the Adult's job to speak for the Child.

INNER CHILD: But what if my fear overpowers you, the Adult?

ADULT: What are you afraid of? What do you think your boss will do?

INNER CHILD: Get angry, I guess, because I know he's not going to fire me.
      ADULT: What would you like me to do to take care of you with the anger? What do you need from me?
INNER CHILD: I guess I need not to cry. I cry too easily. I can't cry at work or I won't be seen as someone who can do the job.
      ADULT: I understand your pain and you have a right to it. You also have a right to cry, but I understand why you don't want to cry in front of this person. So what would you like me to do? Would you like me to say, "Excuse me" and go to the bathroom so I can be there for your pain?
INNER CHILD: Well, maybe. But I'd really like you to tell him not to yell at me.
      ADULT: I'd be willing to tell him that it's not okay for him to yell because it's too upsetting and you just can't work that way. I could say, "I want you to know that yelling is not acceptable and I'm going to walk away now. When you're ready to talk without yelling, then let's talk."

The dialogues above illustrate two points. First, when the Adult does the speaking in the world for the Inner Child, the Child feels safe and loved. Quite often, however, the Child is afraid to have his or her feelings exposed. Thus it can be very helpful to visualize the Child behind the Adult, as the Adult takes action on behalf of the Child's feelings. When Jessica was afraid to take action, she was trying to speak from her Inner Child's vulnerability ("I'm afraid I'll cry.") instead of from her Adult's strength ("I want you to know yelling is not acceptable.")

The other important point is that in both cases, the action planned to meet the Inner Child's needs establishes the individual's personal boundaries. When you set your boundaries and then firmly stand your ground, it's a very powerful thing to do. If you keep the Child behind you—not taking things personally and not getting intimidated, while you assert your boundaries and state your truth—that is loving behavior. It certainly promotes your own growth and sense of empowerment, and you've done all you can to affect a negative situation. Now it's up to the other in the interaction to choose to be open to learning or closed and protected.

If that other person retaliates by being defensive rather than with a learning response, then your challenge is to stay connected or bonded in that confrontation or conflict. When you can do that—stay open in external conflict and connected within—you will still have ups and downs in your life, but your sense of self-worth and inner power will endure.

Heading for "Home": The Bonded or Connected State

What we're headed for here is Inner Bonding, the state where the Adult and the Inner Child are connected. When we are connected, we feel grounded, centered, secure—the feelings we associate with feeling that we're finally "home"—the ideal state, the safe haven where protections aren't necessary, actions do not have to be guarded, and love is unconditional. To find our way to those feelings of "home," we need to learn how to stay connected within the context of our everyday lives (as opposed to, for example, the designated safe environment of a therapist's office).

In the connected or bonded state, we're conscious of the gut-level feelings of our Inner Child, and the rational thoughts of our Inner Adult at the same time. Also, we're conscious of both the external and internal environments at the same time. That means the Adult is aware of and present for the Child's inner experience of what is happening externally, as well as the Child's sense of whether or not the Adult is in the intent to learn or to protect.

> The internal experience, not the external circumstance, determines whether or not the Adult and Child are connected.

Staying Connected

Learning to tune in to your internal experience takes time. It takes time and practice to develop the ongoing consciousness: "Am I being a Loving Adult to my Inner Child?" Among the key factors is awareness of discomfort. Once you heed your body signals of discomfort, then you begin questioning what the discomfort is about, asking your Inner Child what is needed, and deciding what would be the loving thing to do.

When most people feel discomfort, they resort to some habitual way of getting rid of the pain. They grab something to eat, have a drink, bury themselves in the newspaper, get angry with their mate, or watch TV. They repeat whatever it is they have learned to use to take away the discomfort, rather than try to find out what *they* are doing that is causing it.

> To stay Inner Bonded in conflict, you must be willing to feel your Child's pain.

> To stay Inner Bonded in conflict, you must stay in the intent to learn.

How Your Adult Causes Your Pain

Whatever we do to cause our emotional discomfort comes from our Adult; that is, our Adult is thinking or doing something to cause it. We may have frightening thoughts, such as "What if I fail?" for example, and so we feel afraid. Or our behavior may be the cause, such as caretaking someone or trying to get someone else to caretake us.

Our emotional discomfort is not caused by what someone else is doing to us. As soon as we believe that, we're making ourselves victims again and immobilizing ourselves. Consequently our thoughts and behaviors will be centered around either overtly or covertly trying to control someone else, making that person responsible for fixing our feelings. When we're doing that, we're not taking responsibility. But as soon as we bring the question back to ourselves and ask, "What am I doing to cause my pain?" that's when we have the opportunity to find out what else we can do.

A personal example may help illustrate the point here. As long as I was caretaking others, I was always unhappy and often ill. I always believed the other person was causing my distress. When I started to move out of caretaking others and began taking care of myself, I believed that I would end up alone and I was very much afraid, which is why I was caretaking in the first place. Therefore every time I chose to take care of myself rather than give up myself to caretake someone else, I felt terrified; but I also felt good inside, even when others got mad at me.

Along the way it looked as if my belief of ending up alone was accurate, because my husband and I separated when I stopped caretaking him. Now, after being apart for two years, we are in the process of healing our relationship, and I feel less alone than I ever have. Taking care of myself and not giving myself up in the face of others' demands still sometimes feels scary, but I feel unhappy only when I caretake others and ignore my own needs. I have found that the price of giving in to others while ignoring myself leads to my feeling very depressed; my Inner Child just goes dead when I discount her. I've learned that the fear I feel at taking care of myself is much better than the deadness and emptiness I feel when I don't. It is my choices alone that create my feeling empowered and joyful or victimized and miserable, regardless of how the other person responds.

> Protecting yourself from feeling your pain is unloving behavior.
>
> Opening to learn about your pain is loving behavior.

Your Inner Adult does not set out to cause you pain, but rather to protect you from it. However, in order to protect you from feeling pain, the Adult closes to your Child's experience of the external events. As we've seen, protecting yourself from pain by trying not to feel it only causes more pain, not less, because the Inner Child's experience of the discomfort is already there, and it doesn't go away by pretending it isn't there.

> When your Adult disconnects from your Inner Child feelings, the feelings are not released or resolved.

> When your rational processes do not recognize your pain, your emotional experience of it exists in the same or greater degree.

Relationships between Our Adult, Our Inner Child, and Others

Usually when we are unloving to others—when we lash out in anger, caretake them, or withdraw, for example—our primary motive is not to cause the other pain, but to get them to alleviate our own pain. Ironically, we are actually sabotaging our chances to get what we hope for.

Jessie, a client of mine in his late thirties, is a man who has suffered from deep jealousy whenever he is involved with a woman. If he thought she might be flirting with someone else, he would go into a rage. As he explored these feelings with his Inner Child, he discovered how he felt replaced by his younger brother in the eyes of his mother. Being replaced caused him to experience deep shame.

Jessie never felt good enough, so when he thought his wife was interested in another man, this shame would come up. The pain of this was so great that he covered it with his rage. As he faced his shame and began to heal it, he realized that he needed to let go trying to control his wife. In order to do so, he had to face a deep-seated false belief: "If I let go of control of her, I will lose her." Yet letting go was the only loving action he could take. The other loving action he needed to take was to reassure his Inner Child that even if his wife did leave him, he would still be all right, because his Adult would be there to take care of him. Ironically, the more he lets go, the better he feels about himself and the more loving he is to his wife, who in turn is more loving to him.

Our unloving behavior in any interaction is going to make the other person less likely to want to help us, maybe even hurt us back instead. Not only that, this attempted manipulation assumes that another adult can know how our Inner Child is feeling. Further, even if people know how we're feeling, they can't fix us. Whether or not others know or want to help, we must change our own feelings through our own thoughts and behavior.

Curiously, even though we may understand this principle, we will still act as if *our feelings* and resulting behavior can control *another's thoughts.* For instance, we may break into tears, and our unspoken hope is that "If I cry, he will decide to help me." Or we may shout out our frustration at our spouse with the tacit logic: "My shouting will make her understand how stressed I've been at work lately."

Most of us interact with others as if *our thoughts* and resulting behavior could change *their feelings,* but our internal systems don't work that way. If someone tries to soothe your nerves by telling you not to worry, that message enters your thought process or Adult; then your Adult decides whether or not this thought transmits any help.

These internal dynamics are not hypothetical; these are simply the ways our thinking and feelings processes operate. It is important for us to remember these dynamics so that, as we try to stay bonded and to meet our needs, we will know what works and what doesn't.

The Home Stretch: Staying Bonded in Conflict

The goal of Inner Bonding Therapy is to live as much of our lives as is possible in the connected, bonded, or Higher Self state. When everything seems to be going our way, this can be comparatively easy. However, when there is conflict in our relationships with mates, spouses, children, employers, and so on—and there always will be—the task of staying connected with our pain and open to learning is much more difficult.

Conflict begins when your Adult receives an upsetting message from an outside source that threatens to violate your personal boundaries. For example, let's use the example of an overtly upsetting message: "You're so selfish!" The moment you hear that accusation is your moment of choice to protect yourself and disconnect from the distress, or to stay open to learning and connect with your feelings.

First, because our protections are so often automatic, let's assume your choice is to protect yourself. Here's what a diagram of the interaction might look like:

By Other Protected		Self Protected/Disconnected		To Other Protected
"You're so selfish!"	⟶	A: Ignores Child IC: "I am angry!"	⟶	"I am not!" You're always too critical!"

Any number of various feelings and responses could result, but the principle is still the same. As you can see, the Adult has abandoned the Child in distress by ignoring the pain, which is unloving behavior. Then the abandoned Child has launched a counterattack, which is also unloving and which will probably result in further retaliation and more pain.

If we rerun the scene with the Adult choosing to stay open to learning, the interaction looks considerably different:

By Other Protected		Self Open/Connected		To Other Open to learning
"You're so selfish!"	⟶	A: "How do you feel?" IC: Blamed A: What can I do to help? IC: Tell her I don't like being blamed and that if she thinks I'm selfish we can talk about it.	⟶	A: I'm not available to being blamed. If there is some- thing you're upset about, I'd like to talk about it.

As you can see, the Adult has been loving to the Child by recognizing and responding to the feelings and taking action. The Adult has also been loving to the other by being honest, not counterattacking, and staying open to learning. Another thing that becomes evident is the contrast in inner power between the disconnected response ("No, I'm not! You're always too critical.") and the connected response ("I'm not available to being blamed. If you're upset, let's talk."). There is some strength shown in defending yourself, but there is much more strength evident in the statement of your feelings and your open invitation to discuss the person's reasons.

The more we consider our choices and the consequences of our behaviors, the more we realize that too often we do not have what we'd
hoped for in our relationships because our own actions brought about the
exact opposite. We hope for sympathy, so we get angry. We want stress
relief, so we yell at our spouse. We want our loved ones to act in loving
ways to us, so we act in unloving ways to them. That's the great paradox
of protection. Our protections do not shield us from pain; they only cause
more of it. The only things our protections keep us from are the things we
want most of all in life—the love of ourselves and love of others.

Now that we know this, the choice is ours.

In Part 1 we have explored the principles of Inner Bonding Therapy
and what happens when you do and don't choose to be loving and open to
learning .

In Part 2 we will take a look at loving behavior in a number of specific
instances. I hope you read all the stories. Many of these situations will
not apply to you directly, but the concepts behind the information and processes are not just specific to the situation. They apply to everyone. I hope
that by reading first about Inner Bonding Therapy in general, and then
about specific examples of the process in action, you will be able to begin
to connect with your own feelings and to become a loving Adult to your
Inner Child.

Part 2

BECOMING A LOVING ADULT
TO YOUR INNER CHILD

CHAPTER 6

The Big Challenge: Loving Your Inner Child with Your Spouse

There are no insurance policies when it comes to primary relationship. There is only process.

Embracing Each Other
HAL STONE, PH.D., AND SIDRA WINKELMAN, PH.D.,

Our first primary relationships are those with our parents and siblings. These are the relationships that teach us how to interact with those closest to us. When our parents were unloving Adults to their Inner Children and to us, we learned to be unloving Adults to ourselves and to others. We then transferred these patterns to our next primary relationships—with our spouses, lovers, and children.

In our most important relationships, we often find it difficult to stay connected as a loving Inner Adult. We frequently expect our spouses or lovers, and later even our children, to be the nurturing adult to us that we have not learned or chosen to be. In essence we hand over our Inner Child to them, thus abandoning ourselves. When our spouses or lovers do the same with us, we then have a codependent relationship. As two abandoned Inner Children, each blames the other for the lack of love and connection in the relationship because neither is taking responsibility for choosing loving behavior.

Because of the many conflict situations that can arise, the marriage relationship presents us with one of our biggest challenges regarding loving ourselves and another: maintaining the balance between narcissism and empathy.

When a couple comes to a therapy session, they generally state that poor communication is their major problem. As we talk together, it becomes apparent that struggles for control enter into almost every conversation. The issues over which they are in power struggles are often about money, time, sex, affairs, work, or responsibilities regarding chores or children. These conflicts tap into each partner's fears and insecurities, and often lead them to abandon their Inner Child and operate either from the position of narcissism (taking) or caretaking. For example, here's a typical disconnected, controlling narcissistic response from a person whose spouse has just refused an invitation to have sex:

"You're always tired. What about my needs?"

This, of course, generally leads the other partner to respond in an equally disconnected way—by giving in, resisting, getting angry, or withdrawing.

A connected response comes from a person who is Inner Bonded and taking responsibility for the Child's feelings of rejection, rather than allowing the Child to act out. For example:

"Honey, this happens a lot and I'd like to understand it. Can we talk about it?"

If the other partner doesn't want to talk, the one who initiated the conversation would be there internally for his or her Child's feelings, exploring what the Child needs from the Adult to feel lovable and worthy in a rejecting situation, rather than making the partner responsible for the Child's feelings.

The following pages relate examples of different conflict situations. The purpose is to illustrate the principles of Inner Bonding Therapy in action and to show that through Inner Bonding each of the conflicts can reach a loving resolution. Occasionally, throughout the dialogues, I have inserted my interpretation of the speaker's comments in italics to help point out the dynamics or intent present. Other interpretations are possible as well, but these were mine at that time.

Susan and Donald

The Situation

Susan and Donald came in for therapy because Susan had found out that Donald had been having an affair and Susan was planning on leaving the marriage. This was not the first time Donald had strayed, but it was the first time Susan had decided to leave. Typically Donald was beside himself with remorse and fear of losing Susan.

Susan and Donald were in their mid-thirties and had three young children. They were both teachers; she taught kindergarten and he was a high school humanities teacher. It was evident to me in the first session that these two people still deeply loved each other; yet their marriage was being destroyed because each of them functioned as an abandoned Child, which resulted in a codependent relationship.

Susan had become the emotional and sexual caretaker of the relationship. She gave herself up to Donald in many ways, particularly making love when she didn't feel like it and spending time with Donald when she wanted to do other things, such as read, paint, or exercise. She gave herself up to protect herself from the rejection and resulting aloneness she felt when Donald shut her out with his angry withdrawal if she didn't do what he wanted.

Donald was a "taker" on the narcissistic side of codependence, and pursued time and sex with Susan and other women as a way to fill himself up from the outside. He was sexually addicted, that is, he used sex as a way to feel worthy, lovable, and adequate. He made Susan responsible for his sense of worth. When she didn't perform in the way he felt he needed, he sought sex elsewhere.

Susan's Exploration

As Susan began to work with her Inner Child, she saw clearly that her Inner Child believed that she was undeserving of love and support, and that her worth was in pleasing Donald. Susan's parents were both alcoholics who had completely ignored her emotional needs. She grew up feeling very alone, and learned to caretake her parents as a way to maintain some sense of connection with them. When she was sixteen years old, she met an older man who flattered her and gave her the attention she so desperately needed. He used and abused her sexually, constantly threatening her with rejection if she refused him sex. This relationship went on for a number of years, further eroding her already fragile sense of self. When the man finally left her, she was devastated. Soon after that she met Donald.

Susan's Adult had no idea that it was her responsibility to take care of her Inner Child, having had no loving role-modeling from any adults. When she met Donald, she was an abandoned Child, hoping he would finally give her the love and security she so desperately wanted.

During the first session, Susan made a firm decision to separate from Donald and continue to work on the relationship with him. She was much too angry and untrusting to spend time with him other than in the therapy sessions. At the end of the first session I referred Susan to Adult Children of Alcoholics (ACoA) and Codependents Anonymous (CoDA), and she started going immediately.

We decided it was best for Susan and Donald to work individually for a while, until Susan was no longer so angry. In the next few sessions Susan was able to vent her anger and sense of betrayal and to see that her Inner Child was really angry at her Adult for giving her up so much and making her responsible for Donald's feelings. As she took more responsibility for her own choices, her anger and blame toward Donald gradually diminished.

Donald's Exploration

When Donald first came in for therapy, he was not open to dealing with himself. He was there only out of fear of losing Susan, hoping I would help her see that he "had learned his lesson and would never stray again." He did not want the separation. Here are Donald's own words, along with my labels and comments inserted in italics:

> I really love Susan. I never meant to end up in bed with this woman. It just sort of happened. *(Closed to learning; denial of responsibility.)* She was really nice to me and came on to me in a way that Susan doesn't. It's really mostly Susan's fault because she ignores my needs so much of the time. I think Susan has a sexual problem. *(Abandoned Child; blaming Susan and projecting his problem onto her.)* She's not really turned on very much of the time. If she would deal with her problem so that my needs get met, it would make it easier for me not to look at other women. *(Making her responsible for his choices.)* But I know I won't stray again, because now I realize how much I love Susan and I don't want to hurt her. *(Denial that he has a problem that needs healing.)*

Donald's comments were very typical of the view presented by someone who is on the narcissistic side of codependence: "It's not my fault and I won't do it again."

When I asked Donald about his childhood, he answered defensively, "My parents loved me." Donald's wall was so thick I wondered what he was protecting against feeling and knowing.

I explained to Susan and Donald about sexual addiction and referred Donald to a Twelve-Step program, Sex Addicts Anonymous (SAA). He was resistant to going, stating that he was not a sex addict, that he was just a normal man with normal sexual needs. I explained to him that anytime one's sexual needs were more important than the relationship and were causing problems in the relationship, the possibility of sexual addiction existed. Despite the fact that he was angry with me for this diagnosis, he consented to attend one meeting.

Donald came to the next session in a much more open frame of mind, having seen himself in the stories of several of the men at the SAA meeting. I told Donald that there were good reasons for his sexual addiction and that the reasons lay in his past. We began Inner Bonding work in the sessions, and within a few weeks Donald's childhood memories began to emerge.

Because Donald had been brainwashed by his parents never to "air dirty laundry," it was hard for him to tell the truth about his past. He felt, as has every abuse survivor that I've worked with, that he was betraying his parents. Nevertheless he pushed forward, and the following story finally emerged.

Donald's father was a brutal man who beat him with a belt for the slightest infraction. Donald was a sensitive and creative child, interested in music, art, and poetry, not the "man's man" his father wanted him to be. As a result of his father's abuse, Donald learned to push his Inner Child underground and to "act" as his father wanted him to act. Donald had completely lost touch with the creativity and aliveness of his Inner Child, and felt deeply shamed about his core self.

Donald's mother was a sexually promiscuous woman who was also regularly beaten by the father. She was very seductive with Donald, wanting to see him naked and often commenting on his penis. I explained to Donald that even though she never touched him, she sexually abused him in covert ways. Donald learned from his mother that his worth lay in being sexually attractive to women. This false belief, coupled with his shame-based, low self-esteem, was at the heart of his sexual addiction.

Like Susan, Donald had no functioning Adult when it came to relationships. As he worked with his Inner Child at home and in the sessions, his Adult began to see that his Inner Child had much more worth than just sexual attractiveness. Over time his natural warmth, aliveness, creativity, and inner knowingness emerged. However, it was still hard for him to stay connected to his Child and feel the pain of the aloneness when Susan did not do what he wanted her to do. The old rejection from his parents was very deep, as it is in so many of us, and the willingness to feel that pain in present situations presents our greatest challenge.

The only way the Child can feel that pain is if the Adult is present, letting the Child know we can handle the pain. Without the Adult, the Child is thrown back to the unbearable pain of the past, and moves into protecting against it in whatever ways have been learned. Donald had learned to become angry, withdraw, and seek outside sex as a way to control Susan and not feel the aloneness.

Donald's angry withdrawal and sexual acting out tapped into Susan's fears of rejection, and she had learned to comply to protect herself from her pain of aloneness.

The Loving Behavior: Susan

After about a month of individual sessions, Susan and Donald began joint sessions. A few weeks later Susan decided to move back in with Donald. Both Susan and Donald saw that the loving behavior for each of them was to act as a loving Adult for their Inner Child when the feelings of rejection came up. For Susan this meant that she needed to be willing to support what her Inner Child wanted to do in any given moment, even if Donald got angry and withdrew.

Susan had to be willing to set her own boundaries, saying no to love-making when she didn't feel like it. If Donald then became angry and withdrawn, she had to let her Inner Child know that she was not responsible for Donald's feelings. She had to be willing to exercise or paint or read when she wanted to, even if Donald wanted her time; and she had to let her Inner Child know that she was there for her to help her handle the pain when Donald chose to disconnect from her rather than lovingly support her. Susan had to be willing to let her Child know, each time Donald withdrew from her, that she was deserving of his love and support, rather than to shame her Child by telling her that she was selfish, bad, or wrong for doing what she wanted to do and not caretaking Donald.

I have found that many people use the word "selfish" in a very distorted way. One of my clients told me that her husband told her she was selfish when she didn't want to watch violent movies with him. Whenever they would go to pick out a video, he would pick one out without asking her what she wanted, and she would go along with it. One time, after beginning to work on her codependence, she told him that she didn't like his choosing a video without asking her, that she didn't like violent movies, and that she wanted to watch something she liked once in a while. He got furious and told her she was being selfish. I told her that he was the one being selfish, expecting her always to give herself up for him and not caring about what she wanted.

Webster's *New World Dictionary* defines selfish as "too much concerned with one's own welfare or interest and having little or no concern for others." I don't think it is possible to have too much concern for one's own welfare. After all, we are our own responsibility. However, when we are not at the *same time concerned with the welfare of others*, then we are being selfish. We are being selfish when we expect others to give themselves up for us rather than being willing to take full responsibility for ourselves. If I accuse my friend of being selfish because she is not doing what I want, instead of supporting what she wants while taking care of myself, I am being selfish.

Susan needed to understand that when Donald accused her of being selfish because she wanted to exercise rather than make love to him in the morning, it was really Donald who was being selfish. He was not caring about and supporting what Susan wanted for herself, nor was he willing to take responsibility for his own feelings. Making someone else responsible for our feelings is selfish.

I explained to Susan that Donald telling her she was selfish was "crazymaking." Crazymaking occurs when one partner lies and blames in such a way that he or she is really turning things around—that is, we accuse the other person of doing what *we* are doing. It was Donald who was being selfish and crazymaking by telling Susan she was selfish. Susan was terrified of being selfish, since her parents had often accused her of that (in the same crazymaking way), and would often capitulate under Donald's crazymaking. Being loving to her Inner Child meant telling her Child that doing what she wanted was not selfish and that Donald was crazymaking.

The Loving Behavior: Donald

Donald needed to let his Inner Child know that each time Susan didn't want to make love or spend time with him it was not because he was unlovable or undesirable or unworthy, but because Susan had other interests that were important to her. He needed to help his Inner Child not take Susan's behavior as a personal rejection, for only then could he be loving and supportive of Susan. The only way his Inner Child would not feel rejected and shamed was if his Adult was there for him each time to explore his beliefs and teach the truth. The next evening Donald wrote the following dialogue:

ADULT DONALD: I can feel your pain because Susan doesn't want to make love. Why is this so painful for you?

CHILD DONALD: If she loved me, she would always want to make love when I do. (*False belief*)

ADULT DONALD: So you believe that when a woman loves a man she always wants to make love to him?

CHILD DONALD: Right. If I was good enough, she would always be turned on to me. (*False belief*)

ADULT DONALD: Not always wanting to make love with you means that you are not good enough. Is that what you think?

CHILD DONALD: Yeah. You've always told me I wasn't. (*His Child is telling his Adult how he shames him.*)

ADULT DONALD: Well, I was wrong. You are good enough—even if Mom and Dad didn't think so. I really like who you are. You are very smart and creative and sensitive. You're very much like Dillon [Donald and Susan's oldest son], and you know I think Dillon is a wonderful person. A woman does not need to be turned on to Dillon for him to be lovable and wonderful. *(Donald is telling his Inner Child the truth.)* Susan really does love you, but right now she wants to exercise. It has nothing to do with you not being good enough. Do you care about what Susan wants?

CHILD DONALD: Well, right now I do, because you are caring about me. But when you ignore me or tell me I'm no good, then I need Susan to take care of me and I get mad at her when she doesn't. But right now I want to go hug her and tell her I love her and that I'm glad she decided to exercise.

ADULT DONALD: Why are you glad that she decided to exercise?

CHILD DONALD: Because I like it when you talk to me the way you are talking to me right now. If Susan and I had made love, I would have felt good for those moments, but I feel really good deep inside when you love me. If you were there for me every time I felt bad, I wouldn't need her so much and be angry when she wasn't there. Do you think she would mind if we exercised with her? I'd like to do that.

ADULT DONALD: Well, let's find out!

By being loving to himself, to his own Inner Child, Donald was then able to be loving to Susan.

Patti and Roger

The Situation

Patti and Roger, both in their late forties, came in for therapy because of conflicts over money. Patti is a dentist with a very successful private practice, and Roger is an emergency room physician. Both earn excellent salaries and have for the last ten years of their twenty-year marriage.

Patti initiated the therapy, and Roger reluctantly agreed to come along for only one session. Patti described the conflict as she saw it:

Roger has always been uptight about money—not necessarily about his spending it, but about me spending it. When he wants something he goes out and buys it, and I always support him in whatever he wants. He's not reckless with his spending and we certainly have enough to buy what we want. I'm not reckless either; yet whenever I buy something—whether it's new clothes, furniture for the house, or even tires for my car—I get Roger's anger and disapproval, and I'm sick of that.

I earn as much money as he does and he has no right to try to control what I spend. Why can't he just support me like I support him? I'm tired of feeling guilty and afraid whenever I spend my money, which I don't do very often because I can't stand his reaction.

Then Roger presented his view of the situation:

Patti is right. I have been very uptight about money, and we've spent a lot of time talking about why. I was taught in my family that women were always out of control when it came to spending and that it was the man's job to set the limits. I realize now that isn't true, yet every time she spends it touches off some fear in me and before I know it I'm angry at her. After we talk about it I always apologize, and I really understand how she feels. I don't see why she still sees it as a problem between us. (*Denial about his lack of recovery regarding his beliefs, fears, and need to control.*)

Patti responded:

Yeah, we talk and talk and nothing changes. You keep doing the same thing over and over and apologizing over and over. It still feels to me like you want to control me more than you want to support me.

Roger said that he was willing to keep trying to deal with it differently. I described the Inner Bonding process to them, and explained to Roger that whenever he felt afraid of being out of control, his Adult abandoned his Inner Child and his Child took over. His Child's way of protecting himself was to get angry at Patti. I told Roger that if he was willing to dialogue every day with his Inner Child, his Adult could learn to stay present when he was afraid. Roger said he would think about it.

Patti came in alone for the next session. Roger had told her that he was not interested in therapy or Inner Bonding. It was clear that he did not see the situation as a problem for him and was not motivated to deal with it.

The Exploration

It was apparent from the first session that Patti's intention was to get Roger to change, and she was now frustrated that Roger would not deal with "his" problem. I pointed out that it was really her problem, since she was the one who was unhappy. She was operating from the false belief that Roger's behavior, rather than her own choices, was causing her unhappiness. We had the following dialogue:

MARGIE: Patti, how is money handled in your family?

PATTI: Everything we earn goes into a joint account. We have one checkbook that we share, and Roger pays the bills. Even if I don't tell him about something I've bought, he finds it out when he goes through the checkbook or pays the credit card.

MARGIE: What has stopped you from setting up your own account and putting a certain portion of your earnings in that account each month? That way Roger knows ahead of time the amount you are taking for yourself and doesn't have access to what you spend it on. There must be a good reason you've chosen not to do that.

PATTI: Yeah, Roger would hate that. He would be furious. My independence seems to frighten him.

MARGIE: And what if he is angry and frightened—how does that make you feel?

PATTI: Well, as his wife, I don't think I should do things that I know really frighten him. *(False belief: I am responsible for his feelings. Patti feels empathic toward Roger's feelings, ignoring her own. Patti is on the caretaking end of codependence.)*

MARGIE: It sounds like you take responsibility for the fears of his Inner Child and ignore the needs of your own Inner Child. Then you expect him to change and support the needs of your Inner Child.

PATTI: Well, I support him in what he wants. Why shouldn't he support me in what I want?

MARGIE: Certainly it would be loving if he did, but you have no control over that. You have given him the job of nurturing your Inner Child and you are not doing that for yourself, for instance, when you don't buy what you want. Instead, you abandon your Child to nurture his. Then when you do buy something and he gets angry instead of supporting you, you abandon yourself again by making him responsible for your feelings instead of standing up for your Inner Child.

PATTI: But in a loving relationship doesn't each person nurture the other?

MARGIE: Yes, but not at the expense of yourself. A loving relationship is when you each nurture yourself and support and nurture each other. Neither of you is nurturing your own self. Neither of you is taking responsibility for the feelings and needs of your own Inner Child. He makes you responsible for his fear by trying to control you, and you take responsibility for his fear by ignoring the needs of your Child and then blame him for your unhappiness.

I explained to Patti that in their codependent system, she was on the caretaking end and Roger was on the narcissistic end regarding the issue of money.

PATTI: Does that mean I have the right to take care of my needs even if he is upset about it?

MARGIE: Of course. His upset feelings are his issue to deal with, just as your upset feelings are yours. Perhaps if he is upset by your choice to take care of yourself, he would be motivated to deal with his Inner Child, or perhaps not. You have no control over that. But you do have control over your own choices; and you not only have the right, but you have the responsibility to take care of the needs of your Inner Child.

The Loving Behavior

Patti decided to set up her own bank account. She added up her usual monthly expenditures, the ones that Roger gave her a hard time about, and opened a checking account. She told Roger about her decision and about the amount that she had decided on. As she predicted, he was upset, saying that it wasn't fair for her to have her own account when he didn't have his own. She told him she was perfectly willing for him to have his own account and to take the same amount out for himself every month.

Roger grumbled a bit and then stopped, realizing that there was nothing he could do. Patti was surprised that it was so easy. She reported there was a great lessening of tension between them about money, and that she was finally able to spend her own money without feeling guilty and afraid.

Patti realized that the money issue was not the only issue over which she had abandoned her Inner Child and taken responsibility for Roger's feelings. As she shifted her beliefs from feeling responsible for his abandoned Child to taking responsibility for herself, many other issues in their relationship began to move toward resolution. One issue, however, moved into greater conflict and finally brought Roger into therapy.

The Situation: According to Roger

Patti and I have always had a good sex life, when we have sex. But Patti never seems to really want sex. I've told her there is something wrong with her sexuality, but nothing ever changes. (*Roger is blaming instead of being in the intent to learn about the good reasons Patti has for not feeling turned on to him.)* She tells me she doesn't feel sexual unless we are emotionally connected, but I think that's just an excuse. *(Roger is in denial about Patti's true feelings.)* I feel so connected to her after we make love. *(Roger believes Patti should feel as he does, which is often true of the person on the narcissistic end of codependence.)*

Lately Patti has refused to have sex with me, saying that she will not make love again until she feels loved by me. I feel really manipulated by that. *(Roger has no empathy for Patti's feelings. He is only concerned about his own wants.)* She knows I love her and she is just withholding to control me. *(Roger projects his own intent to protect onto Patti rather than accepting that Patti is attempting to take good care of herself.)* If she keeps on this kick, she is going to destroy our marriage.

The Situation: According to Patti

From the beginning of our marriage, Roger has withdrawn and been angry at me whenever I don't want to make love. He does the same thing with sex that he did with money—he tries to control me. I have no freedom to say no without him being mad. I've told him over and over that if he would just try to understand instead of withdraw, things would get better. But again he would rather control than support me. That makes me feel unloved, because he doesn't care about how I feel. He tells me he can't sleep or that he feels bad about himself when we don't make love a lot, but am I responsible for that?

I've abandoned my Inner Child a lot and made love when I didn't want to just to please Roger so he wouldn't be mad at me, and I'm not going to do that anymore. I'm not going to make love until it's what I want, and why would I want to when Roger is mad at me all the time? Roger always has sex on his mind. No matter what we do together, he sees it as a prelude to sex and is then angry if sex doesn't happen. I never feel relaxed around him or have fun with him because I know that at the end of the evening, if we don't make love, he will be mad.

I explained to them, as I had with Susan and Donald, about sexual addiction, and Roger responded just as Donald had: "That's ridiculous. I'm not addicted. I just have normal sexual needs." I explained that anytime we use something outside of ourselves for our good feelings, rather than our Adult giving them to our Child, we are addicted to that thing.

Some people use substances to feel good and take away the pain, others use things and activities. Still others, like Roger, use people, needing their love, approval, romance, or sexuality to feel whole.

Roger made Patti responsible for his good feelings about himself, for his wholeness and connection to himself. The only way he knew to feel connected to himself was through sex. Patti had taken responsibility for

Roger's feelings by having sex when she didn't want to, because she believed it was her responsibility and because, as an abandoned Inner Child, she was dependent on or even addicted to his approval and afraid of his disapproval. Now, through Inner Bonding Therapy, she no longer needed outside approval nor feared disapproval and was no longer willing to caretake his abandoned Inner Child.

Patti was being loving to herself by not making love when she didn't want to. She was also being loving to Roger, because she was acting from her truth and therefore giving him an opportunity to face his own fears. Of course, Roger could not yet see that Patti was being loving. He just accused her of being selfish.

I told Roger that I wanted to work with him alone, and recommended that he attend SAA (Sex Addicts Anonymous). He agreed to come in for sessions alone, but refused to attend SAA. It took another six sessions before Roger accepted that he was truly sexually addicted and finally went to SAA.

The Exploration

Roger came from a home where his father was gone most of the time and was emotionally absent when he was around. His mother was a narcissistically needy, seductive, and controlling woman who clung to Roger for her needs. Roger was her "little man" from infancy on. Roger's mother tried to meet all of Roger's needs. She clearly implied through her behavior that it was not Roger's responsibility to meet his own needs, and further, that he was incapable of meeting them. She wanted him dependent on her as a way of tying him to her.

Roger was never affirmed for any act of independence, and the only personal quality that was valued by his mother was his looks. As a result Roger grew up believing that he needed a woman to make him whole. He was emotionally and sexually dependent on Patti for his sense of worth and well-being.

It took Roger a long time to begin Inner Bonding work. His Adult just didn't want the job of taking responsibility for his Inner Child. His Adult was operating from the false belief that he was incapable of taking care of himself. Neither of Roger's parents took care of themselves emotionally, so he had no role-modeling to draw from. In addition, his mother's caretaking of him convinced him that he could not take care of himself. Roger was deeply committed to this false belief, and his fear of failure kept him locked into his narcissistically dependent behavior.

In addition, he was convinced that his Inner Child was just an empty being with nothing there of true value. The only dialoguing he would do for months was in my office. In the back of his mind he kept hoping that if he held out long enough, Patti would give in and caretake him again.

Fortunately she stuck to her decision to no longer caretake Roger, sexually or in any other way, and their marriage grew more and more distant. Even though Roger was attending both SAA and CoDA meetings, there was no real change. He was able to talk about the fact that he was sexually addicted and emotionally dependent, but he still was not willing to do anything about it. He was unwilling to take responsibility for loving his Inner Child. It was not until Patti decided to separate that Roger began to dialogue in earnest.

The Loving Behavior

In the six months that Patti was gone, Roger finally took the plunge into personal responsibility. With all hope gone of Patti doing it for him, facing the risk of failure was less frightening than facing the risk of losing Patti forever. Through the Inner Bonding process, Roger discovered a wonderful, though lonely little boy inside of him—playful, intelligent, creative, caring, and frightened. Slowly he began to listen to and care about meeting the needs of this abandoned Inner Child. As he practiced Inner Bonding on a daily basis, the inner void that always needed filling from the outside began to fill from the inside.

When Patti saw that he was truly working with himself, she moved back into the house, but not into a sexual relationship with Roger. It took many more months of Inner Bonding before Roger was filling himself enough within for the love to flow out toward Patti. At that point his sexuality became an expression of that love rather than a pull for love, and Patti's sexual feelings for him returned. As Roger learned to support his own inner needs rather than make Patti responsible for them, he was also able to support Patti in the things that were important to her.

Roger and Patti were creating a whole new marriage.

Beth and Dave

The Situation

Beth and Dave sought therapy because Dave discovered that Beth was having an affair and was not sure he wanted to go on with the marriage. Beth did not want the marriage to end—primarily because of finances and the children, not because she loved Dave.

Beth and Dave had four children, ranging in age from three to ten. Dave worked for a large munitions firm, and Beth did part-time marketing research at home. Dave was a workaholic who rarely came home before eight every evening. Beth complained constantly about Dave never being home, and Dave claimed he didn't come home because there was nothing to come home to—Beth was drunk every night and on the phone all evening. He said she had started drinking within two years of their marriage, and before that he was always home early. Beth denied being an alcoholic and refused to attend Alcoholics Anonymous (AA) meetings. She claimed she drank because Dave was never around—she was always waiting for him and always angry because he wasn't there.

They were caught in an intense power struggle: Dave blamed Beth for his never being home, and Beth blamed Dave for her drinking and running around with other men. She claimed she was not turned on to him sexually because he was so parental and controlling with her, and he said he was parental and controlling because she was so irresponsible, especially driving drunk with the kids in the car. She claimed she never did that, that she never would do that, and that he had no right to accuse her of it.

Beth came to the second session clearly drunk. I confronted her with it, and she lied about it and denied it. She didn't want to come to the session and didn't want to work on the marriage. She just wanted things to go along as they were. Dave said he would leave if she didn't work on the marriage, so she agreed to another session. I told her I would try one more session, but that if she didn't agree to attend AA and deal with her alcoholism, I couldn't work with her.

Beth came in drunk again to the third session. She blamed her drinking on being pushed by Dave for closeness when she didn't want to be close to him. She again refused to even talk about attending AA. I spoke to both of them about the disastrous effects on their children of her drinking and his being gone so much, but again she was in denial about how much she drank. She finally admitted that she felt too lonely and alone when she didn't drink, and was not willing to feel that pain. Her abandoned Child needed the alcohol to survive the pain, because her Adult was completely absent and had no intention of showing up. I told Dave that I would work with him individually.

The Exploration

MARGIE: Dave, why are you staying in this marriage?

DAVE: Well, I care about Beth and I'm hoping she will change.

MARGIE: From what you've said, she has been this way the last twelve years of your fourteen-year marriage. What makes you think she will change?

DAVE: I don't know. I guess I keep thinking that if I can get her to see what she is doing that's causing us problems she will stop doing it. *(Dave is operating from a false belief about being able to control another's intent and behavior.)*

MARGIE: And what happens when you try to "get" her to see things your way?

DAVE: She shuts me out and won't talk to me. She never wants to talk to me.

MARGIE: Maybe that's because you are constantly trying to get her to see things your way. You said you were going to try coming home earlier. What's happened with that?

DAVE: I have been coming home early and nothing is changed. She still drinks every night and doesn't want to have anything to do with me.

MARGIE: How does that feel?

DAVE: It feels awful. That's why I come home late.

MARGIE: Dave, if you believed that there was nothing you could do to make Beth change, what would you do?

DAVE: I would leave the marriage.

Dave was staying because of his hope that he could find some way to change Beth. That hope dies hard in most of us. We want to believe that there is some way we can change another's intent. It was evident to me that Dave was available to working with his Inner Child and learning to be a loving Adult. It was equally evident that Beth was completely closed to taking any personal responsibility, and therefore no change would occur. Dave was not yet ready to accept this truth. He needed more Inner Bonding work before he could accept that he was helpless to change Beth. Dave did this work, and after a few months came in ready to explore the loving behavior toward his Inner Child and his children.

The Loving Behavior

DAVE: I know I have to leave. My Inner Child deserves to be with someone who loves him and wants to be with him, not someone who does everything she can to push me away. I know now that I can't change her and that she doesn't seem to want to change.

          What I don't know is what to do about my children. I haven't been very involved with them. I think I've taken out my anger at Beth on my kids. I think I resisted spending time with them because she was always blaming me for never being around. But now that I'm getting to know my Inner Child, I seem more connected to my kids.

It scares me to leave them with her, and I do want more time with them, but I also don't have the time to be with them a lot. And they probably want to be with her because she is the one who has been with them the most.

MARGIE: You need to decide how much you want to see them. What would be comfortable for you at this point?

DAVE: I don't know yet. I'm going to work on it with my Inner Child.

Dave did leave Beth, and he came up with an arrangement that felt good to him regarding the children. His relationships with his children steadily improved when he was no longer in the power struggle with Beth. As the children began to ask to spend more time with him, and he was no longer available to blame, Beth finally decided to get some help. Dave reported to me that she did go into therapy and was attending AA. At this time Dave and Beth were having minimal contact, speaking only to make arrangements for the children. Dave knew that even though Beth was changing, it was too early to attempt a friendship. He expressed the hope that he and Beth would get back together someday, but he knew he could not count on that and was moving on with his life.

Andrea and Stanley

The Situation

Andrea came in for therapy by herself initially, because she was feeling lost within herself and lost in her relationship with Stanley. Stanley was a freelance writer. Until recently, he had worked at home for most of their eight-year marriage. Andrea, fair and round, was a violin teacher who worked part-time at home. Six months before Andrea came in for therapy, Stanley had accepted a full-time job as a writer/editor for a large publishing company. His boss, a woman, was quite demanding of his time.

Until this job came along, Stanley had been the emotional caretaker in the relationship. While he was not turned on to her sexually (*a common experience for caretakers*), he was always there for Andrea through her many depressions and rages. Now he was gone most of the time and Andrea felt abandoned. (*The primary feeling of the person on the narcissistic side of codependence when the caretaker is no longer available.*)

Andrea pictured Stanley as a selfish and self-centered man. (*It is common for narcissists to project their own self-centeredness onto their partner, which is crazymaking for the partner.)* I asked her if Stanley would be willing to come in for a session alone, and she said yes.

Stanley, tall and a bit overweight, with prematurely white hair, willingly appeared at the next session. He was anxious and distraught over the problems in his marriage. He loved Andrea and could not understand why she was so angry with him over his new job. He wanted her support in doing something that was important to him; he had always supported her and could not understand why she felt threatened. He was trying every way he knew to pacify her, but nothing was working. He felt like he had to quit his job to save his marriage and was feeling very resentful over this.

Stanley's Exploration

When Stanley learned the concept of codependence, he immediately saw the problem clearly. He saw that he had always been a caretaker in every relationship he had ever had—his parents, friends, lovers, and now his wife. He realized he had always picked needy people as friends and lovers.

As we began Inner Bonding work, it became readily apparent that Stanley really liked his Inner Child. He greatly valued his sensitivity, caring, creativity, and talent. He always felt happy and peaceful when he was alone with himself, but it was his deep-seated false belief, learned in childhood from both of his parents, that he was responsible for other's feelings.

Stanley never saw his parents take care of their own feelings within their relationship. They constantly pulled on each other and blamed each other for their unhappiness. As the middle child, Stanley's role in the family had always been the peacemaker for his parents and siblings.

The Loving Behavior: Stanley

Stanley was deeply delighted with the realization that he was not responsible for Andrea's feelings. He saw easily that in taking responsibility for her, he had unwittingly helped perpetuate her dependency. He had always thought of himself as a loving and giving person, but he could see that caretaking Andrea was unloving to her and to his own Inner Child.

Stanley resolved in that first session to begin unhooking from the codependent system. I warned him that things would get worse before they got better, since it was likely that Andrea would act out even more when she was unable to pull him into the system. He had no control over whether

Andrea would decide to take responsibility for herself, or would leave the marriage and seek another man to take care of her. He had to be willing to lose her in order to give up the caretaking and have a chance at a really good marriage. Although he did not want to lose her, he did not want things to go on as they were and was willing to risk any outcome.

Stanley decided that whenever he felt Andrea pull on him to make her pain and misery go away, he would ask her if she wanted his help in working with her Inner Child. If she did, he would assist her in her exploration; but if she just wanted him to fix her, he would quietly walk away and do something fun for his Inner Child. As he imagined doing this, he could feel the guilt rising up from within his Inner Child. He saw that he constantly had to reassure his Child that he was not responsible for Andrea's feelings, and that belief had been a lie.

Stanley came in two weeks later feeling much more inwardly powerful. He felt he had done an excellent job of not caretaking, and as I had predicted, things were getting worse. He was very worried about Andrea, as she was somewhat suicidal, although he did not really think she would kill herself. I told him that if she got worse, she might have to be hospitalized, but that there was a good chance her veiled threats were manipulations to pull him back into the system.

Andrea's Exploration

Andrea's original reason for entering therapy had been to get Stanley into therapy so he would work on himself, see how selfish he was being, and move back into caretaking her. She didn't really believe she needed therapy—things had been fine before Stanley took his new job, so it must be all Stanley's fault. However, once Stanley pulled back even more from his caretaking, her terror of abandonment escalated and she came running back to my office, furious at me for the way I was dealing with Stanley.

MARGIE: Andrea, I really understand how frightened and hurt you are. I'm wondering how your Inner Child feels about how your Adult is handling her feelings. Would you ask her? (*Note: I keep an assortment of stuffed animals and dolls in my office for clients to use for role-playing. It often helps them begin their inner dialogues.*)

ANDREA: (*Getting her tears and anger at me under control, speaking to a large stuffed bear*) Andy, how are you feeling?

CHILD ANDY: Scared and angry. Stanley doesn't love me anymore.

MARGIE: Now ask her how she feels about how you are handling these feelings.

ANDREA: I don't want to ask her. I know I'm not there. I don't know how to be. I don't know what she needs. (*Andrea does not want the job of loving her Inner Child.*)

MARGIE: Ask her what she wants from Stanley.

ADULT ANDREA: Andy, what is it you really want from Stanley?

CHILD ANDY: I want him to want to spend time with me and listen to me and hold me and tell me he loves me and talk to me and be real nice to me.

MARGIE: Andrea, those are the things your Child needs from you. Whatever you are trying to get from Stanley is what your Inner Child needs from you. Are you willing to give those things to her?

ANDREA: I guess so.

MARGIE: You don't sound very enthusiastic. There must be a good reason you don't want the job of being a loving Adult to your Child. Do you have any idea what it is?

ANDREA: If I do that for myself, why do I need him?

MARGIE: Are you saying that it is Stanley's job to make you happy, and if you make yourself happy, you won't need him anymore?

ANDREA: Well, why else would you want to be with someone?

MARGIE: I think there are two main reasons people are in relationships. One is to get love and the other is to give love. If your intent is to get love, you'll probably always feel empty, because you haven't filled yourself up from inside and you have no love to give.

When your intent is to learn to be loving to yourself and others, to fill yourself with love and share that love with another, and when his intent is the same, then there is a lot of love and joy shared.

It seems to me that you believe your best feelings come from outside yourself rather than from loving yourself and others. If that's true, then of course you would not be motivated to learn to be loving to your Inner Child.

ANDREA: But I do feel good when I get the love.

MARGIE: Of course you do—in the short run. You've gotten your "love fix" and it feels good, just as alcoholics feel good in the short run when they drink. But later, when the alcohol wears off, the self-esteem usually goes down the drain.

It's the same with you. You feel good as long as Stanley is giving you what you want, and you feel horrible when he isn't. You are addicted to his love; you are dependent on it. But when you give it to yourself, then you feel good in the long run, not just for the moment. Only when you love your own Inner Child will she know she is lovable is a deep way, a way that no one can take away and that is not dependent on anyone. But the only way you're going to know this is to try it.

The Loving Behavior: Andrea

MARGIE: Andrea, how would you feel about giving your Inner Child what you want Stanley to give her for one week and see how it feels?

ANDREA: *(Still not totally convinced, but willing to try)* Okay, I'll try it for a week.

The next week, we had the following dialogue:

ANDREA: I'm doing better. I've been talking to her a lot, but there is still something I'm not doing right. I'm still in a lot of pain and I don't know why.

MARGIE: How about asking her?

ANDREA: Okay . . . I've been asking and I don't get an answer, but I'll try again. *(Looking at the bear)* Andy, why are you in such pain? Can you tell me? I really want to know.

CHILD ANDY: I know you're really trying, but I don't think you like me very much.

MARGIE: Andy, would you tell Adult Andrea why you think she doesn't like you?

CHILD ANDY: She never says anything nice to me about me. That's why I like to be with Stanley. He really likes me. He thinks I'm pretty and talented, but big Andrea doesn't and Mom and Dad never did.

MARGIE: Does big Andrea treat you like Mom and Dad did?

CHILD ANDY: Oh, yes! They always told me I wasn't good enough, just like she does. *(She was shamed by her parents, and her Adult continues to shame her.)*

MARGIE: Okay Andrea, what do you think of what your Child is saying?

ANDREA: She's right! I never say anything nice to her. I was taught never to say nice things about yourself—it's vain and self-centered.

MARGIE: Sounds like you've been operating from a false belief that has kept you from really seeing and valuing your Child. She needs you to be an accurate mirror for her in order to know her own worth and have high self-esteem. Are you willing to spend time with her telling her who she really is—all the beautiful and wonderful things about her?

ANDREA: Yes. I can feel how hard that is for me—how I'm always trying to get that from others. And I can feel how much she wants that. And even when others do give it to me, like Stanley, it never really goes in. I never really believe it. I guess I won't believe it until I give it to myself.

MARGIE: That's right! How can your Child believe good things others say to you when your Adult doesn't say them to her? That's why you could get it forever from Stanley, but it won't sink in until you give it to yourself.

ANDREA: God, that feels really right! My little girl is feeling better already!

Nothing happens overnight, of course. Andrea spent many months struggling with accepting the responsibility for her Inner Child, taking two steps forward and one back. In addition to telling her Child who she is, Andrea eventually learned to act in her Child's behalf. She saw that telling her Child who she is and how much she loves her was not enough; she had to take good care of her Child in many ways, physically, emotionally, and spiritually, for her Child to experience feeling loved by her Adult.

As Andrea took more responsibility for her own good feelings and Stanley took responsibility for his and not for hers, their relationship slowly got better and better. Their codependent relationship became an evolving relationship, where each supported themselves and the other in their highest good.

Loving Your Inner Child with Your Spouse

One of the popular myths in our culture is that when we fall in love, "it will be forever," and "we two will be one"—we will feel complete and at last there will be an end to our aloneness. Of course, that isn't true, as all people who are in love and get married discover sooner or later.

The most important thing we can learn about loving each other is the paradox that we must learn to love ourselves first. Without self-love and self-acceptance, we will always tend to choose to protect ourselves, instead of opening to love. For a strong and lasting partnership, both of us must be connected to our own inner feelings, as well willing to be open to learning about the other's. Even so, as the epigraph says at the beginning of the chapter, there are no insurance policies for our relationships, only process. In other words, there is no end to the need to work on our own growth and on the ways our individual lives fit together. Still, if both wife and husband stay bonded within and open to each other, there is no limit to the potential for richness and joy.

CHAPTER 7

Starting Off Right: Loving Your Inner Child with Your Lover

Learning how to love my child is learning how to love the world.
The Magical Child within You
BRUCE DAVIS, PH.D.

When we first fall in love, things always seems to be perfect. As new lovers we are always certain that our love is different, our love will last forever. It's so easy to believe this when everything feels so wonderful.

After a few months, though, fears usually start to set in, and very often a codependent system begins to develop. When our Adult and Inner Child are not bonded, the seeds for a codependent relationship are sown even before we meet—we cannot just put aside the fears that create codependence, no matter how much in love we feel. Sometimes a relationship will be working well right up until a couple gets married, because the fears of abandonment and engulfment may only be associated with the commitment of marriage. Most committed relationships, however, show the symptoms of codependence within the first six months of meeting.

Lovers have some of the same conflicts as spouses. Like spouses, lovers suffer from fears of loss of self, loss of other, of not being enough, of not being adequate. They may fight over time; over triangle relationships, when one partner is married or in another committed relationship; over money, sex, or each other's children. Difficulties over responsibilities concerning money and chores often arise when one partner moves into the other's house.

Lovers who are not in a committed relationship often feel very insecure and their insecurity leads them to act out their narcissism or caretaking.

Without Inner Bonding, lovers will continue to act out their fears with codependent behavior, often going from one lover to the next and never understanding why it never works out.

Alexis and Brendan

The Situation

Alexis, an advertising executive in her mid-thirties, short, round, blond, with sparkling blue eyes, had been in a relationship for six months with Brendan, who was also in advertising and in his mid-thirties. Alexis had been in therapy with me for some time before she decided to have a session with Brendan. Here is what she said about the difficulties that she didn't know how to resolve:

> Whenever Brendan mentions anything about sex with his ex-wife, I get really hurt. I've asked him not to talk about it to me, but he still does sometimes. *(Belief: Brendan is responsible for my feelings.)* I think it's rude and insensitive of him to continue to do that, and I don't know what to do about it. *(Belief: I can control what he does by making him wrong.)*

I asked Brendan what he was feeling about the situation:

> I try to remember not to talk about that, but sometimes it just comes up in the course of our conversation. I don't know what to do. One of the reasons my wife and I split up was that there were so many things I wasn't allowed to talk about that I felt I was always walking on eggs. I tried to be careful of her feelings, but it got so I couldn't stand to be around her. In my own therapy I realized I was caretaking her. I don't want to do that with Alexis, but I don't know what else to do. I really don't want to hurt her. *(Belief: I'm responsible for Alexis's feelings.)*

I spoke with Alexis about the fact that her upset feelings were coming from her own fears and beliefs, and that instead of trying to get Brendan to change, she could explore her own feelings. I told her that if she kept trying to control Brendan and he kept trying to comply, they would eventually end up just like Brendan and his wife. I asked her if she was willing to dialogue with her Inner Child, and she was.

The Exploration

ADULT ALEXIS: *(Speaking to a doll)* Why does it upset you so much when Brendan talks about sex with his ex-wife?

CHILD ALEXIS: *(Turning the doll around and becoming the Child)* I get scared he will leave me. *(Beliefs: I can't handle the pain; I can't take care of myself.)*

ADULT ALEXIS: But why?

MARGIE: Does it remind you of anything in the past? Anything with your father? *(Alexis had done extensive work on incest and abandonment issues related to her father.)*

CHILD ALEXIS: Well, Daddy had sex with me and with other women, and then left me to be with other women.

ADULT ALEXIS: So when Brendan talks about his ex-wife, it reminds you of what happened with Daddy?

CHILD ALEXIS: Yes. If Brendan liked sex with her, then he will leave me and go back with her. I'm scared that he liked sex with her better than with me.

MARGIE: It sounds like your Child believes she is not good enough to keep Brendan.

ALEXIS: You're right. I just realized that I've always believed that my father left me because I wasn't enough for him, especially sexually.

The Loving Behavior

MARGIE: So what would it look like to be loving to your little girl right now Alexis?

ADULT ALEXIS: *(Speaking to her Child, looking at the doll)* I understand why you are afraid. But it's really not the same thing, because Brendan is not Daddy. Brendan loves you, and talking about his ex-wife doesn't mean he doesn't love you. It doesn't mean he is going to leave you and go back to her. When he talks about sex it doesn't mean he liked it better with her than with us. He's told us lots of times that he really loves our lovemaking.

But even if he did leave, we would be all right because I'm here to take care of you. I couldn't take care of you when you were a baby, because I was too little; but now I'm big and I can take care of you. *(Alexis is telling her Child the truth about the false beliefs that she can't handle the pain and can't take care of herself, as well as reassuring her Child that Brendan is not like her father.)*

CHILD ALEXIS: But I wasn't good enough for Daddy, so maybe I'm not good enough for Brendan. *(Belief: I'm not good enough.)*

ADULT ALEXIS: Daddy did not leave because you weren't good enough—he left because he was a sick man. You were a sweet, lovable little girl and you still are. Daddy left because he had lots of problems. He didn't know how to love. It had nothing to do with you not being enough. Daddy was not supposed to want and need you sexually, and you weren't supposed to meet his needs. You were just a baby. *(She is beginning to confront the core shame-based belief of not being good enough. This belief needs to be confronted over and over until the Inner Child no longer believes it. This false belief has been the main cause of Alexis's being upset with Brendan.)*

MARGIE: So what do you need to do next time Brendan talks about something that upsets you?

ALEXIS: I guess I need to talk like this with my Inner Child and find out what she is feeling and why *(take responsibility for her own feelings)* rather than get mad at Brendan *(make Brendan responsible for her feelings).*

The Situation

Alexis then brought up another issue: Sometimes Brendan withdrew from her. When she would ask him why, he would just say he was "tired." She knew that wasn't the real reason, and she wanted to know why he withdrew and why he wouldn't talk to her about it.

The Exploration

BRENDAN: I withdrew last week because I felt pressured by you to make a decision about getting a divorce. *(Brendan and the woman referred to as his ex-wife had been separated for a few years, but neither of them had ever taken the action to get a divorce.)*

ALEXIS: Why didn't you just tell me to back off?

BRENDAN: I didn't want to hurt your feelings.

MARGIE: It sounds like you were taking responsibility for her feelings again.

BRENDAN: Yeah, I guess I was. I did that the other night too when I didn't want her to sleep over. I needed some time alone, but I was afraid if I told her that she would be hurt.

ALEXIS: So instead you were so cold that I left early anyway. I'd much rather you had just told me you needed some space.

BRENDAN: But I feel so bad when you get hurt.

MARGIE: That's a hard one, isn't it? In order for you to be honest about what you want, you need to change your belief about pain and being responsible for another's pain. Sounds like you see pain as bad.

BRENDAN: Yes. It feels really bad. I don't like to be in pain, so I don't like it if someone I care about is in pain from something I've done. *(Brendan has fears and false beliefs about pain.)*

The Loving Behavior

MARGIE: But pain is not bad, even though it hurts. Emotional pain is a teacher. It's there to let us know that there may be false beliefs that need exploring and to tell us that we may be behaving in a way that isn't good for us. It's the Inner Child's way of letting us know that we are not taking good care of ourselves. If Alexis was in pain because you needed space, her Adult would not be taking good care of her Child by allowing her Child to feel rejected by your legitimate needs. It means that she is operating from a false belief that says, "If he needs space from me, he must not love me," or, "If he needs space from me, I must be doing something wrong, or I must not be good enough." Her pain gives her an opportunity to explore and heal these false beliefs.

   If you caretake her by not being honest and by giving yourself up, you rob her of the opportunity to learn. Being honest about your own wants and needs is always loving, even though it doesn't seem so at the time.

BRENDAN: I see that, and I see where I need to do some work with my Inner Child. This one is really hard for me, but I don't want this relationship to end up like my first marriage. I want to be able to be honest.

Resolving his fears of pain and the belief that he is responsible for Alexis's pain is a process that takes time. For Brendan it means doing what it is he is afraid of, that is, being honest about his wants and needs, and being there as a loving Adult to reassure his Inner Child that he is not bad or wrong when Alexis is in pain or gets angry as a result of his honesty. As he does this over a period of time, his own fears of pain and of being wrong when someone else is in pain will gradually diminish. If anything is to change within him, his Adult has to be willing to take the action of being honest.

ALEXIS: I can see where my work is, too. I guess as long as we each stay open to doing our own work, we'll be okay. I can see that if I want Brendan to be honest, and I do, I have to take responsibility for my own pain rather than blame him.

Even if Brendan does manage to be honest with Alexis, if she continues to make him responsible for her feelings, he will eventually get tired of this and leave the relationship if he is taking good care of his Inner Child. It is not loving to ourselves to stay in a relationship where we are blamed for another's feelings. If Alexis did that, she would prove to herself that she is not good enough, her original false belief. But if Brendan is honest and Alexis takes responsibility for her own pain, their relationship will grow and deepen as they each grow.

Bridget and Homer

The Situation

Bridget, red-haired and freckled, is a therapist in training. As part of her training, she attended a one-month, intensive residential workshop on hypnosis, where she met Homer and Homer's girlfriend, Sally. As Bridget explained to me:

> Homer and I became friends early in the workshop, and when it became apparent to me that we were heading toward becoming lovers, I asked Homer to tell Sally what was happening. It felt uncomfortable to me to be sneaking around with Sally in the workshop. He said no, that there was no point in hurting her since we didn't know where all this was leading. I went along, ignoring the warning voice of my Inner Child.
>
> We did become lovers, and now we are all back in town and I'm feeling awful. Homer still wants to see me, but we have to sneak around. He make lots of excuses about why he can't spend more time with me, and he's constantly breaking our dates.

The Exploration

I asked Bridget to dialogue with her Inner Child:

ADULT BRIDGET: *(Talking to a large stuffed bear)* What are you feeling right now?

CHILD BRIDGET: I'm really mad at you. You didn't listen to me and take care of me. You gave me away to Homer and now I feel so alone and sad.

ADULT BRIDGET: I thought you loved Homer.

CHILD BRIDGET: I do, but you shouldn't let me get involved with a liar. It hurts too much when he lies to me.

ADULT BRIDGET: Well, I think he loves you too much to lie to you.

MARGIE: Bridget, your Adult seems to be having trouble looking at the truth. A man who will lie to his girlfriend will also lie to you. Again, you are not listening to what your Child knows, your own inner wisdom.

BRIDGET: But he told me that he loved me like he had never loved anyone before, and that he was going to tell Sally as soon as he knew we were really going to be a couple. That's why I agreed to become lovers with him. But now it seems like he wants both of us.

MARGIE: Would that be okay with you?

BRIDGET: Yes, if Sally knows so we don't have to sneak around. But I hate the sneaking, and I guess I am feeling lied to.

Bridget recognized that her Adult had given her Child away to Homer because Homer was so sweet and loving and her Adult believed that Homer could take better care of her than she could of herself, a false belief. She realized she had abdicated her personal responsibility and had instead made Homer responsible. Now she was angry at him for abandoning her, when in fact she had abandoned herself.

Bridget explored her false belief that someone else could make her happy, that someone else could take away her pain and be a better parent for her Inner Child than she could be for herself. She saw that she was expecting Homer to be all that her parents had not been, rather than being willing to do that for herself. She realized that her aloneness was more from the inner abandonment then from the outer one.

Also, Bridget saw that she was feeling like a victim of Homer's choices. She was waiting around for his calls and hated having to hide their relationship. Bridget was angry at him for making Sally more important than her after he had told her how important she was to him and how much he loved her. She felt helpless to do anything about Homer's choice to continue to be dishonest, and it was clear to her that the arrangement was not making him unhappy.

The Loving Behavior

Bridget was very much in love with Homer. It was the first time in years that she had connected so deeply with anyone on so many levels—emotional, intellectual, and sexual. She felt if she lost him she might never find another man with whom she felt so compatible, and she was tired of being alone.

A painful choice had to be faced: Was she willing to lose herself to keep him, or was she willing to risk losing him to retain her own integrity? Her Inner Child made it clear to her that losing herself was not worth having any man. As much as she loved him now, if she continued to give herself up, the anger she was already feeling would eventually replace the love.

Through her dialogue with her Inner Child, Bridget came up with the behavior that felt most loving to her Child: She decided to tell Homer that she was not willing to see him anymore until he was honest with Sally. Also, she did not believe he was merely protecting Sally's feelings, but was really protecting himself; if she went along with it, she was colluding with his and Sally's codependent relationship.

Homer was quite surprised by her decision and tried to talk her out of it, but she stood her ground. She told him not to call her for one month and at the end of that time she would hear his decision. Bridget went through much grief at letting go of the relationship, but she also felt very inwardly powerful. Her self-esteem went up significantly as well.

At the end of the month, Homer called to tell her that he still loved her. He said he realized that she was right about his relationship being codependent, and that he was going to go into therapy to deal with it. He made it clear that he was not going to do anything different regarding his relationship with Sally at this time.

Bridget then worked with her Inner Child to help her accept that she had to move on with her life and not wait for Homer. If she waited with the hope that he really would go into therapy and "see the light," she would again feel like a helpless victim. She accepted that she had fallen in love with a man who did not want a committed relationship with her and realized she had actually known this from the beginning. She chose to ignore it because of her false belief that Homer could take care of her better than she could. She decided she no longer wanted to do this in future relationships.

A couple of months later, Homer called Bridget and wanted to see her. Bridget agreed. Seeing him again brought up all the in-love feelings. She ended up in bed with him, convincing herself that things would be all right.

Days passed, and Homer didn't call her. Bridget realized that she had again abandoned her Inner Child. She had heard her Child's inner voice before she made love with Homer, saying, "Wait, this will hurt me," but chose to ignore it. Now her Child felt that Adult Bridget had not protected her and was feeling depressed.

Bridget saw that much of the depression in her life had come from not listening to and protecting her Inner Child from painful situations. She saw that her Adult was still having a hard time wanting and accepting full responsibility for her Child, a common experience for most of us.

Two weeks later Homer called to tell her that their relationship was over. Bridget's self-esteem took a nose-dive and she came into her next session feeling awful.

BRIDGET: I feel that his rejecting me means I'm unworthy. I've been working with my Inner Child, telling her that she is worthy and that his rejecting her does not mean that she is not worthy, but that feeling of unworthiness is still there. I don't know what to do.

MARGIE: Bridget, I'd like to act as your Child for a moment and to speak to you. Is that okay? *(Bridget nods.)*

(Margie speaking as Bridget's Child): "Of course I feel unworthy, but it's not because Homer rejected me. It's because you don't listen to me and you don't take good care of me. If you thought I was worthy, you would listen to me when I warn you about things and you wouldn't pick men for me who are unavailable to me. I'm never going to feel worthy until you listen to me and take better care of me. If you thought I was worthy, you would pick a man who would love me. It's you who makes me feel unworthy, not Homer. If you thought I was worthy, you wouldn't have picked Homer for me."

BRIDGET: *(Tears streaming down her face)* That's right. I pick men who are just like my mother—dishonest and unavailable—and then I think they are responsible for my lack of worth. I can see that for my Child to feel worthy I have to treat her differently—by picking men who are loving instead of rejecting.

Dina and Nick

The Situation

Dina and Nick came in for therapy together because they were fighting all the time and couldn't figure out why. They knew they loved each other and wanted this relationship, yet found themselves breaking up at least once a week.

Dina, in her early thirties, had been married before and had two young daughters. Tall and dark, she had worked as a model before having children. She had been quite successful in her work, had received a fair amount of money from her divorce, and was receiving child support. She wasn't wealthy, but she had enough money without working to support herself and her children.

She had met Nick about a year before coming in for therapy. Nine months after meeting, they decided to move in together. Nick moved into Dina's house, and that was when the problems started.

Nick was five years younger than Dina and was working as a manager in a supermarket. Before meeting Dina, he had gotten himself into debt through unwise use of credit cards and was spending most of his money paying this off. Dina and he had agreed on what he would contribute to their expenses, but he never seemed to have the money. In addition, he made commitments to do chores around the house, but never seemed to get around to them.

When these things happened, Dina would blow up and Nick would get silent or leave the house. Later they would try to talk about things and Nick would promise to do better, but soon the same things would happen. Dina's anger was getting more and more intense and Nick was doing less and less all the time.

Dina's Exploration

Dina's father died when she was three years old, leaving her mother with very little money. Her mother worked long hours and was generally bitter and angry when she was home. Dina's mother would yell at her, criticize her for even very minor infractions, and often hit her. When her mother wasn't abusing her, her older brother was. Dina grew up feeling unloved and unprotected, always waiting for Daddy to come and make things better.

Dina learned as a little child to caretake her mother as a way to avoid some of the punishment. In her first marriage Dina was also a caretaker, allowing her husband to abuse her, never standing up for herself. Her husband would yell and criticize her, just as her mother did, and Dina responded just as she did as a child, always trying to do better. She was devastated when her husband finally left her.

With Nick she started out as the financial caretaker. When he did not give her what she wanted emotionally in return for the financial caretaking, she took on her mother's role, the narcissistic end of the codependent system. She became the one to yell at and criticize Nick; and the more he allowed it, the angrier she got.

As Dina became immersed in her Inner Bonding work, her grief at the loss of her father and being so abused by her mother and brother surfaced. For weeks she cried deeply, allowing the old pain to move through her and be released. She realized she had always thought it was her fault that her mother and brother abused her and that she had hated her own powerlessness. Now she was projecting this hatred onto Nick, abusing him as she had been abused. She saw that she had even begun to take her rage out on her own children.

Also, Dina realized that she did not value her Inner Child; she had treated her in much the same way she had been treated by her mother and brother and believed her lovability lay in caretaking Nick financially. She was afraid he would leave her if she didn't support him, and at the same time she resented him and felt used.

Nick's Exploration

Nick also came from an abusive childhood. His father had been brutal with him, often flying into out-of-control rages. Nick was not only afraid of his own anger, because he had no role-modeling for setting limits on it, but he was also terrified of Dina's anger. As soon as she yelled at him, he became a frightened child, immobilized and withdrawn. He couldn't fight back, not only because he did not know the limits of his own anger, but also for fear of losing Dina. He felt deeply bonded to her, as she did to him. In spite of their problems, they had fun together and cared deeply for each other.

Nick was also afraid of being controlled by Dina, as he had been by his father. He entered the relationship with a lot of resistance, which he had developed as a child in response to his father. As soon as Dina and he moved in together, his resistance to helping her clicked in and he started withholding by not giving her money or doing chores. She further exacerbated his resistance by getting angry when he didn't do things her way, confirming to his Inner Child that she was just like his dad.

Nick and Dina were both operating as abandoned children, as are all couples locked into a codependent system.

The Loving Behavior: Dina

DINA: What should I do when he says he is going to do something and he doesn't do it? How do I take care of myself in that situation? I guess I don't know what to do besides getting angry. I don't feel so angry anymore, but I still don't know how to respond.

MARGIE: What goes on with your Inner Child when Nick doesn't follow through?

DINA: I guess I feel rejected. I feel like he doesn't care about me, that I'm not important to him.

MARGIE: Maybe your Adult needs to let your Child know that Nick's behavior is not a personal rejection, but that it's coming from his own fears he had long before meeting you. If you didn't take his behavior as a personal rejection, then how would you feel?

DINA: Well, I still wouldn't like it. I want him to carry his own weight. But I can see that if I don't take it personally, then I would be interested in why he is behaving that way.

MARGIE: So when you don't take his resistance personally, you could move into an intent to learn with him and explore his beliefs.

But what if he is not open to that? What would your Inner Child like you to do then?

DINA: I don't know. I'll ask her. *(Looking at her bear)* How would you like me to take care of you when Nick doesn't want to talk about things?

CHILD DINA: *(She turns the bear around and sinks into being little. Her voice is slightly higher.)* Well, just tell him how we feel and then let's go do something else. I don't like to be with him when he's withdrawn.

DINA: I guess that's the hard part for me. I always want to get him to see what he is doing. It's hard for me to just leave it and go do something else.

MARGIE: Have you ever tried it?

DINA: No.

MARGIE: Will you?

DINA: Yes.

Dina came in the following week much encouraged. Leaving Nick alone when he was closed and resistant rather than yelling or lecturing opened the space for him to initiate the discussions and even to do more of the chores. She saw that as soon as she tried to control him, he became more entrenched in his position—a classic power struggle. She found that walking away rather than engaging him was a real challenge for her. It was hard for her to give up that attempt at control. Giving up the control became possible only when she showed up as a loving Adult for her Inner Child. As soon as her Adult abandoned her Child, allowing her to believe she was being personally rejected, her Child immediately moved into her addictive need to control.

The Loving Behavior: Nick

NICK: I don't know how to get myself to do the things I've agreed to do, especially when Dina yells at me.

MARGIE: What does your Child feel about these responsibilities?

NICK: Trapped and controlled. I just want to get away.

MARGIE: How does your Adult feel about them?

NICK: Well, I guess my Adult sees them as my responsibility and that I do want to carry my own weight.

MARGIE: It sounds like your Child is in charge. Where is your Adult when these feelings of being trapped and controlled come up?

NICK: I don't know. Not there.

MARGIE: So as soon as your Child feels trapped and controlled, your Adult abandons your Child and you then resist. What do you think your Child needs from your Adult when he has these feelings?

NICK: I don't know.

MARGIE: Nick, is it your choice to be in this relationship?

NICK: Yes.

MARGIE: Is it your choice to want to be an equal partner?

NICK: Yes.

MARGIE: Then how are you being trapped and controlled?

NICK: I'm not really . . . Oh, I see. I'm letting my Child think I'm trapped and controlled like I was when I was little.

MARGIE: Right!

NICK: So when I feel that way, I need to tell my Child that this is our choice, that Dina is not Dad, and that I want to be here and do these things.

MARGIE: That's right. You've let your Child run things based on false beliefs of the past rather than coming in with the truth from your Adult. The truth is you are not trapped—you do have choice.

NICK: That's right! So if I repeat that to my Child each time I feel trapped, maybe I will be able to get some things done!

Nick found that remembering to tell his Child the truth took a lot of practice. His habit of retreating was so deeply entrenched that it took many months of consistent work before he was able to remember to show up for his Child at the time he was feeling trapped. By doing his Inner Bonding work daily, he slowly learned to be more present in each moment, more aware of his feelings and of how to handle them.

Dina and Nick's codependent system did not change overnight, but it did change due to both of them being deeply committed to their Inner Bonding work.

Candace and Peter

The Situation

Candace and Peter, both in their late thirties and both writers, came in for therapy only four months after they met. They were already caught in a codependent system that threatened to destroy their relationship.

Candace complained that Peter didn't spend enough time with her, while Peter complained he needed more time with his work and friends—

that Candace needed too much from him. He was on the verge of ending the relationship when Candace suggested they came in for therapy.

The Exploration—Peter

When Peter was twelve years old, his father died suddenly of a heart attack, leaving his mother feeling helpless and distraught. Peter was the oldest of four children and the only son. Peter's mother clung to him for comfort and support, putting him in the position of the caretaker. In addition, his mother's energy was somewhat seductive, an energy that frightened Peter and from which he emotionally withdrew.

Peter, left without a father and with only his mother to rely on, learned to take care of her as a way to feel safe. By being there when she needed him, he was able to ensure himself that she would be okay, that he would not lose her and be left alone. Looking back, Peter realized that he lost himself and allowed himself to be smothered and controlled by his mother out of his fear of losing her.

In his previous relationships, Peter had chosen women who did not make demands on him and with whom he did not feel emotionally connected. By dating women he could not really fall in love with, he ensured himself that he would not be smothered and controlled by them. But inevitably he got bored with them and would move on to another relationship. He had been married twice, both times to women he did not love, but with whom he felt safe from being engulfed.

Now, for the first time, he had fallen madly in love, and all his fears of being controlled and smothered were surfacing.

Peter, a screenwriter, was a man of great talent. He not only loved his work, but had many hobbies and activities that were important to him, such as mountain climbing and cross-country skiing, which he liked to do with his friends.

Within weeks after meeting Candace, he began giving up some of the activities that were important to him and not having enough time for his work. He found himself caught, just as he had been with his mother, between his fear of losing Candace and his desire to pursue the other things that gave him pleasure. As much as he loved Candace, he was ready to leave the relationship. Whenever he expressed his desire to spend time with friends or be alone, Candace would get hurt or angry. When he gave in he felt trapped and resentful; and when he didn't he felt guilty because he believed that he was responsible for her feelings.

The only way he knew to deal with his trapped feelings was to leave the relationship. However, each time he had decided to leave, he felt depressed and missed Candace. Each time he came back into the relationship, he felt trapped and smothered.

MARGIE: Peter, it could be that your Inner Child is not happy with either of those choices.

PETER: But I have no other choices.

MARGIE: That's not true. You can stay in the relationship and deal with your feelings of guilt and being engulfed. Both are coming from within your abandoned Child, and from false beliefs from your childhood. I heard two of those beliefs as you were talking to me: "If I do what I want, I will not be loved," and "I'm responsible for others' hurt feelings when I do something they don't want me to do."

These are beliefs that your mother taught you and that you absorbed as a way to survive, but they don't serve you well now. When you learn to be there for your Child's fear by telling your Inner Child the truth, you can feel free within the relationship. A healthy relationship allows intimacy and freedom to pursue other interests, rather than intimacy at the cost of personal freedom.

PETER: That would be nice, but it wouldn't work here. I want to date other women and Candace could never be okay with that.

MARGIE: Why do you want to date?

PETER: Just to see what else is out there.

MARGIE: Peter, you've been dating a long time. You know what is out there. Is it possible wanting to date is just a way to give your Child freedom because you feel so trapped?

PETER: Maybe. I never really want to date when I pull back from Candace. Then I just miss her. But when I'm back with her all I can think about is dating.

MARGIE: So, it seems like the idea of dating gets you out of feeling trapped. Do you do any drugs or alcohol?

PETER: I used to smoke grass a lot, and I find myself doing it more since I've been with Candace. I don't know why.

MARGIE: Peter, dating and grass are addictive ways of taking away the feelings of being engulfed. They are the ways your Inner Child has learned to deal with these feelings when your Adult is not there to take care of him and teach the truth.

PETER: Yeah, they do get me out of those feelings, but I don't get what it means to take care of my Child when Candace is hurt or angry.

MARGIE: Well, I'd like you to spend time dialoguing with your Inner Child this week about your beliefs that you are responsible for others' feelings and that others won't love you if you do what you want. I'd like you to explore your memories of situations with your mother. I'd also like you to go to some Codependents Anonymous meetings. Are you willing to do that?

Peter did spend time dialoguing and going to CoDA meetings. Over the next few months, we continued to explore his childhood experiences, including the terror and grief he felt when his father died. Because his mother was so dysfunctional, Peter never got to feel his own feelings of fear and loss, and now he allowed his Inner Child to feel and grieve, which is what leads to the healing of pain.

The Loving Behavior: Peter

Eventually, through much practice with dialoguing, Peter was able to be there for his Inner Child when he felt trapped and responsible.

PETER: It's getting easier to do what I want to do without feeling guilty, and it's getting easier to tell Candace what I want to do without sounding hard and rejecting. In the past, because I was so afraid of her reaction, I was very distant when I'd tell her what I wanted. She felt rejected as much by my distance as by what I wanted to do.

Now, most of the time, I can gently and lovingly tell her what I want. When she gets upset, I can tell her I don't like her lack of support without feeling guilty. It's amazing—when I don't act lovingly and I abandon my Child, I immediately want out of the relationship or I want to date or go smoke grass. That's when I realize my Adult isn't there.

The Exploration: Candace

When Candace was four years old, her father left her mother for another woman. Candace's mother blamed Candace and her younger brother for his abandonment. Candace had been very bonded to her father and couldn't understand why he left her. She rarely saw him and concluded that she was not good enough for him.

When she was an adult, she found out from her father that her mother did everything possible to keep him away, including lying, telling him that Candace didn't want to see him. Her father had participated in some illegal actions in his business, and her mother threatened to tell the police about it if he came around. So Candace rarely saw him after he left.

In addition, her mother would lie to her, telling her that her father was coming. Candace would sit at the window for hours waiting. When he didn't come, her mother would degrade him and call him names, further eroding Candace's trust in men.

Even though Candace now had a good relationship with her father, she had enormous unexpressed grief within her Child over his original departure. It took months of dialoguing before her Inner Child felt safe enough to let her in on the deep pain of that abandonment. As she slowly opened to the pain, she saw that her whole life had been centered around avoiding that abandonment pain, that her hurt and anger were the ways she had learned to attempt to control the men in her life so they would not leave her. As long as she was unwilling to feel the abandonment pain, she had to protect against it with her controlling behavior.

She had been terrified to feel that abandonment pain, fearing that it would overwhelm her, that it would be endless, that it would make her crazy. But as she learned to be there for the pain of her Inner Child, she found that she could handle it when her Adult was present. Knowing this enabled her to grieve and heal much of her old pain. However, she found that she was still hurt and felt abandoned whenever she wanted to be with Peter and he had other plans.

The Loving Behavior: Candace

CANDACE: I feel really happy only when I'm with Peter.

MARGIE: Candace, isn't there anything else in your life that you really enjoy doing, that really gives you pleasure?

CANDACE: Well, I really enjoy my work when I'm doing it, which as you know I haven't been doing the last few months. (*Candace was a freelance writer who often worked on others' books as a ghost writer. She had finished a book a few months ago and had not been working.*)

MARGIE: What do you enjoy doing when you're not working and not with Peter?

CANDACE: Nothing. I've never had hobbies, and I don't really know how to plan things for myself. My mother never took us anywhere or helped us to do anything.

MARGIE: You seem to be very dependent on Peter for everything. It sounds like you have not been a very good Parent to your Inner Child. She needs you to make up to her for all the things your mother and father never did. Would you ask

	her what she would like to do with her free time other than be with Peter?
CANDACE:	Okay. *(Talking to a doll)* Candy, what would you like to do with our free time? Are there things you always wanted to do and never got to do?
CHILD CANDY:	Yeah, you know there are. I always wanted to learn karate and take accordion lessons. You know I always wanted to do that when we were little, and Mom would never let us.
CANDACE:	That's right! I could still do that, couldn't I?
MARGIE:	Of course. And if you get involved in things that are very compelling to you, things that give you a lot of pleasure, then you might even be happy when Peter is busy, because it will give you a chance to do the other things that are exciting for you. Maybe the reason you've been pulling on Peter so much is that you aren't working and have nothing else to fill your life but him. What about spending time with friends?
CANDACE:	I always neglect my friends when I'm in a relationship. I guess that's not a good idea, is it? I even cancel dates with them when Peter wants to do something with me. It's amazing they're still my friends.

Candace found that when she took responsibility for making herself happy rather than relying on Peter, as well as taking responsibility for any abandonment feelings that came up, she was able to be much more supportive of his work and other outside activities. Not surprisingly, when she let go of trying to control Peter and get him to be with her, she found he wanted to be with her more often.

Loving Your Inner Child with Your Lover

As you can see from the examples about spouses and lovers, when both people are willing to do their Inner Bonding work, codependent relationships can move into recovery fairly quickly. You can also see from the examples that it is possible to shift a codependent system when only one person is willing to do the work, but we never know whether the relationship will get better or fall apart.

Whenever one person changes, the other has to change in some way. There is no guarantee that when you decide to do your own work your partner will eventually open, but that is always possible. It is equally possible that your changing can lead to the end of the relationship. It is always true that in order to be there for ourselves, we have to be willing to risk losing the other. Very often one partner is initially unwilling to do their Inner Bonding work, but comes in for therapy as the other partner changes. When we are unhappy in a relationship and our partner is unavailable for inner work, we have to decide if it's worth remaining unhappy to maintain the relationship or if we'd rather risk losing the relationship to find our own wholeness.

CHAPTER 8

What Are We Responsible For?
Loving Your Inner Child with Your Parents

"But you've lost your childhood," Tallis said. "That can never come back."

Mr. Williams stood and walked around the fallen stones . . . "I don't believe that," he said. "That it's lost, I mean. It's hard to remember the events of childhood, sometimes . . . But the child still lives in the man, even when you're as old as me."

Lavondyss
ROBERT HOLDSTOCK

As we become adults, those of us whose parents are living may find that our role with them reverses and we become the parent, especially when our parents age or are alone. In addition, we may never have moved beyond the belief that we need our parents' approval, or we may believe we are responsible for them. Sifting through our behavior to determine what is codependent and what is loving can be an ongoing challenge.

Common issues with parents include how often we call them, how often we visit them, or how much time we spend with them. Financial issues are frequent problems with parents who are alone or who have little income. Many of us are faced with decisions regarding taking care of ailing parents in our home or putting them into a retirement or convalescent home. If we feel truly loved by our parents, these decisions can clearly be made with a loving intent; but if our parents were absent or were physically, emotionally, or sexually abusive, these decisions become more difficult. Rachael, a client in her mid-thirties who had been violently abused by both parents, had this dialogue with me when she found out her mother was in the hospital with a heart attack:

RACHAEL: Should I go home and see her?

  MARGIE: Do you want to?

RACHAEL: No, I hate her.

  MARGIE: Then why would you go?

RACHAEL: I feel an obligation to go.

After working with her Inner Child, Rachael realized it would be abusive to herself to go. She realized that she needed to address the beliefs that created the sense of obligation and guilt.

What are we responsible for regarding our parents? If they acted in very unloving ways to us, what does it mean to be loving to ourselves with regard to them? These are important questions to which there is no single right answer; what is right is different for each one of us. We can discover our own right actions through Inner Bonding.

Oleg and His Parents

The Situation

Oleg, in his mid-twenties, came in for therapy because he was suffering from obesity. This had been a real problem since he was sixteen.

Oleg was the only child of older, Russian-born parents. His mother, a closet alcoholic, was rarely available to meet his emotional needs. His father was sometimes affectionate and sometimes proud of him, but in general was a very strict disciplinarian. His early memories are mostly of his father, who was sometimes loving and often harsh.

When Oleg was fifteen years old, his father was in a near-fatal car accident, from which he emerged with severe brain damage. When he came home from the hospital, he still looked like Oleg's father but he didn't feel like his father. His father's body was there, but no one was "home" most of the time. His mother responded to this situation by drinking even more, and Oleg was left to handle everything. So Oleg pushed down his own feelings and decided to be "strong," as his father had taught him to be. He soon found that eating large quantities of food was a satisfying way to stuff his feelings of aloneness and rage.

Now, at age twenty-four, Oleg was still living with his parents, and his compulsive eating was completely out of control. He felt responsible for taking care of his father because his mother's drinking was also out of control.

The Exploration

MARGIE: How do you feel living in your parents' home?

OLEG: I hate it. I wish I could move out, but everyone in my family would be mad at me if I did. They all feel it's my responsibility to take care of my father.

MARGIE: Who would take care of him if you didn't?

OLEG: I don't know. I guess my mother would have to.

MARGIE: I wonder how your Inner Child feels about this? *(After explaining the Inner Bonding process, I hand him a doll and a bear and ask him to choose the one his Child most identifies with. He chooses the doll.)* Ask your Child, from your Adult, which is a circle of energy between your head and your heart, your mind and your compassion, how he feels about living with your parents.

OLEG: *(He stares at the doll awhile, clearly uncomfortable and embarrassed about talking to a doll.)* Okay. How do you feel about living with Mom and Dad?

MARGIE: Now turn him around and pull him into your stomach. Focus in your stomach, in your body, and let yourself feel little. Now pretend your Adult is sitting in that chair opposite you and he has just said, "How do you feel about living with Mom and Dad?"

CHILD OLEG: *(Tears welling up immediately)* I feel invisible. Nobody sees me. Nobody cares about me. I never get to have any fun. I feel so alone and helpless. I wish I could have my dad back, or I wish he were dead. I *hate* that he is there but he's not. *(Oleg sobs for a few minutes.)*

MARGIE: Now turn him back around and move back into your Adult. How do you feel about what he's saying?

OLEG: I'm really surprised. I haven't cried in years.

MARGIE: I would say that indicates you haven't been aware of his pain. Do you have an awareness of using food so you wouldn't feel his pain?

OLEG: I haven't been aware of that. I'm just aware of feeling anxious and wanting to eat.

MARGIE: Ask your Inner Child how he feels about you as a Parent— if he feels you are there for him or not.

OLEG: *(To the doll, still looking embarrassed about talking to a doll)* How do you feel about me as a Parent? Am I there for you?

CHILD OLEG: You don't care about me. You never ask what I want. I don't think you like me very much.

MARGIE: Oleg, I think that when your Child feels unloved by you, he
            feels alone and empty inside. I think he has learned to fill
            that emptiness with food. But what he really needs is your
            love. Ask him if he'd like to move out and have your own
            place to live.

OLEG: (*To the doll*) Would you like to have our own place to live?

CHILD OLEG: Yeah, I would love that! But don't we have to stay and take
            care of Mom and Dad? (*His Child is operating from false beliefs
            about responsibility.*)

OLEG: (*To the doll*) I don't know. I would like to leave too, but I don't
            know if we can. (*His Adult has the same false beliefs.*)

I told Oleg that before he could make that decision, he needed more
awareness of his codependent and addictive behavior. I asked him to attend some ACoA meetings, and a few sessions later I asked him to attend
some CoDA meetings. He did, and found these meetings were tremendously helpful in giving him a new perspective on his situation.

Oleg and I spent many months exploring all the ways he had learned
to ignore, deny, and stuff away the feelings of his Inner Child, as well as
his false beliefs concerning his feelings. Some of these were:

Crying is weak.

If I cry and show my weakness, no one will like me.

I'm responsible for others' feelings.

If I open to my feelings, I won't be able to function.

I'm always supposed to know what to do in every situation.

I have to be perfect to be lovable.

If I need help, I'm weak and unlovable.

Oleg became acutely aware that he ate compulsively whenever he felt
alone inside. He also became aware that he felt alone whenever he ignored his feelings and did not take responsibility for them, the feelings of
little Oleg. He finally realized that little Oleg felt trapped in his dysfunctional household.

The Loving Behavior

Slowly, over the weeks and months, Oleg became committed to dialoguing with his Child every day. Through those dialogues he was able to
reach the conclusion that he needed to move out.

Little by little he began to share his new awareness with his mother, and finally he confronted her with her alcoholism. He told his mother how much her drinking had affected him in his life, and suggested that she start attending AA meetings. He made it clear to her that, whether or not she chose to take responsibility for her own behavior, he was moving out. Shortly after that Oleg found an apartment.

Oleg then started attending Overeaters Anonymous (OA) meetings to gain much-needed support to change his eating patterns.

His father's brain damage was such that every once in a while he would become lucid for a few minutes. During one of those times, just before Oleg moved out, he was able to tell his father that he loved him, and to feel some resolution of this lengthy, difficult problem. As a result of Oleg's move, his mother finally made the decision to attend some AA meetings.

Oleg learned to be a loving Adult to his Inner Child by dialoguing every day, and felt supported by his Twelve-Step programs. Eventually he was able to change his entire relationship with food. He no longer stuffed himself in the middle of the night, or shoveled in huge quantities of food without even tasting it. He no longer ate sugar, having realized his addiction to it. Occasionally he still binged, but now saw it as an opportunity to learn how he was not loving his Inner Child.

Linda and Her Mother

The Situation

Linda grew up with a very critical mother and a very passive father. Her mother was constantly shaming her by telling her she was ugly, stupid, and no good. No matter what Linda did, she could not please her mother. In spite of this Linda, now in her late thirties, was married with two daughters and had a successful business. Nonetheless she constantly battled the critical Adult in her own head.

Linda now lived two thousand miles away from her mother. When she talked to her on the phone, which she did every Sunday, she still received a barrage of criticism. Her mother believed she had the right to tell Linda how to raise her daughters, how to deal with her finances, how to manage her husband, and how to run her life. This had been going on for years. Linda knew she didn't like it, but she had no idea how to deal with it.

Linda had originally entered therapy with her husband, Eddie, to deal with marital problems. In the course of therapy this problem with her mother emerged.

The Exploration

MARGIE: How do you feel about your mother?

LINDA: Well, I love her, but I don't like her very much. She's my mother and I want her in my life. I just don't want it to be like this.

MARGIE: Have you ever told her how you feel?

LINDA: I've tried, but she gets so defensive and hurt. She cries and then gets even more critical.

MARGIE: How do you feel when your mother gets hurt and cries?

LINDA: I feel so guilty. I just can't do that to her.

MARGIE: In other words, you feel responsible for hurting her feelings when you try to speak your own truth about your feelings?

LINDA: Well, I am responsible, aren't I? *(The false belief behind the caretaking side of codependence)*

I explained codependence to Linda and suggested that she attend some CoDA meetings and do some reading on codependence, which she agreed to do. A few sessions later we had the following discussion.

The Loving Behavior

LINDA: I've been going to CoDA and reading, and I now see that I'm not responsible for anyone else's feelings. But I still don't know how to take care of my Inner Child when my mother starts criticizing me.

MARGIE: Linda, what would you do if your mother treated one of your daughters that way?

LINDA: She has done that when we've gone there to visit. I've told her if she wants me to visit, she has to be nice to them.

MARGIE: And what's happened as a result of that?

LINDA: Oh, she treats them much better than she treats me.

MARGIE: So, you can stand up for your children, but you can't stand up for yourself? How come you can't say the same thing in your own Inner Child's behalf?

LINDA: I just never thought of it. Even when I think of it now, I can't think of the words to say.

MARGIE: Well, let's practice. I'll be you and you be your mother, okay?

LINDA: Okay. Let's see . . . *(Acting as her mother, talking in a hard, parental, critical tone of voice)* I hope you're not working too hard. A mother needs to be home with her children. I never thought you would be a mother who would neglect your children. I don't know how Eddie stands it with you so busy all the time. You don't even have time to come visit me.

MARGIE BEING LINDA: *(Soft tone of voice)* Mother, I don't want you to talk to me that way. It feels really awful.

LINDA BEING HER MOTHER: *(Angry)* What way? I don't know what you are talking about. You always were too sensitive.

MARGIE BEING LINDA: *(Staying soft)* Mother, I'm no longer available to be criticized and ordered around by you. If you can't talk nicely to me, I'm going to hang up. *(Setting her boundaries)*

LINDA BEING HER MOTHER: *(Threatening tone of voice)* Don't you dare hang up on me.

MARGIE BEING LINDA: *(I make a gesture of hanging up the phone.)*

LINDA: Oh God! I can't do that! That's so mean! *(Many of us have been taught that we are being mean and unloving when we set our personal boundaries.)*

MARGIE: Are you saying that your Inner Child is not deserving of your protection? That it's okay for your mother to be mean to her?

LINDA: I don't know. I'll have to think about this.

The next week Linda came in all smiles.

LINDA: Well, I did it, just as we talked about. And guess what! The day after I hung up on her, she called me and we had a really nice conversation. Once she started in on me again, and I told her she had to stop or I would hang up again—and she stopped! I can't believe it! I also can't believe that I let her do that to me all those years. Now I might actually look forward to visiting her.

Linda did visit her mother a few months later, and she had the best time she had ever had. When she was allowing her mother to mistreat her, she was not only being unloving to herself, but to her mother as well. It is never loving to others to allow them to treat us unlovingly. By being honest and taking care of her own Inner Child—by setting boundaries instead of trying to protect her mother's feelings—Linda gave her mother an opportunity to shift her behavior. Her mother had not realized her behavior was harming Linda until Linda told her. During her visit Linda was able to share with her mother much of the pain she had felt as a child. Her mother had always thought she was being helpful, because Linda had never told her about her pain.

Anne and Her Father

The Situation

Anne grew up in a household where her father was a tyrant and her mother was compliant. Anne was always a rebellious child and often got into trouble with her father. He would punish her by forcing her to stay in her room after school for months at a time, especially when she was a teenager and he feared her involvement with boys. Anne left home at eighteen and made her own way in the world. She had married and divorced, and through the years her relationship with her father had slowly healed. He was no longer angry at her and had learned to respect her. She had worked with her Inner Child on her relationship with her parents and now, at forty years of age, had come to forgiveness toward them. She decided to visit them in Montana.

The visit went fairly well, yet Anne realized that she still had unresolved fears concerning her father. She didn't sleep well while she was there and needed a light on. Her father made efforts to be close to her, yet she found herself keeping him at a distance, not really knowing why.

The Exploration

MARGIE: What were you afraid of?

ANNE: I felt like he was going to come and get me. I feel like he's really angry at me still, and that somehow if I shut all of the lights out in the house I wouldn't be able to protect myself from him. I was afraid he would come and yell at me and kill me for being who I am. But that's crazy, because he likes who I am now and he's not angry at me anymore. I don't know what's going on.

MARGIE: Anne, it sounds like you are projecting onto your father your unloving Adult's anger at your Inner Child. It's really your own unloving Adult, who's been patterned after your father, who tries to kill your Child. Your Adult shames her and doesn't appreciate and value her for who she is. See if you can get into being that father part of you—that critical, angry, shaming part of you that wants to kill you, that part of you that doesn't like who you are.

ANNE: That sounds interesting! Not with her, though (pointing to the bear she used to represent her Inner Child).

MARGIE: Yes, do it with her. You do it to her unconsciously all the time anyway. Now we're just trying to make it conscious.

ANNE: Okay. But I'll put her over there (points to a chair across the room, walks over and puts the bear on the chair), and I'll stand up and do this. Okay. Here goes (yelling at the bear): You stupid bitch, you're just no good! You're not good enough and I don't like the way you do things. You don't do them fast enough for me and you're not smart enough and you never do what I say and I don't like you sometimes and you make me mad and you're responsible for my feelings—you're responsible for taking care of me—I'm not responsible for taking care of you—*and* you're really demanding. Demand, demand, demand, demand—all you want is for me to take care of you all the time and you know what? You don't ask for simple things like normal people. You're always asking for big, big, big things and that's hard on me.

MARGIE: Is that what's essentially wrong with her?

ANNE: *(Anne's Adult speaking to Margie)* She's unmanageable. She wants too much. She always wants too much and you'd think she'd want little things but no, no, no, not her. And it's a real stress and strain on me and plus she doesn't do what I say. Never has done what I told her—has a mind of her own—thinks on her own.

    (Talking to her Inner Child again): And you really make me mad. You make me look bad sometimes. I don't like that. And you make me take risks. I hate taking risks. You make me take risks all the time and I don't like that. Risks. Risks. Risks. Risks. That's all our whole life has been about and I pay the consequences, not you. I do.

MARGIE: Now be your Inner Child and put critical Anne over there.

ANNE: Okay, but I want to tell her something first. *(Anne's loving Adult talking to the bear, holding her in her lap, soft tone of voice)* You can be really you. That's not all of me that's there. I'm here and she's not going to hurt you. You can say what you want to say. Okay, I'm going to sit on the floor so I can connect better to being little.

CHILD ANNE: That really hurts when you talk to me in that tone of voice. I hate it when you've got your hands on your hips. You know I have dreams and I have wishes and I support you. Why can't you support me?

MARGIE: *(Talking to Child Anne)* When she *(the unloving Adult)* is judging you and angry at you, how does that make you feel about other people?

CHILD ANNE: Then I'm angry at them. I'm angry at them and I dislike them and I want them to get away from me and I'm critical of them—I'm super critical of them because they're not perfect either. I'm not perfect.

MARGIE: *(To Child Anne)* But you don't really want to know that it's your own Adult judging and being angry at you, do you? You want to think it's your father, don't you?

CHILD ANNE: Yeah. The only thing is that I get really scared when I'm in that house. I feel like he's gonna come and get me for all of the bad things I ever did. ·

MARGIE: *(To Child Anne)* I wonder what you're afraid Daddy's gonna come and punish you for?

CHILD ANNE: For not listening. I'm afraid that because I didn't listen to him, he's gonna pay me back for it. I'm waiting for him to pay me back for not listening to him and not doing what he said.

MARGIE: *(To Child Anne)* Does your Adult tell you are bad because you didn't listen to him?

CHILD ANNE: Yeah.

MARGIE: *(To Child Anne)* Not listening to Daddy does not make you bad.

CHILD ANNE: But in Daddy's mind I was the worst person in the world.

MARGIE: *(To Child Anne)* And your unloving Adult is still telling you that's true.

CHILD ANNE: Well, tell her to stop.

MARGIE: *(To Child Anne)* You tell her.

CHILD ANNE: Okay. *(To her unloving Adult)* Stop doing that! Stop doing that! Stop doing it more! I know you're stopping but stop doing it more! Stop it! I'm not bad. Tell me I'm not bad. I need to hear it twenty thousand times a day. You tell me I'm bad and then you tell me I'm not and then you go back and forth. I need to hear from you all the time that I'm not bad. I'm not wrong. And I didn't do anything wrong at home. What did I do that was so awful?

ADULT ANNE: *(Now being loving)* Nothing. You were really a good little girl. I'm so sorry that I keep acting like Daddy with you and shaming you.

MARGIE: When you were being the critical parent, your voice and everything was not like an adult—it was like a child, an Adult Child. Are you aware of that?

ANNE: Yeah, and I noticed the way I was standing. I was going like this—*(demonstrates hands on hips like a pouting kid)*.

MARGIE: The whole thing was like being an angry kid. Often our unloving Adult is patterned after the abandoned Child of our parents. The unloving Adult is actually an Adult Child, a Child who had to be an Adult. Your Mom and Dad were the adults, but they both acted like an abandoned Child, so your Adult patterned herself after their abandoned Inner

Children. Now, when you are being critical, you are an unloving Adult acting like an abandoned Child.

ANNE: Criticizing my own Child.

MARGIE: Right!

ANNE: Okay. Boy, the feelings are really strong! When I was doing it, I was embarrassed that it was so right there.

MARGIE: But that's what you absorbed from your parents and that's what you continue to do to yourself. Then you project it out onto them or other people.

The Loving Behavior

ANNE: Okay, so how do I heal the unloving Adult?

MARGIE: With your Higher Self or Higher Power. Your Higher Self or Higher Power needs to deal with your critical, ego Adult. Why don't you talk to your unloving Adult right now, from your Higher Self?

ANNE: Okay. That's kind of neat. Okay, my Higher Self. I have to envision a critical parent and how I would talk to her.

(Puts a pillow on a chair and talks to unloving Adult): Taking risks is a normal part of life. It is a loving thing to do for yourself and it is important to us and that . . . (Anne stops talking to her Child and talks to me.) I don't know how to talk to her. I'm scared to talk to her. I don't know what to say to her without criticizing her for being such a schmuck.

MARGIE: Try to see her as someone who wants to love but doesn't know how. She is an Adult acting like an abandoned Child, and she is coming from the belief system of an abandoned Child.

ANNE: Okay, listen now. The beliefs that you have are not correct. First of all, little Anne was not a bad person because she did not listen to Dad. The truth is she had a right to be who she is and express who she is in the world and be proud and be happy about that. There is no reason to feel bad about her because she didn't listen to Dad. Dad is not going to hurt us. Daddy is not God and we are not going to be punished for not listening to him. We have a right to be who we are.

I know it's scary taking risks for the little girl, but it is better to take risks and be happy than to not take risks and be miserable. And I know you think she's demanding, but she's a creative, wonderful, talented, little girl. She needs the room to grow and explore and be. That's who she's always been and that's not bad either. That's just who she is.

You don't have to do everything she wants to do all in one day. You're putting that on yourself. She's not saying do it for me right now or else the world is going to end. You think you have to do it right now and you don't. You can pace yourself and you can work at it. You're putting that big load on yourself. Don't blame her for it, please.

And you don't have to worry about being massacred for not doing or listening to what a man says. You are not a child anymore. He can't hurt you. He's not going to hit you. And no male is going to do that because we won't let them.

MARGIE: How does that feel?

ANNE: It feels fine.

MARGIE: Good. What you're doing here is speaking the truth to the ego, the fragmented, separated, disconnected part of you that operates from the false beliefs of the past.

ANNE: Can I, in my dialogues, write to my unloving Adult?

MARGIE: Yes, it is the Higher Self's job to speak to the unloving Adult and the abandoned Child—the ego voices—and to teach them.

ANNE: Okay. I'm feeling like I can distinguish who my abandoned Child is, and I can write to her; but I can't always grab this unloving Adult.

MARGIE: Well, let's say someone yells at you and your Child reacts with a scared feeling. If your loving Adult comes in and says, "It's okay. This person is having a bad day or is threatened. You haven't done anything wrong," and reassures the Child, the anxiety goes away. But if the anxiety continues, it could mean two things. Either your unloving Adult has come in said, "They're treating you that way because you're a jerk and you don't listen and you do things wrong and you take too many risks," and so on, or it could be that your Child already has those beliefs and the Adult has not come in to tell her the truth.

ANNE: Okay, then help me with something that I've been going through for the last two days. I realize that I'm telling my Child she's bad. I write to her as soon as I'm aware of shaming her, and I take my pad everywhere. I reconfirm with her that she's not bad, she's not wrong, and I value her.

MARGIE: But you also need to address the part of you that has said she is bad. You need to speak to the unloving Adult, the Adult Child.

ANNE: So, write to that one, too?

MARGIE: Yes. You're trying to heal the false ego beliefs. The ego beliefs are coming from both the Adult and Child aspects. If you are only speaking to the Child, you may not be addressing the part of you that has the false beliefs. The unloved Child absorbs the beliefs from the unloving Adult, which you got from your parents. So you want to address the false beliefs of your ego aspect. Sometimes that means addressing an Adult aspect, sometimes it means addressing a Child aspect. It depends on where it feels the belief is lodged.

ANNE: So it's really that you're addressing the ego, but you separate it out into the head part and the feeling part, in order to make it more tangible so that you can address it.

MARGIE: That's right. You know, you can deal with feelings over and over. But if the beliefs don't shift, if the thought process doesn't shift—which is the Adult process—the feelings are never going to really be permanently different. The feelings of the Child come from the thoughts of the Adult. When the Adult thoughts are negative and unloving, the feelings of the Child are anxiety and aloneness.

ANNE: I get it. But if you come in as a loving Adult with loving messages, why doesn't that shift the beliefs of the unloving Adult?

MARGIE: Because you've dealt with the beliefs on a feelings level. You haven't addressed them on the level of your thought processes.

ANNE: But just to have those thoughts you're counteracting the thoughts of the ego.

MARGIE: But you're counteracting thoughts without hearing the ego's beliefs. You need to hear the ego's thoughts. When you get that feedback and hear that argument, then you can confront the false beliefs and see the truth.

ANNE: Do you mean it's like saying to an abandoned Child, "You're an okay kid," and at the same time telling the kid to shut up and not say, "But I don't feel like an okay kid"?

MARGIE: That's right. You need to give your unloving Adult the chance to argue back and say, "Well, you're telling me this, this, and this, but what I believe is this, this, and this . . . and why are you right?" Then you keep coming in with the truth of the Higher Self, and eventually the beliefs shift.

ANNE: That's good, I like that.

MARGIE: Don't forget that when you're dealing with your Child you're dealing on a feeling level. But you've also got the thought level, the intellect.

ANNE: But isn't that the loving Adult?

MARGIE: Not necessarily. Your thought processes or intellect can come in as the unloving Adult just as well. So when you are talking to the feelings of the Child, the unloving Adult intellect may be interjecting a little, and then everything you are telling your Child doesn't sink in. It's like repeating affirmations and they don't sink in . . . because you haven't addressed the belief system, and the belief system may be coming from your intellect or from your feelings.

ANNE: After you talk to your little girl, you say, "Okay, I just talked to my kid and how does that feel?" If it worked and you felt better, then there is no need to address the Adult. But if it didn't feel better, then you need to say, "Okay, now we need to deal with the unloving Adult."

MARGIE: Right.

ANNE: But sometimes it feels better for about three or four or five minutes.

MARGIE: Well, then address it when it is not feeling better. The feelings come from the thoughts. If you're sitting in your living room and you suddenly get the thought that you've made a bad investment and you're going to lose all of your money, what are you going to end up feeling?

ANNE: Awful. Terrified.

MARGIE: Okay, you weren't feeling terrified before you got the thought. The thought generated the feeling. If you're sitting in your living room and you get a vision of enormous success and prosperity and you see yourself as wonderful and beautiful and you're really into that, then what are you feeling?

ANNE: Great.

MARGIE: The feeling comes from the thought. So, if you're telling your kid all this good stuff and she feels great for five minutes and then she doesn't feel great, that means there's a thought that's come in from the unloving Adult. And those thoughts have to be addressed. Those are the false beliefs that are governing your life.

ANNE: Okay, I see now where I did that this morning. A client called me and he wanted me to do some extra work. I went into feeling bad and wrong, so I wrote to my little girl about valuing the work she has done. But my head was saying something like, "Well, you really haven't worked that hard. You've been screwing around." And then I was trying to tell my little girl that I value the work she has done, while the other part of my brain was saying, "Well, well, well, you know you didn't do a lot of work and you deserve that . . ." That was going on in my head all the way over here. One part of me was saying, "I value you," and another part was saying, "No, no, no." But the truth is, I have done good work.

MARGIE: So you need to address that part that has the false beliefs and challenge those beliefs by looking at past successes.

Anne, how are you feeling about your father right now?

ANNE: *(Smiling)* I can see that he is not the issue at all. All my recent experience with him tells me that he likes me and is proud of me. That's the truth. And I'm not feeling scared of him now. I guess I just shifted my belief about him, didn't I?

Martin and His Father

The Situation

Martin is in his early forties and runs a successful children's clothing manufacturing company. However, through some bad investments, he found himself in debt a number of years ago and has been working hard to pull himself out of it. He is married and has two children.

Martin's parents split up when he was a small child and he rarely saw his father. His mother remained single, and Martin grew up a very lonely only child with fantasies of a loving father that never got fulfilled.

After he was married and had his first child, his father, Chuck, came back into his life. Chuck had always had a hard time earning a living and was not working when he contacted Martin. Martin, anxious to heal the relationship with his father and to have a grandfather for his child, hired him to run personal and business errands for him. For a while this seemed to work out fine, but after a year or so Chuck slowly stopped doing his work.

Since he couldn't seem to find another job, Martin kept supporting him, even though it put a strain on his own financial situation. At the time he came in for therapy, he had been supporting his father for years and was feeling trapped and resentful. He had threatened numerous times to stop supporting him, but never actually did.

The following exploration occurred after about a month of therapy. Martin, initially uncomfortable working with a doll to represent his Inner Child, had overcome his uneasiness and had been dialoguing with his Inner Child consistently at home.

The Exploration

MARGIE: From what you've said, I'd guess you feel trapped and resentful because you feel you have to support him—that you have no choice. Is that right?

MARTIN: Well, I know I don't have to, but I'm afraid of what would happen to him if I didn't. I'm afraid he would end up on the streets or kill himself.

MARGIE: How would you feel if that happened?

MARTIN: Terribly guilty.

MARGIE: Would you miss him?

MARTIN: Yes.

MARGIE: So you wouldn't just feel guilty, you would also feel sad. Why would you miss him?

MARTIN: Well, I never had a father as a child. I like being with him and seeing him play with my children.

MARGIE: Sounds like the little boy in you likes having a father around. Would you ask your Inner Child how he feels about your father?

MARTIN: Okay. (*Picks up the doll and sets him on his lap*) How do you feel about Dad?

CHILD MARTIN: (*Turns doll around and lets himself feel little*) I love him. I was always sad when I was little that he wasn't there, and now he is there and I don't want him to go away again.

MARGIE: How do you, the Adult, feel about him?

MARTIN: Well, I like him and I'm glad that we've been able to have a relationship. And my children like him too. But I also feel used. I feel like I'm the parent and he's the child and I don't want it to be that way. I just wish he would get a job. I hate it when he comes around asking for extra money beyond what I give him monthly. I never seem to be able to say no to him, and then I always feel angry and resentful after giving him more money. (*This is a typical feeling resulting from the choice to caretake.*) Plus, I put myself under too much financial pressure when I do that.

MARGIE: The chances are he will not get a job as long as you are supporting him. Why should he? From what you've said, he never really wanted to work, and as long as you are supporting him he doesn't have to. But I can also understand that you are afraid of what will happen to him if you stop giving him money. Your Adult feels responsible for him and your Child loves him and wants him in your life. Perhaps the real issue here is the extra money you give him. So the question is, how can you best take care of yourself in this situation?

The Loving Behavior

Martin saw that cutting his father off financially would not make himself happy, yet continuing to completely support him was also making Martin unhappy. He decided that he would slowly cut down on the amount of money he was giving him, ultimately giving him just enough to live on. That way he knew he would not end up living in the streets or killing himself, and perhaps it would even give him the incentive to earn some of his own money.

Martin realized that a big part of the issue was that he was giving his father what his father wanted rather than what Martin wanted to give. He saw that he was caretaking his father and that caretaking was causing his resentment. He realized that he did not feel resentful giving him enough money to live on, that he was willing to continue doing that as long as he lived, but it was giving him the extra money that caused his resentment.

Martin had no expectations of his father getting a job and was willing to accept his father being upset with him for cutting down the money. Martin's Inner Child felt secure that he would still have a father around, and his Adult no longer felt resentful. His resentment had come from his inability to say no to his father's demands for extra money.

The question of how much responsibility to take for aging parents is one that many of us face. We need to dialogue with our Inner Child to see if we are giving out of fear, obligation, or guilt, or out of love. When we give out of love, we never feel resentful. Martin loved his father and realized that he was giving him basic support out of love. But the extra money was coming from fear and guilt, which always leads to resentment.

Loving Your Inner Child with Your Parents

It is my belief that we do not "owe" it to our parents to take care of them, any more than I believe my children "owe" it to me to take care of me. Hopefully, when we are faced with that responsibility and choose to take it on, we can find a place within ourselves that comes from love. Or, if we choose not to take on the responsibility (if for many good reasons we feel it would be unloving to ourselves to take it on), that we accept that choice without guilt.

Being loving to ourselves means doing what feels best to us. If giving to our parents feels best and we are doing it out of love, then we are not being codependent. But if we are giving out of fear, obligation, or guilt, we are being codependent—and we will always feel angry and resentful about this kind of giving. It would be unloving to ourselves to force ourselves to give in codependent ways. Many people had parents who were horribly unloving and abusive to them as children, but who now expect to be taken care of. When this is the case, giving to these parents may be being abusive to oneself.

Regardless of your relationship with your parents when you were growing up, roles change now that you are an adult. Your ability to provide care change, and your feelings change, becoming sometimes more, sometimes less loving. In the end, only you can know what you are responsible for. You can determine what is right and loving for yourself through Inner Bonding dialogue, both with your Inner Child and with your Higher Power.

CHAPTER 9

Becoming Role Models for the Future: Loving Your Inner Child with Your Children

It is vitally important to learn when your Inner child needs attention.
Homecoming
JOHN BRADSHAW

No matter how hard we try to be good parents to our own children, we will always make mistakes. However, in order to avoid making the kinds of mistakes our parents made by modeling unloving behavior and giving us messages and beliefs that came from their own inner disconnection, we can truly understand and put into practice loving self-parenting.

If we have an authoritarian Inner Parent who is constantly shaming our own Inner Child, we might find ourselves projecting this onto our children, emotionally abusing them with yelling and criticism. Or we might put aside our own Inner Child, putting ourselves last, not taking good care of ourselves because we believe our children are more deserving than we are. If we have a permissive Inner Parent, one who is absent or indulgent with our Inner Child, we might find ourselves being absent or indulgent with our children, allowing them to behave in ways that are harmful to themselves or others.

People who operate from a completely abandoned Inner Child because the Adult is absent have no Adult to set limits for themselves and may abuse their children emotionally, sexually, or physically. Child abuse occurs from a rageful abandoned Inner Child with no functioning Adult to create appropriate boundaries.

Even when we try hard to be good parents, when we are not being loving to our own Inner Child, we are teaching our children to be unloving to themselves.

As parents we are faced with many challenges, such as when and how to discipline, when to set limits and when to let go, when to help and when to stand back, as well as how to meet our own needs while also meeting our children's needs. We can't possibly know how to handle all these situations in loving ways when we are out of touch with our inner feelings, reactions, and needs. When facing these challenges, most parents respond from their primary codependent position, their narcissism or their caretaking.

Let's take the example of Brad, age fourteen. He states at the dinner table that he has a paper due in school the next day and doesn't want to do it. His narcissistic father responds, "Get to work, Brad. Don't make me ashamed of you. I don't want your teacher thinking I got a dumb kid." His caretaking mother offers to help him and ends up doing it for him, which Brad knew would happen if he complained. Neither response is loving; both responses come from the parent's internal disconnection.

A loving response in this situation would be an intent to learn: "Brad, there must be a good reason you don't want to do the paper. Do you want to talk about it?" In order to respond with an intent to learn, his parents must not have an investment in Brad succeeding—that is, their worth cannot be attached to how well Brad does in school. Only through Inner Bonding and defining their own worth can they truly be loving and supportive to Brad.

Karen, Thomas, Hilary, and Alana

The Situation

Karen and Thomas had originally come to my office for marriage counseling. One day, after I had not seen them for quite a while, they called about a problem with one of their daughters. I suggested that they all come in for a family session.

Hilary, ten years old, clearly dominated the session. Outspoken and vivacious, she was constantly cutting off her parents and her older sister Alana, age fourteen. When any of them objected to being interrupted, Hilary would whine and pout, saying, "Nobody ever lets me speak." All three of them would give in to her at this point.

Karen and Thomas were worried because Hilary was afraid to be alone—not alone in the house, but alone in her room or alone in the kitchen or wherever she was. She always wanted to be with Alana, and

Alana was getting frustrated. She wasn't getting any time to herself, or time to be with her friends without Hilary.

Karen worked part-time as an illustrator, and Thomas was a very hard-working and successful chiropractor. Because they both worked, they had a housekeeper to take care of the house and children when they weren't there. The housekeeper, along with the rest of the family, constantly catered to Hilary's demands. Hilary would yell, cry, and pout when she didn't get her way, and everyone would put aside their own needs to shut her up. As a result, she never learned to take responsibility for herself and was becoming more and more unpleasantly demanding. She was in total control of the household.

By the end of the first session, Hilary was quite upset with me because I set boundaries by not letting her interrupt when others were speaking. Surprisingly, when I asked her if she wanted to come back, she said yes. I told her that first I needed some sessions with her parents.

The Exploration

MARGIE: Why are the two of you afraid to say no to Hilary?

THOMAS: I'm not afraid to say no, but I'm not around a lot. I work long hours so I have kind of let Karen manage the child-raising. I'm not the one who Hilary usually comes to when she is unhappy.

KAREN: It's been hard for me to say no to both of my daughters, but it hasn't been a problem with Alana. She has always been such a responsible child, even when she was little. I guess I feel like a bad mom when I say no. (*False belief: It's unloving to say no to your child if it upsets your child.*)

In previous sessions, when I had worked with Karen and Thomas on their relationship, we had explored Karen's background. Her father had died when she was two years old, and her mother had become a street person. Karen had been put into numerous foster homes, where she was often badly abused. She was finally adopted when she was six by an older couple who had no children.

Because she had so little mothering when she was very young, Karen was determined to be a good mother to her daughters. She wanted to give them everything that she didn't have, to be there for them in the way she had wished someone had been there for her. The problem was, though, that in not taking responsibility for her own Inner Child and in taking responsibility for Hilary's feelings, she was teaching Hilary to be a narcissistic codependent.

MARGIE: Karen, how does your Inner Child feel when you ignore her and give in to Hilary? Would you ask her now?

KAREN: Okay. *(Talking to her stuffed rabbit)* How do you feel when I give in to Hilary?

CHILD KAREN: I feel just like I always felt when I was little—like I don't count. Other kids who had parents mattered, but I never mattered. Hilary matters, but I don't matter to you. She's much more important to you than I am. Sometimes I hate you. You let Hilary walk all over me.

It soon became apparent through more dialogue with her Inner Child that Karen had never accepted responsibility for her own Inner Child. It also became clear to her that unless she was willing to accept it now, nothing would change with Hilary.

MARGIE: Karen, how would you feel about trying to take care of little Karen instead of Hilary this week and see what happens?

KAREN: Well, I can try. But Hilary is going to hate it.

MARGIE: How will she ever learn to show up as a loving Adult for herself when you don't show up as a loving Adult for yourself? She needs a role-model.

KAREN: Okay, but I don't know what to do when she gets upset.

MARGIE: What are the things she does when she is upset?

KAREN: She pouts, or cries, or has a temper tantrum, kicking and screaming; or she whines and talks incessantly, trying to convince me to do what she wants.

MARGIE: What are the things she gets upset about?

KAREN: Not getting to be in Alana's room with her, not having someone make her a snack, not having someone play with her when she doesn't know what to do, not being able to watch TV when everyone else wants it off, not getting to go over to her friend's house across the street as much as she wants because she hasn't gotten her chores done.

The Loving Behavior

MARGIE: Karen, ask your Inner Child what she would like you to do for her when Hilary is manipulating you to caretake her.

KAREN: Okay. *(To the rabbit)* How can I take care of you when Hilary is angry or crying and trying to get me to do what she wants?

CHILD KAREN: I don't like to be with her when she is like that.

KAREN: Okay, so she wants me to get her away, but I don't know how to do that. Sometimes I have to make dinner and I can't just get away.

MARGIE: How would you feel about having a walkman and earphones handy with music or interesting tapes ready? That way you could turn up the volume so you couldn't hear her. Or, if you weren't cooking, maybe you could go in your room and lock the door and turn on loud music or the TV so you don't hear her. Does that sound okay?

KAREN: Won't she feel rejected?

MARGIE: If she does you can make it clear that you love her, but you don't like being around her when she acts like that. Thomas, how do you feel about this?

THOMAS: I think it's great. It's basically what I do, but I can see it doesn't have any impact when I'm the only one who does it. I think we have to make sure Alana and the housekeeper do the same thing. I think if Hilary's behavior stops working for her, she will stop acting like that.

MARGIE: Right. Are you willing to try it, Karen, and ask Alana and the housekeeper to do it, too? I'm not asking you to be mean to Hilary. I'm asking you to be loving to yourself.

Karen agreed to try. Two weeks later, she came for a session alone. She had worked very hard at taking care of herself; and while she could not yet do it all the time, she was feeling much better about things. She had experienced some intense feelings of inner joy at taking care of herself, especially when she was able to get beyond the guilt of not caretaking Hilary. Hilary, after being very angry for the first week, soon found out that escalating her obnoxious behavior got her nowhere. She was actually beginning to learn to make herself happy by herself.

Karen noticed that Alana wanted to spend more time with Hilary than she had before. The four of them even spent some enjoyable family time together over the weekend, something they had not been able to do in a long time because there had always been so much tension. I continued to work with Karen once a month for the next few months, helping her explore other areas where she had not been loving to her Inner Child. More and more, Karen saw her own Inner Bonding being reflected in her daughter's behavior.

Hilary and Karen had two more sessions together. I taught Hilary the Inner Bonding process. She was resistant to being a loving Adult to her

Inner Child, but was able to do it in a role-play when I played her angry, blaming Child. Once Karen saw that she was capable of being there for herself, she felt better about backing away from the caretaking. Karen became aware of the fact that whenever she did not take care of her Inner Child, Hilary would abandon herself as well. Recognizing this proved very important in motivating her in her own Inner Bonding process.

Annette, Marvin, and Todd

The Situation

Annette, a dance teacher, and Marvin, a successful architect, had been married for eleven years. They had been in various forms of therapy for years because of violence in their relationship, but Marvin had continued to physically abuse his wife. Annette was planning on leaving the relationship, but decided to give therapy one more try.

Both worked diligently with Inner Bonding, and within a few months Marvin had control over the anger that led to the violence. He learned to take responsibility for his Child's anger and to discover the beliefs and behavior that led to the anger. He learned to act in his Child's behalf rather take his anger out on Annette. Annette, who had felt very much the victim in the relationship, had begun to learn what it meant to take her own power and take care of her abandoned Child.

They were in the midst of dealing with many other related issues in their relationship—time, money, sexuality—when the issue of six-year-old Todd, their only child, came up. On a Saturday afternoon a few days before their session, Todd stayed home with Annette while Marvin was out doing errands. Todd had spent the whole time trying to hit Annette. She tried to talk to him, she yelled at him, she tried to hold him, but nothing would stop him. She was quite distraught in the session as she talked about it. I asked her if this was the first time this had happened, and she admitted that it was a fairly frequent occurrence. She said she had tried over and over to find out why he was so angry at her, and he refused to talk about it. I asked if she ever hit Todd, and she said no. I asked them to bring Todd with them to the next session.

The Exploration

It quickly became apparent that Todd would not talk to me in the presence of his parents. He just sat quietly with his eyes cast down and a feeling of pain about him. I asked him if it would be all right with him if his parents left the office for a while and I talked to him alone. He nodded.

MARGIE: Todd, you can tell me anything you want and if you don't want me to tell your parents, I won't. It will be up to you. Okay? *(He nods his head, still not talking.)* Are you angry at your mom? *(Again, he nodded)* Are you angry at your dad? *(He shakes his head no.)*

Do you know why you are angry at your mother? *(Again he nods.)* Would you tell me? *(Silence)* Does your mom yell at you? *(He nods.)* Does she hit you? *(Again he nods.)* A lot?

TODD: *(Looking straight at me, struggling not to cry.)* She yells at me a lot, and sometimes she hits me a lot.

MARGIE: How does she hit you? With her hand? With a belt?

TODD: With her hand. She gets so mad sometimes she just starts hitting. Then she's sorry and she holds me.

MARGIE: Is that why you hit her? *(He nods.)* Can I tell your parents you told me this?

Todd hesitated a minute and then agreed. I gave him a hug and told him he had a lot of courage. When Annette and Marvin came back into the office, I told them what Todd had said.

ANNETTE: *(Defensive)* I don't hit him very often. It's hardly ever happened.

MARGIE: Annette, in Todd's experience you hit him a lot. Remember when you first came here for therapy and you told me Marvin hit you a lot? He became defensive and said it happened only about once a year? *(Annette nodded.)* And I'm sure you remember me telling Marvin that in your experience it felt like all the time because the threat of it was there all the time. You never knew when it would happen or what would trigger it.

Todd feels the same with you. And hitting is the only way the two of you have taught him to deal with anger. Marvin, you taught him to hit by hitting Annette; and Annette, you taught him by hitting him. You both abandon yourselves when you are angry and allow yourselves to harm others. If you want Todd to learn other ways of expressing anger, then both of you have to role-model other ways, which I know you are beginning to do. Annette, I want you to consider the possibility that some of your anger at Todd is really anger at your father *(who also hit her a lot)* and anger at Marvin. Would you work with your Inner Child about this at home? *(She nods.)*

The following week Annette came in by herself.

ANNETTE: You were right. I'm enraged at both my father and Marvin. My Inner Child is also furious at me for letting Marvin hit me and for hitting Todd. What do I do with this anger?

MARGIE: Let's see if you can get some of it out right now. Imagine that your father is sitting in that chair, and you can say anything you want to him without punishment. What would you say? Let yourself be little, the little girl in you.

ANNETTE: *(Tears welling up)* Oh Daddy, I loved you so much. How could you be so mean to me? How could you hit me and hurt me? I was just a little girl. I tried so hard to be good.

MARGIE: Annette, where is the anger?

ANNETTE: I don't know. I always just start to cry when I think about my father.

MARGIE: Try putting Marvin there in the chair.

ANNETTE: I don't feel angry at him either. He's been so great lately. I think it's myself I'm mad at. I think my Child is very angry at my Adult.

MARGIE: Okay, then be your Child and put your Adult in the chair.

CHILD ANNETTE: *(Shouting)* Why do you always let people hurt me? What's the matter with you? You're supposed to take care of me and protect me. I don't like you. I hate you. Where are you when I need you? *(She starts to cry.)* Oh God, I'm really angry at my mother for letting my father hit me and not protecting me, and now I'm acting just like my father acted with me.

(To her Adult from her Child): How could you let me hit Todd? You're supposed to be there for my anger and help me deal with it. And how could you let Todd hit me? Do something! Do something!

(Back into the Adult mode): God, that's the problem. I don't know what to do with my anger and I don't know how to stop Todd from hitting me. What do I do?

The Loving Behavior

MARGIE: Annette, do you still feel angry?

ANNETTE: No, I feel better. I feel calmer.

MARGIE: Whenever you feel angry, why not try doing what you just did? You could go in your room and lock the door and yell at whoever you're angry at—Todd, Marvin, either of your parents, or your-self—until the anger feels dissipated. It worked for you here. Don't you think it would work at home?

Annette agreed, and then I asked her what Todd did that triggered her anger.

ANNETTE: It's usually things like interrupting me when I'm busy, or not listening to me.

MARGIE: It sounds like it's a control issue with him. You feel angry when you feel he's controlling you or not letting you control him?

ANNETTE: Yes. Because my dad had total control over me, and so did Marvin. I was afraid of both of them. I'm going to try to be aware of that. But what shall I do when Todd tries to hit me and he won't stop and talk to me about it?

MARGIE: What would your Inner Child like you to do?

ANNETTE: She'd like me to get her away from him.

MARGIE: You could go in your room and lock your door until he is ready to stop. Or, if you are busy in the rest of the house, you could put him in his room for a few minutes. If he won't stay there, try putting a hook lock on his door, just for the next month or so, until he realizes he can't hit you anymore. But never leave him in there for more than five minutes at a time. Let him know that as soon as he can stop hitting you, he can come out.

This is a boundary issue for both of you. Both of you need to learn to respect each other's boundaries. Hitting is always an infringement of boundaries—when he does it to you and when you do it to him. How would you feel about that?

ANNETTE: I'll try it. So, I lock myself in my room when I feel angry and out of control, and I lock myself in my room when he is angry and out of control, or I lock him in his room.

MARGIE: And the more you can go into your room rather putting him in his room, the better. That way, you're setting your own boundaries without trying to control him.

Annette and Marvin each kept working on taking responsibility for their own anger. Within a few weeks of the above session, they began to see a change in Todd. I told them about hitting the bed with a pillow, or a rolled up towel, or a plastic bat when they were really angry, and asked them to teach that to Todd. Todd really liked that. All of them were finding appropriate ways of expressing their anger, rather than dumping it on each other.

Any time we allow our children to abuse us, we are being unloving to ourselves and to them. However, it won't work to abuse them in order to stop them from abusing us or abusing siblings. I'm reminded of the cartoon showing a father spanking a child and saying, "I'll teach you not to hit kids smaller than you." Clearly the father is teaching exactly that—that when you are angry or frustrated, it is appropriate to express it by hitting someone smaller than you. Often hitting between siblings can be traced back to the children being hit by the parents. "Oh, I just spank him once in a while, when he really deserves it," many parents will say. Hitting is hitting, whatever you want to call it. If you don't want your children to hit others, then don't deal with your anger by hitting them.

Older teenage children can sometimes become extremely abusive to their parents—stealing, living at home without working or going to school, using drugs, or being verbally or physically abusive to their parents. If their parents have been overly permissive, allowing their children to violate the parents' boundaries, the children grow up with no Inner Adult to set limits on their behavior. They may be very self-centered and self-indulgent, having no regard for their parent's rights or anyone else's. The book *Toughlove*, and the Toughlove classes, teaches parents how to start being loving to themselves, which may mean setting very strong limits for their children.[1]

The best situation is for parents do their Inner Bonding work before having children. Hopefully, more and more people will realize the importance of this before having their children. But it is never too late to do our own work, and it is never too late for it to have a positive effect on our children, even if they are adults and no longer living at home. In the last six years, through my own Inner Bonding work, I've gone through major recovery from caretaking, and I can certainly see the positive effects of my changes on my adult children.

Lynn, Ben, Amy, and Ryan

The Situation

Lynn, Ben, Amy, and Ryan came in for therapy because the school had recommended it for nine-year-old Amy. Amy was not only having a hard time concentrating in school, but she was constantly getting into fights with the other children and ended up hitting and biting them. Even when she had a friend at home with her, the friend would often end up somehow getting hurt during play with Amy. Lynn and Ben stated that this had been going on since preschool. They had been to different therapists and tried different things, but nothing had worked. Their baby, Ryan, was almost a year old, and they were concerned that Amy would hurt him.

Ben informed me that he would not be available for most of the sessions. He traveled a lot in his work and just did not have the time. In addition, he did not feel this was his problem. Since he was gone most of the time, he felt certain that Lynn was responsible for the problem. I told him that I did not necessarily see it that way, but that I accepted his decision and would work with Lynn. I asked Lynn to come with Amy for the next session.

The Exploration

The first part of the session was spent with Amy, trying to get a handle on the source of her anger. The essence of it was, "Nobody likes me. My mom doesn't like me, my dad doesn't like me, my teachers don't like me, and the kids at school don't like me." *(Belief: I'm not lovable.)*

MARGIE: When you feel someone doesn't like you, is that when you hit them?

AMY: I try not to, but sometimes I just get so angry I can't help it.

MARGIE: Why do you think your mother doesn't like you?

AMY: Because she is always yelling at me and she never wants to be with me. She spends all her time with Ryan.

MARGIE: Are you angry at Ryan?

AMY: No, I love Ryan. He so cute! I like to play with him when Mom lets me. She thinks I'm going to hurt him, but I won't.

MARGIE: Why do you think your dad doesn't like you?

AMY: Well, I guess he likes me, but he's never home. Sometimes he's nice to me.

MARGIE: Amy, do you think that when you hit the kids at school, you might really be angry at your mom or dad, but you can't hit them so you hit the kids instead?

AMY: I'm angry at Mom when she yells at me, and I'm angry at the kids at school when they won't play with me. *(Belief: Either I can have control over their liking me or playing with me by getting angry with them, or I can avoid the pain of the rejection by getting angry.)*

MARGIE: Maybe they won't play with you because they are afraid you will hit them. What do you think?

Amy agreed that might be the reason. Then I asked her if I could tell her mom what she had said, and she said yes. I brought Lynn back into the office and told her what Amy had said. I then asked Amy if it would be all right if I talked to her mother alone for a few minutes, and she said yes.

MARGIE: Lynn, how do you feel about Amy?
LYNN: Well, I love her, but I've never felt close to her. I don't know why. I feel much closer with Ryan.
MARGIE: How about when she was a baby? Did you feel close to her then?
LYNN: Not like I do with Ryan.

It was evident that Lynn had never bonded to Amy, and Amy's angry behavior was a reaction to this rejection. We began to explore why Lynn felt the way she did.

Lynn grew up in a very cold and distant family, a family where the girls, she and her younger sister, were supposed to be "seen and not heard." Her older brother, whom she adored, was apparently allowed to be seen and heard. Lynn had no sense of her Inner Child. Her Child had been ignored her whole life, first by her parents and then by Lynn herself. When Amy came along, Lynn treated her the same way she treated her own Inner Child—she just ignored her. She could bond to Ryan because he was a boy and therefore important; but to Lynn, Amy was just "there."

Lynn began the work of learning to acknowledge the importance of her own Inner Child through the Inner Bonding process. Within a few weeks she found that she was feeling closer to Amy. She stopped yelling at Amy about homework and cleaning her room, and started to spend more time with her. Within a few months Amy's behavior showed a dramatic change, and one day she came into a session beaming. Some of the kids had eaten lunch with her that day and played with her at recess!

As Amy's self-esteem rose, so did her ability to concentrate in school. When she was feeling insecure and fearful, it was very hard to concentrate on school work. As she felt safer both at home and at school, her mind wandered less and she was able to get much more work done.

As Todd had in the earlier example, Amy learned appropriate ways of expressing her anger, such as writing it out or hitting the bed with the pillow. She really liked using the pillow as a way to express her frustration; and she found that even when she was feeling frustrated and insecure at school, she was able to deal with it without hitting the other kids.

Richard, Carol, Michael, and Patrick

The Situation

Richard and Carol came in for therapy because they were disturbed over how much their sons Michael and Patrick, ages ten and eight, were fighting. Their sons were in constant power struggles. Michael would want to play basketball, and Patrick would refuse. Michael would tell Patrick to get out of his room, and Patrick would refuse. Michael would tell Patrick to stop following him around when he had friends over, and Patrick would continue to follow him around. Michael would try to control Patrick by yelling at him, and Patrick would resist. Michael would then threaten Patrick or hit him, and Patrick would run to tell their parents. Richard and Carol felt sad that their children weren't friends and wanted to do something about it.

Carol, a physician, worked outside of the home; Richard, a building contractor, had his office in the house. They had a housekeeper to help with the children, but Richard was the one they came to when problems occurred.

The Exploration

MARGIE: How do the two of you handle your children when they don't do what you want them to do?

RICHARD: Well, most of the time we try to talk about it, but lots of times I get frustrated and then I guess I don't handle it too well.

MARGIE: What do you do when you feel frustrated?

RICHARD: Carol and I have talked about that a lot. She's told me that I get a very disapproving look on my face and that I get angry. Sometimes when I'm angry I threaten them with taking away privileges, and other times I guess I try to make them feel guilty by telling them that they don't care about me. Sometimes I just give them an angry look and walk away.

MARGIE: And what do they do when you do those things?

RICHARD: They usually end up doing what I tell them to do.

MARGIE: So you end up getting your way and your controlling behavior works for you. Do you get into this more with one child or with both of them?

RICHARD: Definitely more with Michael, especially when he's mean to Patrick. I guess because he's older, I expect more from him. But I get into hassles with Patrick, too.

MARGIE: It sounds like Michael treats Patrick the way you treat Michael, is that right?

RICHARD: I never quite looked at it like that, but I guess so.

MARGIE: When Michael is mean to Patrick, do you end up blaming Michael for the problem?

CAROL: I think we both end up doing that. Michael is so much bigger than Patrick. I guess we're afraid he'll hurt Patrick.

MARGIE: It sounds like you believe that Michael is completely responsible for the problems between Patrick and him.

CAROL: I guess we make him responsible because he is older, but I have occasionally seen Patrick egg him on in very annoying ways until Michael finally loses it and lashes out at Patrick. Then Patrick comes and tells on Michael, which makes Michael even more angry.

MARGIE: And then you take Patrick's side, which must really infuriate Michael. And on top of it, you have not role-modeled for Michael loving ways of dealing with anger. Michael does what he has been taught to do by you and then gets punished for it. It sounds like Michael is mean to Patrick for many good reasons. He's taking out on Patrick his anger at you—especially you, Richard—for trying to control him and for blaming him. And he's angry at Patrick not only for taunting him with annoying behavior, but for then going and telling on him when he lashes out.

CAROL: I think that's exactly what happens.

MARGIE: Richard, what do you feel inside when you ask your children to do something for you and they don't do it? What is the feeling under the frustration, the feeling that the anger and frustration is covering up?

RICHARD: I don't know.

MARGIE: Well, let's ask the Child in you. *(Richard and Carol had read* Healing Your Aloneness *and were familiar with the Inner Bonding process.)*

RICHARD: *(He picks up the bear and stares at it for a while.)* Richie, what do you feel when Michael or Patrick don't do what we tell them to do?

CHILD RICHIE: I feel like they don't care about me. *(Richard has made his children responsible for his feeling lovable. He is on the narcissistic side of codependence.)*

MARGIE: *(To Child Richie)* Do you feel that your Adult cares about you?

CHILD RICHIE: Sometimes he takes real good care of me, like with work. I really like the work we do. But sometimes he ignores me. Sometimes I don't think he likes me very much.

Richard, Carol, and I spend a number of sessions exploring the codependent system within their family. It became clear to them that Richard was on the narcissistic side of codependence and Carol was the emotional caretaker. By always being there for Richard to bolster his self-esteem and to offer him awarenesses about himself, she perpetuated his dependence on others for his insights and good feelings. Richard realized that he also made his children responsible for his good feelings, and felt rejected and angry when they didn't treat him the way he wanted to be treated. Both Richard and Carol recognized that they were teaching their children to be codependent, just as they were.

MARGIE: Richard, how do you feel after you have been controlling with your children?

RICHARD: Tense, and angry that they only do things for me when I threaten them.

MARGIE: Anytime you feel tense and angry, it indicates that the way you are dealing with your children is unloving to yourself and therefore unloving to them. So let's begin to look at what the loving behavior would be.

The Loving Behavior

MARGIE: In order to help yourself and your children, you need to understand the dynamics of a power struggle. A power struggle exists when one person wants something from the other and will not accept a "no" answer. That's what happens when Michael wants to play a game, Patrick refuses, and Michael tries to coerce him to play anyway. When each one of them is intent on winning and having his way, or at least not losing, the power struggle can escalate into yelling, threats, or violence.

RICHARD: That's exactly what happens between them, at least once a day.

MARGIE: That's right, and they've learned it from you. Richard, you get into a lot of power struggles with both your sons any time you want them to do something and they refuse. You've taught them that when you want your way, and they refuse, you have the right to try to control them with whatever works. Now they do the same thing with each other.

Most people do not want to be controlled and will not say yes to a request until they know they have the right to say no without punishment. So the first thing you need to do is work with your Inner Child about not feeling personally rejected when your boys say no to you. You need to tell your Inner Child the truth—that they are not rejecting you, they are just attempting to protect themselves from being controlled by you.

When your boys say no to you, you need to explore with your Child why it is so important to have them do things your way. Is your sense of worth tied up in having control? If so, you need to work with your Child about what is worthy about him other than having people do things your way.

We spent the next few sessions working on these issues with Richard as well as with Carol on caretaking issues. Richard found he was having fewer problems in dealing with his sons, but they were still fighting with each other as much as ever. Now it was time to deal with them directly. I asked Richard and Carol to sit down with the boys and tell them about power struggles so that they all had the same vocabulary to describe what was happening. They agreed, but said what they really wanted to know was what to do when the boys were fighting or when Patrick came complaining to them.

MARGIE: Once they understand what a power struggle is, they can begin to see that they are both responsible for the fights. It is essential that you no longer blame Michael. It is also essential that you do not move in to solve the problem for them, but only help them solve it when they want the help. Patrick comes to you, not for help, but to manipulate you into blaming Michael. When he comes complaining, you can ask him if he wants help in resolving the power struggle.

RICHARD: What if he doesn't come and complain? What if they are just fighting?

MARGIE: How do you feel when they fight?

RICHARD: Irritated, and sad that they aren't friends.

MARGIE: If you were to take care of your Inner Child when they are fighting, what would you do?

RICHARD: My Inner Child just wishes they would stop.

MARGIE: So you try to stop them, and what happens?

RICHARD: We all end up angry or irritated.

MARGIE: Well, how about saying, "I don't like to be around this fighting. It makes me sad. If you want help with it, let me know," and then leave and put on loud music or go in a room where you can't hear them and close the door.

CAROL: But we're afraid Michael will hurt Patrick.

MARGIE: How badly does he hurt him?

CAROL: Oh, he'll sock him in the arm or push him.

MARGIE: It doesn't sound like he's really violent. If you don't rush in to rescue Patrick, then he might be more willing to receive your help or not egg Michael on to begin with. And if Michael doesn't get blamed, he also might be willing to receive your help. Why not try it and see what happens?

They both agreed to try it. The next week they reported that they had both talked to their sons about power struggles and how sad it made them to see their boys fighting. After the first time they asked Patrick if he wanted their help, he stopped coming to complain. By the end of the week, Michael came to them saying, "We are in a power struggle and we need your help to get out of it." Richard was able to talk to both of them. He heard both sides and was able to help each of them find other ways of handling the problem. Michael burst into tears after telling Richard how bad it felt always to be blamed. Richard and Carol saw that it was impossible for their boys to be friends when Michael was always getting the blame for situations that were equally created.

By doing their own inner work and learning to be more loving to the Inner Child within each of them, Richard and Carol were learning how to take care of themselves around their children. The more loving they were to themselves through taking responsibility for their own feelings and needs, rather than trying to control their children, the more loving they were to their children.

Loving Your Inner Child with Your Children

Parents often come into my office asking how they can get their children to do their homework, stop hitting other kids, brush their teeth, take a shower, eat right, do the chores, get to bed at a decent hour, stop watching so much TV, stop lying, and on and on. My response is that they need to stop focusing on "getting" their child to be different and start focusing on how they are not taking care of themselves. What are they role-modeling? Are they teaching codependence by taking responsibility for their children's feelings, successes, and failures, and by making their children responsible for the parent's feelings of anger, frustration, or aloneness?

Many of us have tried so hard to be good parents, being there to meet our children's needs in ways our parents were never there for us. But have we been there for ourselves? If we are there for our children and not for our own Inner Child, we are not role-modeling personal responsibility, which is the most important thing we can teach our children. Learning to set our own boundaries with our children is a major part of loving parenting and loving self-parenting. Behavior that is unloving to ourselves cannot possibly be loving to our children, because it is teaching them to be unloving to themselves.

It is only when we are willing to do our own inner work and take full responsibility for our own Inner Child that we can change the dysfunctional, codependent parenting that dominates our society. As we become healthy, so will our children and their children, leading to a healthy society.

CHAPTER 10

We Take Ourselves with Us Wherever We Go: Loving Your Inner Child with Your Friends

Our boundaries are our limits; how far we go with others, how far
we allow them to go with us. We can define boundaries only for ourselves. Our boundaries define what we allow to come into our lives.
Codependents' Guide to the Twelve Steps
MELODY BEATTIE

Close friends frequently exhibit signs of codependency in their relationships. While the areas of codependency are fewer because the friends are
not sharing responsibilities such as children or chores, they frequently create emotionally codependent relationships. We take our narcissism and
caretaking with us into all relationships in varying degrees, depending
on the importance of the relationship. The more important the relationship, the deeper are the fears of loss and the more frequently we move into
our protective codependent behavior.

Close friendships can actually have some of the same conflicts as mates
and lovers. These issues include jealousy over the amount of time spent
with other people, the need to be the "best friend," issues over responsibility for each other's feelings, or issues over the need for approval.

For example, here is a typical disconnected codependent interaction on
the telephone between two friends, Mary and Jane:

JANE: Hi. Want to see a movie tonight?
MARY: Oh, I'm sorry, Jane. I can't. I've got a date with Brad.

JANE: Again? You sure are seeing him a lot. We never get time together anymore. I can't understand why you like spending so much time with him. *(With her words and tone of voice, Jane is accusing Mary of abandoning her.)*

MARY: I don't know what you're talking about. You and I just had dinner together the other night. You're just jealous. *(Mary defends and attacks back.)*

If Mary is connected and open, she would respond to Jane's attack with an intent to learn:

MARY: Jane, you seem upset. What are you feeling?

If Jane continues to attack, Mary would have to take care of her own Inner Child:

MARY: Jane, this doesn't feel good. I want support from you, not blame. I'm available to help you with your feelings when you want to let me, but I'm not willing to be shamed by you.

If Jane still stayed closed, Mary would have to say good-bye to her and hang up the phone.

However, if Jane had been connected and open from the start, she would not have been threatened by Mary's choice, and would have responded with love and caring. For instance:

JANE: Oh, Mary, I'm happy for you that you are enjoying Brad. Is there some other time we can get together? I'd like to hear all about him.

Jane could respond this way only if she was connected within. It's the Inner Bonding that heals the insecurity and abandonment fears.

Problems in friendship, as in primary relationships, can occur when one of the friends moves into recovery concerning their caretaking and the other is resistant, threatened, or critical about it. I often hear my clients complain, as they move along their paths toward recovery, "I'm feeling very alone in this. Many of my friends are very upset with my changes. I find myself letting go of more and more of my friends. I never realized that they just wanted me to take care of them." I am able to assure them that this is very common and that they will find new friends, friends who are also in recovery and supportive of their growth.

The examples below are mostly about women's friendships. Since women tend to have emotionally challenging friendships, they more frequently develop problems in their relationships.

Brooke and Pam

The Situation

Brooke and Pam are roommates at a small eastern college. They met in their second year and became best friends. Pam, a music major, had a tendency to be moody and withdrawn. In their first year as roommates, Brooke, a dance major, was constantly putting aside things she wanted to do to try to help Pam work out her unhappiness. As time went on, Brooke felt more and more burdened by Pam's troubles. But when she tried to pull away from taking responsibility for Pam, Pam would shut down even more, cutting off the emotional connection between them that was so important to Brooke.

Pam abandoned her Inner Child by waiting for Brooke to take responsibility for her, and by being upset with Brooke when Brooke didn't want that responsibility. Brooke abandoned her Inner Child by not doing what was important to her—her homework, her dance rehearsals, her time with other friends. She was being unloving to herself in not taking care of her own needs, and unloving to Pam by taking responsibility for Pam's learning process.

The Exploration

Over summer vacation, when Brooke and Pam were not together, Brooke came in for therapy. Brooke, tall and blond with dark, serious eyes, became deeply committed to her own growth very early in therapy.

Brooke discovered that she was making the relationship with Pam more important to her than her connection to herself, that she was caretaking Pam to have some control over not losing the connection with her. As she explored her fears of feeling alone, she opened to experiencing that pain. She discovered that it was a pain she could handle as long as her loving Adult was aware that this pain of her Inner Child was about being alone.

Brooke discovered that it was only when she ignored the pain and her Inner Child felt alone inside that the pain became unbearable. Those were the times that she would move into caretaking Pam to protect against the pain from the disconnection with Pam. She realized that when she paid attention to the pain and fear and spoke lovingly to her Inner Child, she could handle others disconnecting from her.

She learned to say loving words to her Inner Child, like: "I know that this pain and fear you feel is the pain of feeling all alone and the fear that you can't make yourself happy. I know that this is an old feeling, a feeling you had lots of times as a little girl, when you couldn't take care of yourself and make yourself happy. But now I'm here, and I will take care of you. If you need someone to help with these feelings, I will find that help. If you need to be around other people, I will reach out to them. If you need to cry, that's okay, I'm here for you to understand your feelings. Even if Pam disconnects from you, it will be okay because I'm here to connect to you."

At this point in therapy, Brooke asked, "When Pam and I are together again next semester, what is the loving thing to do? Am I being selfish if I don't take responsibility for her unhappy feelings? Am I being selfish if I leave her alone in her unhappiness and go do my homework?"

"You would be selfish," I told Brooke, "if you expected Pam to put aside what was important to her and take responsibility for your feelings and needs, instead of you taking responsibility for them. Taking responsibility for your own feelings and needs, with no intent to harm anyone else, is never selfish. Pam is being selfish and needy (*making another responsible for one's needs*) if she expects you to give up doing your homework or being with your other friends to make her feel better. If she needs more help with her inner process than you have time for, then she needs to find a therapist to help her rather than expecting you to always do that for her."

We explored the difference between being there for Pam when she was there for herself as a loving Adult, and being there for her when she abandoned herself. Brooke realized that, when she had the time, she enjoyed being there for Pam when Pam wanted to explore her own feelings, beliefs, and needs, but felt drained when Pam was moody. When Pam was withdrawn, Brooke would often initiate the discussion by asking her why, and would then feel trapped in the discussion.

Brooke asked me, "Isn't it loving to ask someone what's wrong?"

"It depends on the situation," I answered. "If your friend April, whom you've described as open and responsible for her own feelings, seems down one day, it would be caring to ask her what's wrong. She may not even know she is feeling down or looking depressed and is probably not pulling on you with her moodiness. But your experience with Pam tells you that her moodiness is intended to pull you in. It's not just an outward expression of something that is going on within her. It's a manipulation geared to pull you into taking responsibility for her. Allowing yourself to be manipulated by her is unloving to you and to her."

The Loving Behavior

Brooke understood this and realized that for her, the loving behavior would be to continue with her own plans when she felt Pam pull on her. She realized that Pam might be angry at her or become even more withdrawn, but she was prepared to say to Pam, with softness and caring,

"Pam, I don't want to be around you when you are closed or blaming or pulling on me with your misery and complaints. I care about you very much and I am available to explore with you when I have the time, but I don't want to give up what is important to me anymore. I hope you can support me in taking care of myself as I support you in taking care of yourself." She realized that either the friendship would end, or Pam would decide to take responsibility for herself and support Brooke in taking responsibility for herself and the friendship would get closer.

Brooke was ready to accept either outcome. She understood that she had to let go of being invested in creating a closer relationship in order to take care of herself and not caretake Pam. She knew she could handle the loss of the friendship, even though that was not what she wanted, because she knew she would be there for her Inner Child through her grief at losing a close friendship. She knew she could handle her loneliness when she was connected within.

Brooke and Brian

The Situation

Brooke called for a phone session a few days after school started. Things were going very well with Pam. Now Brooke wanted to explore how to be loving to her Inner Child around Brian. She had really fallen for Brian the previous school year, but realized later that she had abandoned her Inner Child, handing her over to Brian. Her Inner Child had become addicted to Brian's approval.

The relationship had started out as a very nice friendship. When Brian wanted to become sexual, Brooke gave in, ignoring her gut feeling that it was not the right thing for her at that time. Almost immediately Brian's behavior toward her changed from open and caring to closed and abusive, and Brooke found herself trying to be the way Brian wanted her to be so she could keep him. He broke up with her soon after that, and she felt crushed. Then Brian had left school for a semester abroad, so she no longer saw him.

The Exploration

During the summer we had explored why Brooke gave men the power to define her worth. She explored deeply her relationship with her father, realizing that she had never received his approval and was always looking for it with other men. She felt that her father never saw her for who she really was—that he never saw her intelligence, insightfulness, competence, openness, caring, or creativity.

Brooke had often dated much older men, looking for the affirmation she had wanted so desperately from her father. She was addicted to men who were judgmental and afraid to see her, just as her father was. She found herself constantly trying to prove to Brian that she had good taste (he didn't like how she dressed), and that she was intelligent (he often put down her opinions). She realized that she falsely believed that if she tried hard enough, she could have control over what he thought of her. Also, she finally realized that if she wanted to be seen as she really was, she had to pick men who were available to seeing her, not men who were threatened by her as her father had been. As she began to give her Inner Child the affirmation and approval that she had always sought outside herself, her addiction to outside approval began to diminish.

The Loving Behavior

When Brian came back, he began pursuing her again. He told her he had changed, that he had done some reading and thinking and now saw things differently. Brooke felt attracted to him again, but was afraid of getting sucked in the way she did last time. She wanted to know if she should ignore him completely or give him another chance.

As she tuned into her Inner Child, she found that her Child wanted to try to be friends with Brian again, but to take it very slowly and not move into being sexual. Her Inner Child just wanted a friendship at this point, so Brooke decided that she would be available to that and would pay close attention to her Inner Child's experience of Brian in order to know if he was sincere or manipulating. She knew she had to trust her inner experience to know the truth, that being loving to herself meant being open to Brian and to herself, rather than open to Brian and while ignoring herself.

Brooke and Wendy

The Situation

In the same session Brooke wanted to know how to better handle a phone conversation she had recently had with her friend Wendy. She knew she had not been loving to herself in the conversation, because she had felt bad after she got off the phone. She said that Wendy had called her and talked at her instead of to her. Brooke felt Wendy was pulling on her to get her approval, rather than just sharing with her, and she didn't know what to say. She just listened and felt trapped on the phone, because she didn't want to hurt Wendy or get Wendy's anger. As a result Brooke's

Inner Child felt unimportant and empty because Brooke didn't take care of her. She made Wendy's feelings more important than her own and became a caretaker with Wendy, giving herself up.

The Loving Behavior

How could Brooke have taken care of herself and still been loving to Wendy? We explored a couple of options: Brooke could have asked Wendy, with an intent to learn, "What are you feeling? You seem kind of tense." Perhaps this would have helped Wendy tune into her own inner disconnection. Or she could have said to Wendy, again with softness and an intent to learn, "This conversation is not feeling good to me. How is it feeling to you?"

Brooke would have first had to be in an intent to learn within herself to find out that her Inner Child was feeling bored and pulled at, and then she could have been in the intent to learn with Wendy. Of course, she had no guarantee that Wendy would open to learning. Wendy might have protected herself in any number of ways—denying, defending, getting angry. She may have denied that anything was wrong and put it back on Brooke, saying, "I'm fine. It must be your problem." Or she might have become defensive, saying, "I can never do it right enough for you. You're always picking on me." Or she might have become angry at Brooke and said, "Well, if this conversation feels bad to you, fine!" and hung up. Those were the risks that Brooke was unwilling to take at the time, so she gave herself up instead. Now she realized after talking about it that it wasn't worth giving herself up, that she felt worse ignoring her Inner Child, no doubt worse than she would have felt had Wendy been defensive, angry, or in denial. At this point in the session, we had the following discussion:

BROOKE: What would the loving behavior be if Wendy denied that anything was going on with her and got angry or defensive?

MARGIE: When it is evident that a person is not open to learning, how does your Inner Child feel?

BROOKE: She feels shut out.

MARGIE: And if you keep trying to get the other person to open, how does she feel?

BROOKE: Frustrated and battered, like I'm hitting her head against a wall.

MARGIE: So how does she need you to take care of her at that moment?

BROOKE: I guess she needs me to end the conversation. But how do I do that without hurting Wendy?

MARGIE: Brooke, if you take responsibility for Wendy's hurt feelings, then you are caretaking Wendy. If you speak your truth and take care of yourself, you give Wendy an opportunity to learn if she wants to. Wendy can protect against feeling hurt by blaming you for it, or she can open to learning about what her Inner Child is feeling that led to her initial disconnection. You have no control over whether she chooses to protect or to learn, and you have the right to not talk to her when she is protected. So what can you say to Wendy if you want to get off the phone?

BROOKE: I guess I could say, "Wendy, I'd like to talk about this when you're open. I hope you will call me later." But what if she keeps trying to keep me on the phone by blaming me?

MARGIE: Well, what would you need to do if she refuses to say good-bye?

BROOKE: Hang up on her? But that seems mean!

MARGIE: If your intent is to take care of your Inner Child and she is not supporting that by trying to keep you on the phone, then she is the one being unloving, not you. Hanging up is just like walking away from someone who is physically or verbally abusing you. If you had an actual child who was being blamed by someone for something she didn't do, would you make her stand there and take it or would you take her away?

BROOKE: I see what you mean, but that seems awfully hard to do. I don't want her to think I'm running away. (Belief: I can control what she thinks of me.)

MARGIE: Brooke, you have no control over what she will think of you. If she chooses to remain protected, she will probably think you are running away, and if she opens to learning, she will realize that you were just taking good care of yourself. If you are invested in what she thinks of you, you will not be able to take good care of yourself.

BROOKE: So when I stayed on the phone with her, I was trying to have control over what she thought of me rather than take care of my Inner Child. I see that. It's hard to let go of caring what someone thinks of me.

MARGIE: You don't have to let go of caring about what someone thinks of you. You do need to let go of believing you have any real control over what people think of you, or that what they think of you defines your worth. You also need to let go of being willing to give yourself up to attempt to have that control. When you give yourself up to control what someone thinks of you, you are being codependent.

BROOKE: So if she hangs up on me, calling her back and trying to smooth things over would be codependent?

MARGIE: Right. She needs to call back when she is open and wants to explore. There may be a time when it feels appropriate to reach out again and see if she is open. It means tuning into your intent and asking if you are being caring or caretaking. Your Inner Child and Higher Power will let you know which it is because caring always enhances your self-esteem and caretaking diminishes it.

Sometimes we think we are caring because it makes us feel better for the moment, which is what addictions do. What we really are after is the long-term good feelings, not just the momentary good feelings that come from addictive behavior. Just as addictions to food, drugs, or alcohol can make a person feel good for the moment because the substance numbs out the pain of the aloneness, so caretaking makes us feel like there is a real connection with someone and takes away the aloneness for the moment.

BROOKE: I see what you're saying. It's hard to do, isn't it?

MARGIE: Yes, it's hard at first. It takes practice. The more you take care of yourself and the better it feels, the easier it gets.

Heather and Lila

The Situation

Heather, a friend of mine, met Lila in a writing class. They were both in their early thirties, and found they had many interests in common. They soon became fast friends, often meeting in the middle of their work days for lunch. Heather, a single woman, had met Lila's husband, and the three of them often spent time together. Soon Heather and Lila were "best friends," confiding in each other and thoroughly enjoying each other's company.

However, when Lila became pregnant, suddenly she didn't have time for friendship. Heather would call and Lila would be happy to hear from her, but just didn't have time to get together. Lila would occasionally call Heather just to check in. After Lila had her baby, her phone calls to Heather stopped completely. Lila seemed to have no space for Heather in her life, and Heather felt a great sense of loss.

The Loving Behavior

Heather told me that she realized she could take this situation in one of two ways—she could feel angry and rejected, or she could understand that Lila's behavior had nothing to do with her and that she didn't have to take it personally. She had decided on the latter.

She felt her sense of loss and allowed herself to grieve, but realized that it would be unloving to herself and Lila to blame Lila for the situation. Instead, she continued to call Lila occasionally to lend her support, letting her know that she understood how busy her life was and that she still loved her.

Heather felt that as Lila's son got older, Lila might again have more time for friendship. She felt that if she had become angry and blaming, then the possibility for future friendship would not exist. She knew that if she ever really needed Lila, she would be there for her. The bond, which would have been broken if Heather had taken the situation personally and become angry and blaming, was still intact.

Close friendships are often affected by changes in life situations. Often, when two single people are friends and one of them gets married, the unmarried man or woman feels left out, cut off. I think it's sad that many marriages become so exclusive that there is no room for outside friendships except with other couples.

Often one spouse is threatened or jealous of the other's friendship and does controlling things to disrupt that friendship. A woman may want to have time with "the girls" or a man may want to go out with "the boys," and the other spouse feels insecure and threatened, fearing that single friends will influence the spouse in disruptive ways. When one spouse gives up friendships due to the other's insecurities, he or she is caretaking and will eventually feel resentful and trapped.

Continuing one's friendships after marriage and giving the threatened spouse the opportunity to face and grow through his or her fears will ultimately result in a much happier marriage.

Connie and Rona

The Situation

Connie and Rona met as college roommates and became best friends, which continued throughout college and through two of Connie's broken marriages and one of Rona's. They got to know each other's families and felt as if they were sisters.

When Rona met Harlan and fell in love with him, Connie was delighted. She really liked Harlan and the three of them spent good times together. This continued until a few months after Rona and Harlan were married, when Connie received a frantic phone call from Rona one night. Harlan had hit her in an argument and Rona was hysterical. Connie suggested that Rona and Harlan seek out therapy.

The next evening when they talked, Connie asked Rona how things were going and if she had called a therapist. Rona was evasive, said things were fine, that she had exaggerated the situation, and that therapy wasn't necessary.

After that, things changed in their relationship. Rona stopped calling Connie as much as she used to; and when Connie called, Rona was often busy or evasive. Connie felt a wall building between them and was very upset.

The Exploration

Connie came in for her session feeling very angry at Rona.

MARGIE: Connie, what would you really like to say to Rona? If she were sitting here in the office, what would you want to say to her? She's not really here so you can get as mad as you want. Don't hold back. Just let it all out.

CONNIE: Dammit, Rona, what the hell are you doing to yourself? You're a smart woman—you know you can't ignore things like getting hit. How can you do this to yourself? How can you go into such denial? And why are you so willing to let go of our relationship after all these years? Why are you shutting me out? I love you. I want the best for you. Dammit, how can you let this happen? *(Connie starts to sob.)*

   I feel so helpless. I can't stand just sitting by and doing nothing but I don't know what to do.

MARGIE: Helplessness is a very difficult feeling, isn't it?

CONNIE: I hate this feeling. Isn't there something I can or should do to help her? I already know the answer to that. I'm being codependent, aren't I? I'm trying to fix her so she won't suffer and so I won't lose her as a friend. God, Margie, this is hard. I love her so much. I just don't know what to do.

The Loving Behavior

Connie decided that she would make one more attempt to connect with Rona. She invited her out for lunch and Rona accepted. However, Rona called and canceled the day before they were supposed to meet. Connie realized that the only thing she could do was to pull back and send her loving energy to Rona. She went through weeks of grief at the loss of the friendship. Finally she was able to accept that this was the way it was now, that it could change in the future, but that there was nothing she could do to change it.

Loving Your Inner Child with Your Friends

As I said earlier, one of the things that happens very often with people in therapy or recovery programs is that they no longer feel connected to some of the friends they had before entering therapy. As they open and grow, as they become more vulnerable and honest, as they take more responsibility for their own Inner Child, they no longer feel comfortable around people who are abandoning their Inner Child. This experience generally brings about a feeling of aloneness and a fear of never finding friends with whom they feel connected.

My experience is that after a brief period of feeling and being alone, new friends emerge, friends who are also in the process of recovery. I've worked with a number of men who, after they stopped drinking and began attending AA meetings, realized that all their friendships were based on drinking. One man told me that he took all his vacations with his drinking buddies. Now that he wasn't drinking and didn't want to be around drinking, he didn't know who to take vacations with. It was through AA that he made new friends.

Deep friendships often come about through participation in men's and women's groups. It is in groups such as these that people learn that they can be honest, vulnerable, angry, frightened, or in deep grief and experience love and support for whatever they are feeling. Recently in one of Dr. Erika Chopich's women's groups, two of the women who had become friends had a verbal fight with each other in group. Each was going through intense childhood abuse memories and each needed the other to be there as a loving mother; but neither could be there for the other because of their own pain.

As Erika encouraged them to express their feelings, they yelled at each other for the pulling and abandonment they each felt. In this way they were each able to release old anger that was really at their mothers. They found that they could allow themselves to scream like three-year-olds without being rejected. "I've never screamed like that in all my life," said one of the women, laughing. With the tension released, the door was open to explore what was going on in their friendship.

It is through deep friendship that we can heal many of the wounds of childhood.

CHAPTER 11

Power Struggles Follow Us Everywhere: Loving Your Inner Child in Your Work and Professional Relationships

> Will you have the love of power or the power of love?
>
> *the* Darkover *novels*
> MIRIAM ZIMMER BRADLEY

Work and professional relationships can touch off the same fears of rejection and domination and resulting protective responses as primary relationships, and they can deteriorate into codependent relationships when we do not take good care of our Inner Child. A controlling, critical boss or professional person such as a teacher or a doctor can evoke in us the same reactions we had as a child with a controlling, shaming parent.

Power struggles similar to those parents have with children are common in work situations—the boss wants control and the employee is defensive or resistant, or a partner wants control and the other partner is defensive or resistant. Equally common are the typical codependent interactions of control and compliance, in which one person (usually an employee or partner) constantly gives himself or herself up to the other.

Here's a typical codependent interaction between an employer, Mike, and an employee, Jeffrey:

MIKE: *(Hard voice)* I told you to get these bills out by the end of last week. What's the matter with you? Why can't you get things done on time? *(Blaming, shaming, attacking. No intent to learn.)*

JEFFREY: I'm sorry. There were problems with the computer. They'll be done today. I do usually get things done on time. (*Explaining, defending*)

If Jeffrey had stayed connected to his Inner Child and showed up for him as a loving Adult, he would have responded differently:

JEFFREY: Mike, I don't want to be yelled at and blamed. I have good reasons for not getting the billing out on time. When you really want to understand rather than blame, I'd be happy to tell you.

In order to take this step, Jeffrey would have to be in a place within himself where he would rather lose his job than lose himself. It is through Inner Bonding that we can reach that position within ourselves.

Of course, Mike had the option of initiating the discussion with an intent to learn rather than protecting himself with his shaming and blaming:

MIKE: Jeffrey, I noticed that the billing didn't get out last week. I know you generally do things on time. There must be a good reason why that occurred, and I'd like to understand.

It would not occur to Mike to explore with Jeffrey his good reasons unless Mike was in an Inner Bonding process with himself, consistently exploring his own good reasons for his own feelings and behavior. His behavior toward Jeffrey and everyone else in his life reflects his own inner process.

Ali and Nassir

The Situation

Ali and Nassir, both in their late thirties, are partners in a very large and successful import business. They were born in India and met each other as teenagers after moving to the United States. They were working with me individually on marriage and family issues, and both had become very adept at Inner Bonding work. They decided to have a few joint sessions to resolve some conflicts in their business.

The week before making this decision, they had a particularly explosive fight that actually threatened their partnership. They had developed a codependent system, with Ali on the narcissistic side and Nassir on the caretaking side. This had gone on for years. Recently, however, things had changed. As a result of working with his Inner Child, Nassir was no longer willing to give himself up to Ali. One day all his resentment over going along with Ali surfaced and he blew up at Ali, threatening to sever the partnership.

Ali's mode of operating when he didn't get his way was to get very angry and abusive. He would yell at or threaten Nassir or their employees in a mean way. Nassir's mode of caretaking was to look as if he was complying, while lying or withholding information from Ali and then doing what he wanted behind Ali's back—which of course infuriated Ali even more when he would find out. Nassir was terrified of Ali's meanness, whether it was directed at him or at the employees, and would do almost anything to try to avoid it. He didn't realize that all the things he was doing to avoid it were actually making things worse.

When they first came in to see me, Nassir believed that if only Ali would stop being mean when things didn't go his way, their problems would be easily resolved. Ali believed that if only Nassir would be honest and up-front, all their problems would go away. In codependent relationships each person sees clearly what the other is doing and is almost completely blind concerning his or her own behavior. Each believes they are just reacting to the other's unloving behavior.

The Exploration

Nassir started the session by telling Ali how painful it was when Ali yelled at him. He shared with him some things he had never before revealed to him, even though they not only had been business partners for five years, but had been friends for nine years.

NASSIR: When I was little my father would not only yell and scream at me all the time, but was physically abusive as well. He'd take the strap to me for the most minor of infractions. If I tried to stand up for myself, it only made it worse. He was a wild man and I never knew when he would explode. My mother was also scared of him, too scared to protect me. I was terrified of him and cried myself to sleep every night for years. (*At this point Nassir broke down and sobbed for four or five minutes. Ali came over and held him with tears running down his cheeks. Still sobbing, he continued.*)

When you yell at me and threaten me . . . I go back to feeling like that helpless little kid. All I want to do is get away from you. But I also love you, because at other times . . . you are the best friend I ever had. I know I have to learn to stand up for myself around you and not lie and sneak to get what I want.

I know I have to show up as a loving Adult for that terrified little boy, and I think I'm finally starting to do that. That's why I finally blew up. But I don't want to blow up either—I just don't want to give in to you anymore.

ALI: I never knew you were so scared of me. I love you too. You are like the good father that I never had. You know my parents died when I was little. My brother and I were brought up by my grandmother, who used to beat the shit out of me. We were really poor, and the only way I ever got anything was to take it, force it, demand it, like my grandmother did. You really are the father I never had, and I feel really bad when you lie and do things behind my back. But I'm beginning to understand it—I guess I'm like the father you did have. I really never knew you were so afraid of me. I know when I'm yelling I'm also an abandoned Child, with no Adult there to help me get what I want in more loving ways. But I am learning. I've been working with my kid, and I don't think I blow up as much as I used to, do you?

NASSIR: No, which is one of the reasons I finally asked to have a session with you. But you still do it sometimes, and I still don't know how to handle it.

ALI: And I don't know what to do when you say one thing and do another. I feel so betrayed when you do that I just explode. I don't want to do that anymore, but I'm not sure what to do when you lie to me and go behind my back. I want to be a real team with you, not both of us working against each other.

NASSIR: Me too. There are a lot of problems going on in the business that I haven't been able to discuss with you, because I've been afraid you would blow up or try to impose your will on me. I've just tried to solve them myself, but I really do need your help.

ALI: I don't like it when you solve things yourself. I feel left out.

Ali and Nassir spent the next twenty minutes discussing some of the business problems they had not been able to bring up with each other. I could see the relief they were each experiencing as they were able to talk without anger or lies. Then they each again expressed that they needed a plan for handling the situation when one of them was an abandoned Child.

The Loving Behavior

MARGIE: Ali, what would you like Nassir to do when you become angry at him or at any of your employees?

ALI: If others are around, I'd like him to take me aside and ask me what I'm feeling and how he can help me. If it's just him and me, he can tell me that he doesn't like my anger and can we talk about it.

MARGIE: Nassir, do you think you can do that?

NASSIR: I'd like to try. My Inner Child gets so scared that he just wants to run, but I want to try to handle it from my Adult. But Ali, what do you want me to do if I do that and you keep right on yelling?

ALI: I don't know.

MARGIE: Nassir, what would your Inner Child like you to do if that happens?

NASSIR: I guess he wants me to tell Ali that I don't want to be around him when he is being mean and then leave until he calms down. But I'm afraid he will get even angrier.

MARGIE: That fear probably goes back to what happened with your father. And what if Ali gets even angrier? What are you afraid of?

NASSIR: I guess I'm afraid of losing him as a friend.

MARGIE: So, in order to not lose yourself, you have to be willing to lose him. Are you saying that his friendship is more important to you than taking care of your own Inner Child?

NASSIR: I guess it has been, but that's not working for me anymore. So I have to be willing to lose him in order not to lose me?

MARGIE: Yes. That's true in any relationship. If we're unwilling to lose the other, then we will give up ourselves to keep the relationship.

ALI: Why do you think you will lose me if you walk away from my anger? Is it because of your father again?

NASSIR: I guess so. How would you feel if I did that?

ALI: That would be okay. I wouldn't blame you if you didn't want to be with me then. I don't like myself when I'm like that, so why should you?

MARGIE: In fact, Nassir, it is the most loving thing to do. It's not loving to your Inner Child to let him be yelled at, and it's not loving to Ali to support his unloving behavior by staying and listening to it. Walking away lets him know that it's not okay to treat you that way.

NASSIR: Okay, I'm going to try it. This feels hard and scary, but I'm going to try to do it. I'm sure I won't do it perfectly, but I'll try.

MARGIE: Good. Now, what would you like Ali to do when he feels you are lying or withholding information or going behind his back?

NASSIR: I think I want him to ask me why I feel I have to do that. Ask me what I'm feeling scared of. Just don't get mean about it.

ALI: Yeah, I'd like to do that. Now that I understand where your fear comes from in your past, I think I could do that.

NASSIR: Ali, my fear is not just in my past. It started in my past with my father, but you tap into it whenever you are mean. Most of the time when I lie and stuff, I'm doing it because I'm afraid of you.

ALI: You really are afraid of me, aren't you? Boy, that's amazing. I didn't know I was so scary. (*Ali had no way of knowing the effect he had on Nassir, because Nassir never had the courage to tell him before now.*)

MARGIE: Ali, you know your wife and kids have said the same thing. It's important for you to understand that your anger is very frightening to people.

ALI: But I never actually do mean things.

MARGIE: That's not true. You've withheld money from your wife and kids when you were angry at them.

ALI: Oh. Yeah, I guess I have.

MARGIE: Ali, the important thing is to realize that anytime you allow your Child to lash out at people, it is frightening to them. Your abandoned Child can get very mean, just like your grandmother. Weren't you frightened as a child when your grandmother was mean?

ALI: Yes, I hated her when she was like that.

MARGIE: Well, that's how you get, and it scares the people around you.

ALI: I guess I never looked at it that way.

MARGIE: It's your Child acting like your grandmother that scares people. And if you don't want to be like your grandmother, and I know you don't, then you have to show up as an Adult for that Child instead of letting him be mean and abuse people.

ALI: Yeah . . . that's what I'm working on being able to do.

MARGIE: Are you willing to do as Nassir has asked and ask him what he is afraid of when he is lying or withholding?

Ali was willing to try it, and Nassir and he came in again two weeks later. They had spent many hours talking about their feelings and their business problems, and had resolved many long-standing issues. They were both delighted with how things were going and were beginning to build trust again. Ali had not blown up once in the whole two weeks while Nassir was being up-front and honest. Neither had yet to deal with the other's abandoned Child, but both were feeling confident that they could handle it when the time came.

Clark and Audrey

The Situation

When Clark decided to give up working for himself as a freelance artist and take a job with an advertising agency, he made a verbal agreement with Audrey, his boss, that he was free to take vacations when he wanted to. She knew that having that freedom was very important to Clark, and she wanted him to work for her badly enough that she was willing to agree to it.

As Clark quickly found out, Audrey was an unpredictable person, agreeable one day and angry and sarcastic the next. She tended to belittle people when she could not get her way.

After six months on the job, Clark made plans to take a week-long vacation and told Audrey about it. She was instantly resistant, telling him that it was a bad time, that too much needed doing, and that she would have to think about it. She treated him like a bad little boy for even making the request. Clark was quite anxious and upset about the possibility that she would go back on her word.

The Exploration

Clark came in for his therapy session feeling very anxious about the situation. As he explored, he realized that Audrey reminded him of his tyrannical father, who had always yelled at Clark and belittled him. Clark was reacting to Audrey in the same way he had reacted to his father—by being quiet and compliant, a good boy. Clark's mother had rarely stood up for Clark or for herself, and when she did it was always in an angry way.

Clark knew that getting angry at Audrey would only result in his being fired—he had seen it happen to others. He had no idea how to stand up for his Inner Child with Audrey, since he had never seen anyone in his family do that for themselves. He knew he had to be the advocate for his Inner Child, and that his anxiety was not so much because of Audrey's behavior, but because his Inner Child was feeling unprotected by his Adult.

Clark realized that there was an enormous difference between his Adult being an advocate for his Inner Child and *protecting his Child from harm,* as opposed to his *Adult protecting against this responsibility* by disconnecting and leaving the Child to deal with it alone. He saw that whenever he was anxious it was because his Child was left alone to handle a situation.

Clark realized that he had been letting his Inner Child down for the last six months—that he had allowed Audrey to treat him unlovingly all this time, and that the vacation situation was just a symptom of his own unlovingness toward his Inner Child.

The Loving Behavior

What did standing up for his Inner Child look like? Clark knew that if Audrey told him he could not take his vacation, he would have to remind her of her verbal agreement, not in an angry way, but in a kind, adult way:

"Audrey, it is my understanding that we had a verbal agreement regarding my being able to take vacations when I want to. I would appreciate your keeping this commitment to me."

Clark explored various responses if she responded in an angry, blaming, or sarcastic way. He decided that what felt best would be to say, "Audrey, it feels bad for you to talk to me in that tone. Can we discuss this without anger and belittling?" If she continued being unloving, he could say, "Audrey, you seem really upset. Why are you so angry about this?" Or he could say, "I really want to discuss this with you in an open way. Perhaps we can do that later," and end the conversation.

Clark knew he would run a risk of getting fired if he did that, but he felt willing to risk it rather than let his Inner Child be verbally beaten up. He decided that if she didn't agree to his vacation, he would let Audrey know that he was going anyway. He was willing to risk being fired, because he knew he would feel awful on the job if he let her go back on her word.

Clark's anxiety went away when his Inner Child realized that his Adult would really be there to stand up for him. As it turned out, Audrey came in the next day and told him he could take his vacation, saying, "You would have taken it anyway, wouldn't you?" "Yes," replied Clark, and he felt very good knowing that she saw that he was willing to stand up for himself.

Dean and Jason

The Situation

Dean is a personal physical fitness trainer. Jason, one of his clients, is a senior partner in a large legal firm. Jason has a terrible temper, which he periodically unleashes on Dean when Dean lets him down in some way—is late, is rushed, or forgets an important part of the workout. Dean has a tendency to be irresponsible and resistant regarding his management of time, which leads him to be distracted. This is extremely irritating to Jason, who is a perfectionist.

The Exploration

When Dean first came in for therapy, he would respond to Jason's anger and criticism with defensiveness or compliance. His Adult would abandon his Inner Child at the first sign of criticism, and his Child would be left to handle the situation. Dean quickly saw that Jason was similar to his mother, a critical and controlling woman. Sometimes Dean would protect against his mother controlling him by defending and resisting; other times he protected against his fear of her rejection by complying, giving in and doing what she wanted. Now he was doing the same thing with Jason and was feeling terrible about it.

Dean worked hard to establish a connection with his Inner Child. The next time Jason blew up at him, he felt he handled it better, yet he still felt badly afterward. We had the following dialogue in therapy:

MARGIE: How did you handle it when he started yelling?

DEAN: Well, I stayed in my Adult. I told my Inner Child that what Jason was saying had some validity, and that we should hear it without defending. I was able to hear what he was trying to tell me, and I let him know that I understood his feelings and would take a look at the information he was giving me. I felt okay at the time because I didn't get defensive, but afterward it kept bothering me.

MARGIE: Well, let's ask your Inner Child what was bothering him.

DEAN: Okay. *(To the doll)* Hi, little guy. Why are you still feeling upset about what happened with Jason? Is there some way I didn't take care of you?

CHILD DEAN: Yeah. You let him yell at me. I don't like it when people yell at me.

The Loving Behavior

Dean's Inner Child was upset because Dean allowed Jason to abuse him by yelling at him. Dean and I discussed the difference between *content* and *context*. Content is what they were talking about—Dean being late again. Context is how they were talking about it—with the intent to protect or to learn.

If Dean had been willing to stand up for his Inner Child, he would have said quietly to Jason, "I'd be happy to discuss with you anything you are upset about, but I don't want to be yelled at. I'm willing to take responsibility for exploring my lateness and resolve this issue, but I don't want to be attacked for it. Can we talk about it with openness?"

If Jason had kept on yelling, Dean could have said, "I'm not available to be yelled at. Let me know when you are willing to discuss this with me without blaming me," and walked out. Of course, he risked losing Jason as a client, so he had to come to terms with an issue we all have to face at different times in our lives: "Is it better to lose him than lose me, or would I rather give up me than risk losing him?" If he was too afraid of losing Jason, then he would have to accept the bad feelings his Child has from being abused.

Dean realized that he was willing to risk losing Jason rather than allow himself to be verbally beat up; but that he also had a responsibility to deal with his old resistance, which led to his lateness. His lateness was another symptom of his Adult abandoning his Child through indulgence. Instead of his Adult making the decision that he wanted to be on time and taking the responsibility to make sure that happened, he allowed his Child to run the show. His Child was coming from his old resistance to his mother, acting out through lateness the statement, "You can't tell me what to do." It was his abandoned Child's way of not being controlled by his mother and by Jason, but this behavior was not serving him well. To be a loving Adult to his Inner Child meant making his own decision regarding whether or not he wanted to be on time, rather than resisting Jason.

Cassie and Aaron

The Situation

Cassie, tall, dark, and slender, in her early thirties, is a struggling film director. She was working on a documentary film and came in for her session with the following upset:

> I'm really enjoying doing this film, except for the problems I'm having with Aaron, the cameraman. He's fighting me every step of the way. Most of the time when I tell him what I want, he tells me it can't be done, and I know that it can. If I get upset enough, he finally does what I want, but I hate this struggle. Half of the time I give in to him because I get tired of fighting. But I'm always sorry afterward, because I realize that I was right in what I wanted. I just don't know how to handle this situation.

The Exploration

MARGIE: Cassie, before you hired Aaron, did you check him out with other directors?

CASSIE: Yes, and they all said he was a terrific cameraman and wonderful to work with.

MARGIE: Were any of those directors women?

CASSIE: Come to think of it, no. Why?

MARGIE: I don't know Aaron, but maybe he is someone who fears being controlled by a woman and resists that control. Perhaps he had a very controlling mother. What is your first response most of the time when he doesn't do what you want?

CASSIE: I get irritated.

MARGIE: If Aaron is trying to resist control, then he might be afraid you're trying to control him with your irritation. That would put you

into a power struggle where sometimes he gives in and sometimes you do, but the process itself is perpetuating the problem.
It sounds like each time you ask him to do something, he's
afraid of being controlled and so automatically resists.

CASSIE: But I'm the director. I'm supposed to be in control.

MARGIE: Right. But maybe you are asking him to do things in a way that
sounds to him like an order rather than a request. Perhaps you
are using a demanding tone.

CASSIE: Well, yes. I'm telling him what I want. I'm not asking him.

MARGIE: Cassie, knowing you, my guess is that you are telling him what
you want in a fairly hard and parental way. We've talked about
this before—that you have a tendency to be parental, to sound
just like your mother sounded when she wanted you to do
something. And as a child you would resist your mother in the
same way that Aaron resists you.

You can get away with being parental with some people who
are secure enough because they have a strong Inner Adult that
will not allow them to be controlled, so they do not fear losing
themselves. But with others you tap into an abandoned Inner
Child who has to resist to maintain some sense of integrity because there is no Adult saying, "Even though this person is or-
dering us around, we can choose to do what she wants because
this is the job we've chosen and we want to do a good job."

If Aaron had an intact loving Adult, he could choose to follow your orders without a sense of losing himself. But apparently his Adult leaves around a controlling woman, so his
abandoned Child protects by resisting.

The Loving Behavior

CASSIE: So what do I do?

MARGIE: What you need to do is going to be a real challenge for you,
Cassie. You've always believed you had to be tough to get anywhere, and it's worked for you. Yet in this situation it's causing
your problems. You need to soften up both your tone and your
attitude. For example, if you want a scene backlit, how would
you normally say it to him?

CASSIE: I'd say, "Aaron, I want this scene backlit."

MARGIE: What do you think would happen if you said, with a friendly
smile, "Aaron, I want this scene backlit. What do you think?"

CASSIE: So then, what if he says, "No, it can't be done."

MARGIE-AS-CASSIE: "Really? There must be a good reason for that. Could you explain it to me?" See, instead of fighting, you are exploring.

CASSIE: But I shouldn't have to be so careful. I should be able to just say what I want and have him do it.

MARGIE: Perhaps, but that's not how it is. Is it loving to yourself to keep beating your head against his wall, or would it be more loving to accept how he is and work with him in a softer way?

CASSIE: I guess I keep thinking that if I get angry enough he will get that I'm the boss and stop fighting me, but I can see that I'm just making it worse. Okay, I'm going to try doing what you said. Wow! This is going to be hard!

MARGIE: Yes. Sometimes the loving behavior is the hardest thing to do, because we're not used to it. It gets easier with practice.

Alexis and Kathleen

The Situation

Alexis, the advertising executive that we met in chapter 7 when she was exploring her relationship with Brendan, had been working hard in therapy to recover memories of incest that occurred when she was an infant. She had had flashes of memory for months, but was having difficulty recalling complete memories. As a result, I recommended that she have some bodywork, a nonverbal form of therapy designed to release memory that is stored in the body. After only a month of bodywork, Alexis started having more substantial memories.

Alexis was also attending a small professional college, training to become a psychotherapist. On the first day of a new class, the instructor, Kathleen, had the students sit in a circle and share their experiences with their personal growth. After Alexis shared her experience of being in both verbal and body therapy to retrieve incest memories, Kathleen made the statement that perhaps Alexis was going after her memories with a pickaxe. Alexis felt enraged at this, feeling that Kathleen was not seeing how important her process was to her, but didn't say anything to Kathleen. A few days later, when she came in for therapy, she was still angry about it.

The Exploration

Alexis stated in therapy that she felt unseen by Kathleen, and that for some reason this enraged her. As we talked and did some Inner Child dialogue, Alexis recalled that a number of times after her father would sexually abuse her, he would put her back into her crib and leave her alone. She would cry and cry until her mother came home from work and picked her up.

Alexis wanted to tell her mother what her father had done to her, but she was too little—she did not yet have the language. So her mother couldn't see her, couldn't understand why she was crying, why she was feeling so frightened and alone. This made her feel frustrated and enraged, and helpless to do anything about it. She realized that when Kathleen did not see her, it brought up all these feelings from infancy.

The Loving Behavior

Alexis realized that Kathleen was not her mother and that she was not a nonverbal, helpless infant, yet she had acted as if that were true. She felt that she had not taken good care of her Inner Child in the interaction with Kathleen, and wanted to do it differently in the next class. She saw that she needed to stand up for her Inner Child by being in the intent to learn with Kathleen.

Alexis planned what she could say to Kathleen from her Adult desire to learn, "When you told me that I was going after my memories with a pick-axe, I felt angry. I felt that you were not seeing how important my process is to me, and how exciting it is to me to be in this process. It brought me back to not being seen by my mother, and I felt helpless last week to say anything to you about it. I've worked on it this week, and I want you to know that it doesn't feel like a pick-axe to me. I'd also like to understand why you said that to me. Were you seeing something in me that indicated that to you, or were you saying that my process would feel like a pick-axe to you?"

Alexis did just that the next week with Kathleen, and reported that the interaction went extremely well. Kathleen was completely open to understanding Alexis's feelings and to acknowledging that she does go slower in her own process that does Alexis. Kathleen expressed how glad she was that Alexis shared her feelings, and asked her to do so again in the future if the need should arise. Alexis' self-esteem went up a notch when her Adult treated her Inner Child as being worthy of being heard and understood.

We can tell our Inner Child over and over that we love it and we think it is a worthy and important individual; but if we don't take action in its behalf, the words are empty. Alexis not only needed to tell her Child that she had a right to feel upset and to explore her angry feelings, but she needed to stand up for her with the teacher. It is only when we take appropriate action that our Inner Child feels loved and important.

Loving Your Inner Child in Your Work and Professional Relationships

By now it is probably clear that whatever the relationship, whether it be with a mate, a parent, a child, a friend, a coworker, or a professional, the ways we relate with others depend on the relationship we have with our Inner Child. When our Inner Child has unhealed wounds from childhood, we will always project the pain onto the people we relate to, reacting as if these people were like our parents, siblings, grandparents, or others who may have abused us. If we had a very controlling or abusive parent, we may find that we have great difficulties with people in authority.

Some of us find ourselves giving our power away to authorities such as doctors, lawyers, therapists, clergy, or teachers, allowing them to control us as our parents controlled us. I have worked with people who stayed with a doctor, a therapist, an attorney, an accountant, a minister, priest, or rabbi far past the point where they felt they were receiving help because they didn't want to hurt his or her feelings. I have had clients who kept on housekeepers, nannies, gardeners, or secretaries because they were afraid these people would be hurt or angry. This is caretaking rather than taking care of themselves. When you put someone else's feelings before your own needs and allow your needs to go unmet, you are not being a loving Adult to your Inner Child.

Some of us find ourselves extremely resistant to any authority, and we are constantly in power struggles, resisting being controlled by the people with whom we are in work and professional relationships. This kind of automatic resistance or rebellion also gives away our power, since others actually control what we will do because we are determined to do just the opposite of what they want.

In either case we need to take our power back. We do this by becoming a loving Adult for our Inner Child, so that we can stand up for our Inner Child when it is appropriate and make our own decisions about what we do. As always, when we take responsibility for ourselves, our self-esteem goes up another notch.

CHAPTER 12

Personal Power: Loving Your Inner Child When You Are Alone

The first lesson of power is that we are alone. The last lesson of power is that we are all one.

The Woman of Wyrrd
LYNN ANDREWS

Some people find it very difficult to take good care of their Inner Child around others, yet have an easy time making themselves happy when they are alone. These people are generally the caretakers, who shove their Inner Child aside to meet other's needs and pay attention to their own needs only when there is no one else to take care of. Caretakers often feel relieved when they finally have some time alone, time to pursue their own feelings, interests, and hobbies. In fact caretakers often get ill, sometimes very ill, in order to finally have time for themselves. Because they feel so guilty and selfish taking care of their own wants and needs, the only way they can justify it is by being sick.

Many people, however, fear being alone more than anything and have no idea how to feel whole by themselves. Some people are fine when they *choose* to be alone, yet fall apart when left alone. Being left alone can touch off such deep abandonment terror that they feel like they are going to die from it, just as they felt as small children.

Some people know how to take good care of themselves when it comes to playing, yet may let their Child down completely when it comes to personal health and safety. The vast majority of people have chosen to abandon their Inner Child when it comes to healing the pain of the past, which is the source of all other internal and external problems. Without the intent to learn about and heal past trauma and abuse, we will go on abusing ourselves and others without even knowing we are doing it. Our ability to take good care of ourselves and to lovingly handle the difficulties that life presents depends on the degree of recovery we have achieved.

Being Alone

People who live in tribal societies never have to face being alone the way we do in our society. Because we live so separately, in separate houses and separate families, we have to face the difficulties that come with being alone. Whether we are alone because we cannot find a partner, or because we have been left alone through death, divorce, or separation, finding our peace and joy depends upon being willing to be a loving Adult for our Inner Child.

Lenore

The Situation

Lenore first came to see me when her husband, Nate, was dying of cancer. They had been married for forty years, had raised three children, and were just starting to enjoy retirement when Nate became ill.

Lenore was emotionally dependent on Nate. He was the one who had loved her, praised her, made her feel important. She had never sought friends, relying on Nate to meet all her needs. Nate had been the emotional caretaker, while Lenore was on the narcissistic end of codependence. Now, with Nate being so ill, the tables were turned and Lenore was feeling quite lost. She had to take care of Nate, both emotionally and physically. She was angry and felt guilty about being angry with a man who was so sick and dying and who had loved her so well. She also felt betrayed that he was leaving her. It wasn't supposed to happen that way.

The Exploration

Lenore had been brought up by an emotionally caretaking father and a mother who was on the narcissistic end of codependence. Her father treated her and her mother very much the way Nate did, while her mother was always shaming her and yelling at her and was physically abusive at times. Lenore's Inner Adult was patterned after her mother in the way she treated her own Inner Child and Nate, while she acted as her father's had when it came to taking care of her children. She had been a fairly loving mother to her own children, but did not role-model taking care of herself.

In spite of all the years of praise from her father and her husband, Lenore could not truly see her Inner Child. Because she saw her Inner Child the way her mother did, she could never take in the praise. Whenever someone told her she was smart or pretty or good at something, she would unconsciously tell her Inner Child not to believe it. She treated her Inner Child the way she treated people other than her children—detached, intellectual, parental, hard, critical, shaming.

Fortunately she began Inner Bonding work while Nate was still alive, and was able to care for him in his remaining months in a way that did not cause her guilt and regret after he died. We spent many weeks helping her release her anger, which on deeper levels was at her mother and at her Inner Adult. She had always dumped the anger she had at her mother and at herself onto Nate and he had always taken it, being a good emotional caretaker.

When Nate died, Lenore went into deep grief, not as much from losing someone she loved, but from losing someone who loved her. She stopped doing her Inner Bonding work. Her Inner Child felt abandoned and alone, lost and frantic, and there was no Adult there to comfort and reassure. She felt like she was going to die.

Lenore went through months of emotional isolation and panic attacks. Her Adult was either absent or critical, leaving her Inner Child feeling constantly alone and unlovable. She couldn't seem to move through her grief. She finally joined a grief group, which helped remove some of the isolation. But in the group she became the critical parent, telling everyone else how to live their lives, and soon found herself feeling isolated again.

Week after week she came in with one excuse after another about why she wasn't doing her Inner Bonding work. We would do it in the office and she would always feel better by the end of the session, but would come in the following week back into despair.

Sometimes people have to hit bottom before they are willing to take on responsibility for themselves and show up as a loving Adult. Sometimes they hit bottom and still don't show up for themselves and end up dead.

Lenore hit bottom and finally showed up for herself. She finally began the process of bonding to her Inner Child, of reparenting her wounded Child. Slowly, through practicing dialoguing each day, Lenore's loving Adult appeared, at first for only moments at a time. Slowly the sparkle came back into her eyes as she began to give her Child what she had previously received only from others—love.

The Loving Behavior

Using her own concept of good parenting, which she had developed with her children, she began to pay attention to her Child's wants and needs and to take action in her Child's behalf. As Lenore got to know her Inner Child, she found a wonderful and alive little girl there who wanted to meet people and play. She found that she wanted to travel, something that Nate had never liked doing.

She was well off financially, and was able to become part of a group touring ancient mystical sites, something that had always fascinated her. When she returned she became deeply involved in her church and in doing volunteer work with battered women, and through this developed new friendships with women. She had found new purpose, new reasons for being alive.

Lenore was now giving, to herself and others, instead of just taking as she had done with Nate. She told me, just before ending her sessions with me, that she felt happier and more alive than she had ever felt during her whole marriage to Nate. She experienced sadness and regret that she had not been able to give to him in the way she was now giving to others, but grateful that she had at least been able to be there for him in his final months.

Bert

The Situation

Bert's wife left him after thirty-five years of marriage. His wife, Dorothy, had been a caretaker for most of those years, keeping the house clean, raising the children, and catering to Bert's every need. Ten years ago she decided to open her own business, and had done very well at a time when Bert's business was foundering.

Dorothy had always been there for Bert in the first twenty-five years of their marriage; but in the last ten years she had developed close friend-ships with women with whom she spent time. Bert had never developed close friendships with men. He had lived an isolated life, working and waiting for Dorothy to take care of him.

Instead of supporting Dorothy in her efforts to break out of their code-pendent system, Bert did everything he could to keep her in the system. He was angry and sullen much of the time, and blamed her for his busi-ness difficulties, claiming that he couldn't function well because of her lack of support.

Bert had functioned well in life as long as Dorothy was willing to be the loving Adult for his Child, but as soon as she started to be a loving Adult for her own Child and to give up responsibility for Bert's Child, Bert began to fall apart. Instead of rising to the challenge of becoming a loving Adult for his own Child, he sank deeper into his anger, self-pity, misery, and gloom, unconsciously hoping that if he was unhappy enough Dorothy would see the error of her ways and come rescue him. Instead she left him.

When he had lost all hope of pulling her back into the old system, Bert started reading self-help books. After reading *Healing Your Aloneness*, he came in for Inner Bonding Therapy.

The Exploration

Bert's narcissism started in infancy, with a smothering, seductive, narcissistic mother and an emotionally absent father. His mother met his needs without his asking, and at the same time subtly implied that she had to do this because he couldn't do it for himself. Bert grew up believing he had to plug into a woman to jump start himself. He never developed a loving Adult because he never had to; first his mother did it for him and then Dorothy did it.

Bert, like Lenore, had hit bottom, the place where people either get sick and die, commit suicide, end up in the streets, or decide to take responsibility for themselves. In reading and coming for help, Bert had made the decision to heal rather than die. From the moment he finished reading about the Inner Bonding process, he began to dialogue every day. He found that what his Inner Child wanted from him were all the things Dorothy had given him in the past—his undivided attention, concern, and actions in his behalf.

Bert had lived his life mostly unaware of his own feelings and thoughts. When Dorothy would ask him what he was feeling or thinking, he rarely knew. She would end up feeling shut out, something she had complained about throughout their marriage. It was not that he was shutting her out on purpose, but that he was so out of touch with his Inner Child that he really did not know what he was feeling and thinking.

Bert had ignored his Child for so long that it took a long time before he had any real contact with him, but fortunately he was persistent. After about nine months of daily dialogue, his Child finally let him in on his deep fears of inadequacy, of being wrong, and of abandonment. He was able to relive all the subtle ways his parents had created his sense of inadequacy, his mother by doing everything for him and his father by being an empty, inadequate man. He was able to see that his fear of being wrong came from his fear of abandonment, which in turn came from his belief that he could not take care of himself.

Bert went from being flat and unemotional to being filled with emotions. For a while everything made him cry, making him feel very vulnerable. But as he allowed this outflow of feeling, he found that he was feeling more and more full on the inside. He had much to grieve.

The Loving Behavior

Bert began to move himself out of isolation by joining a men's support group and by attending Codependents Anonymous meetings. Through these sources he made men friends for the first time in his life. He began to exercise and get his body in shape, something he had ignored for most of his sixty years.

As he learned to ignite his own energy rather than rely on Dorothy to do it, his business slowly turned around—which certainly helped his sense of adequacy. He had always been convinced that whatever success he had was only because of Dorothy and that he couldn't achieve on his own. Turning his business around without her was a turning point in his growth.

Six months after his separation, he met a woman he was attracted to; but within a few months of dating her, he found that he still tended to give his Child away to her when he was with her. He decided not to date until his inner relationship was more solid.

In the second year after his separation, he found that his relationships with his children were changing, becoming deeper, more meaningful, more fun. He found this deeply gratifying, though he went through much grief at how much he had missed during their growing up years.

Two years after separating, Bert and Dorothy came back together.

And did they live happily every after? Well, yes and no. Life is never without challenges. Learning to take care of yourself alone is not the same thing as taking care of yourself around another person. Dorothy and Bert ran into many conflicts that challenged their commitment to personal responsibility, and sometimes they slipped back into their old system. But because they both did their Inner Bonding work (Dorothy had read the book and come in with Bert to learn the process), they were quickly able to tune in and rectify the situation.

The last I heard they were laughing and playing a lot, something they had not done in thirty-five years of marriage.

Jolene

The Situation

Jolene, twenty-three years old, sweet, bright and beautiful, was stood up by a man she had been out with once before. She had really liked him, had been looking forward to seeing him again, and felt crushed when he didn't show up. She called and left a message on his answering machine, wondering if perhaps he had car trouble but he never called her back. She came in for her session feeling anxious and depressed. She had just recently started her work with me and this was her fourth session.

The Exploration

MARGIE: Jolene, what reasons are you giving yourself for Robert not showing up?

JOLENE: A million reasons have come into my head. I'm not pretty enough. I'm too pretty and he was intimidated. I'm not smart enough. I'm too smart for my own good. I'm boring. I'm too intense. I talked too much about myself. I'm too open on a first date. Or maybe I wasn't open enough, maybe I was cold. Or maybe I was too warm and enthusiastic. I just don't know, but I must have done something wrong! I wish I could figure it out!

MARGIE: It seems that you are taking it personally, believing it is your fault that he didn't show up.

JOLENE: How else can I take it? It is personal.

MARGIE: Do you think it's possible that you are not the only one he had ever done this to?

JOLENE: I haven't thought about that. All I know is that he did it to me and I feel like there is something wrong with me. (Jolene is shame-based).

MARGIE: So if there was nothing wrong with you, then no one would ever let you down? All you have to do is find the right way to be and you can have complete control over others not disappointing you?

JOLENE: Control over . . .? I don't know. I don't see it as control. I just feel that if I were okay, he would have showed up.

MARGIE: But what if his not showing up had to do with his own fears and insecurities? What if he is the kind of guy who is so afraid of rejection that he never dates anyone he really likes? Or what if he is really angry at women and this is his way of expressing it? What if he is terrified of losing himself with someone he likes? The possibility exists that he really liked you; and that liking you set off his own anger, fear, or insecurities and he backed off to protect himself. Does that mean there is something wrong with you, or does that mean that he has a problem?

JOLENE: But how do I know which it is?

MARGIE: Well, which point of view makes you feel better, taking it personally or believing he has a problem?

JOLENE: Well, I feel much better if he has a problem.

MARGIE: Jolene, when you were little and your Daddy was supposed to come and take you out *(Jolene's parents divorced
when she was a baby)* and he didn't show up, what did your
mother say to you?

JOLENE: *(Bursting into tears)* She would tell me it was because I was
a bad girl. Everything was always my fault. Even when
she was late picking me up at school she found a way to
make it my fault. I never could be a good enough girl.

MARGIE: So your mother shamed you and taught you to believe
that if only you could do it right you could have control
over her and your father being there for you?

JOLENE: Yeah . . . I'm always trying to find the right way to be so
people will like me and not leave me.

MARGIE: And were you a bad girl?

JOLENE: *(Still teary)* I don't know. I don't think so. I tried to be good.
I never did anything bad on purpose.

MARGIE: If you had a little girl like you were, would you think she
was a bad little girl?

JOLENE: Oh no! I would love her a lot. I was really cute when I was
little.

The Loving Behavior

MARGIE: If you had a little girl just like you and her Daddy was
supposed to pick her up and take her somewhere and he
didn't show up, what would you tell her?

JOLENE   I would tell her that her Daddy was not a responsible person, that he was not someone we could rely on, and that
it was not her fault he was that way. I would say, "Daddy
doesn't know how to love." I would tell her that I love her
and that her Daddy didn't know what he was missing by
not being with her. Then I would probably take her somewhere special to make up for Daddy letting her down.

MARGIE: And how would you know you were right? How would
you know it wasn't because there was something wrong
with her and that it was really her fault?

JOLENE: I would ask my Higher Power if I was saying the truth . . .
It feels like the truth now. Besides, I don't think it is ever
really a child's fault when a parent is unloving, is it? If I
had a little girl like me whose Daddy didn't show up, I
would know it was his fault, not hers.

MARGIE: Then, if you were going to be loving to your own Inner Child about Robert not showing up, what would you say to her? Why don't you pick up the doll and say it to her.

JOLENE: Okay. *(Looking intently at the doll)* You are a very sweet and smart and pretty little girl. There is nothing wrong with you, and you were fine last week when we were out with Robert. You were you, and being you is fine. You didn't do anything wrong. And I'm glad we found out now that Robert is irresponsible.

I don't want you to have to be with another man like Daddy. You deserve better. *(Pauses, thinking intently)* I've done that to you a lot, haven't I—picked men just like Daddy, and then you always feel bad and think it's your fault. I wonder why I do that?

MARGIE: Why do you think? There must be a good reason.

JOLENE: Yeah . . . Hmmm . . . I never really like men who like me. I always think the men who like me are sort of nerdy. I'm always attracted to the distant, aloof kind, and I always feel bad in those relationships. That's why I came to see you, you know. I'm tired of bad relationships.

MARGIE: Jolene, ask your little girl why she likes those kind of men.

ADULT JOLENE: *(Talking to the doll)* Why do you always go for the distant, aloof kind of men?

CHILD JOLENE: I like it when those men like me.

MARGIE: That sounds to me like you've given away the power to define you to men who are like your Dad. If they like you, then you are okay. You don't see nice, considerate, responsible men as having any power—they're just nerds. What they think of you doesn't count. It only counts when it's a man like your father.

The problem is that men like your father will never like you, because they are incapable of it. They will always do, in one way or another, what Robert did after only one date. Until you take the power back from Daddy and decide to define yourself, you will continue to be hurt by those kind of men. Once you define your own worth and lovability, once you truly value your own Inner Child and see her for who she is, then you will find yourself attracted to men who value you.

JOLENE: That's right! I always feel good when men like Daddy like me, and then I always feel awful when they don't, just like I always felt with Daddy.

MARGIE: Right. That's what codependence is—giving away the power to define yourself.

JOLENE: So how do I take the power back?

MARGIE: By dialoguing with your Inner Child every day and telling her every day who she really is. Why don't you try it right now? Pretend again that she is your actual daughter and reflect to her who she is. Remember how you were when you were a child.

JOLENE: *(Looking at the doll)* Well . . . You are a very cute and pretty little girl. I know you never believed it, because you thought if you were prettier, Daddy would love you. But that's not true. You are very pretty, and you are very smart. You always did well in school . . . And you are very sweet and caring. You have always cared about others' feelings and you have never wanted to hurt anyone or anything . . . And you have a great sense of humor. You always have. You could always make people laugh.

You are a very outgoing little girl, and fun to be with. And you have a lot of talent in writing and playing music. I really appreciate that about you. Your musical talent gives me a lot of pleasure. Whatever you do, you do well. You really are a very special little girl and I'm very glad you are my little girl.

MARGIE: Ask her how she feels.

ADULT JOLENE: How are you feeling?

CHILD JOLENE: I don't believe you. You're just saying that stuff because you're supposed to, but you don't really feel that way about me. You're always telling me I've done something wrong.

MARGIE: Sounds like you treat her just like your mom did.

ADULT JOLENE: *(Tears rolling down her cheeks)* That's right, but I didn't know I was doing that to myself. *(To her Inner Child)* Gosh, I'm so sorry. You don't deserve that. You really are a wonderful little girl and I never let you know that.

MARGIE: That's why she seeks approval from men like your father.

JOLENE: What do I do now—keep telling her how much I love her and how wonderful she is?

MARGIE: Yes, but you also have to take action in her behalf. If you tell her she is wonderful and lovable and you don't treat her that way, she won't ever believe you. If you keep giving her away to men like your father who hurt her, she won't believe you. But if you listen to her needs and give her time for her music and things like that, eventually she will believe you. It takes time. All these years your mother was telling her she was bad and then you took over, so it takes time for that to change.

As you work with her and she feels safer with you, she will let you in on more memories from childhood that hurt her and shamed her and made her feel like she was bad. It's very important to be consistent with your dialoguing. She will not believe you love her if you say you will spend time with her and then you don't. That's treating her like your father did, saying he would be there and not showing up. So it's very important to be consistent and spend time talking and listening to her every day.

JOLENE: I see that. I'm getting excited about this. I can feel my Inner Child getting excited about this. Inside she is saying "Yes, Yes!" She really wants me to spend time with her! I'm going to do this!

Jolene followed through on her commitment. After a while she was actually spending about an hour a day talking and writing with her Inner Child. Because she worked so hard, she made very rapid progress, and within six months met a sweet and caring man she was actually attracted to—much to her own surprise!

We all need to learn not to take it personally when someone doesn't show up for a date or appointment. Not only that, we need to learn to shift gears and use the time in ways that are fulfilling. That also holds true when someone we are counting on spending time with suddenly changes the plans. If the same person cancels or changes plans frequently, we might not want to make plans with that person anymore; but still, good relationships need to have some flexibility.

In order to be flexible for our own sakes, we need to have other pursuits that are exciting and fulfilling for us. For example, when someone suddenly changes plans with you, it's a good idea to have a few things you look forward to doing and for which you never have enough time, whether it's reading, gardening, listening to music, or puttering around the house, whatever you look forward to doing. Then, when someone lets you down, instead of feeling lonely, you can be just as happy as you would have been with the person who changed plans or didn't show up.

All of us need to have ways of making ourselves happy alone so that we do not depend on others for our happiness and do not get angry at others when they change plans. If you are happy only when you are with others, then you need to explore the fears and beliefs behind that codependence.

However, your Adult still needs to make sure that you have enough good friends to call on when you don't feel like being alone, friends you talk to on the phone or go out with spontaneously to have dinner or see a movie or go for a walk and talk. Friends you can take a new class with. Friends who will be there for you in the hard times and hold you when you are in pain.

Personal Health and Safety

When we love and value our children, we try to take good care of them physically, emotionally, and in matters of health and safety. Parents who physically, emotionally, or sexually abuse their children are obviously not protecting them. They are not letting them know they are precious and lovable little beings. Instead the parents are teaching their children to believe they are bad and unlovable.

Some parents do this on purpose, such as parents who are involved in Satanic cults, and may deliberately and consciously set out to destroy the will of their children. Most parents do it unconsciously, acting out on their children their beliefs in their own badness and unlovability. When this was done to us, we tend to perpetuate it with our Inner Child and our own children.

When we do not know that the Child in us is a good and lovable person because our health and safety was not protected by our parents, then we may ignore our own health and safety by not taking care of ourselves physically, emotionally, or financially. We might indulge our Inner Child and physically abuse our bodies through alcohol, drugs, caffeine, smoking, sugar and overprocessed foods, overeating and obesity, bulimia, anorexia, overwork, not enough sleep, lack of exercise, or watching endless hours of TV. We might neglect ourselves by not going to a doctor when something is physically wrong, hoping it will go away by itself, perhaps threatening our very survival. Everyone seems to know someone who found a lump and did not see a doctor for fear it was cancer, and by the time that person did go, it was too late.

Some of us might keep ourselves isolated when we are physically ill or emotionally overwhelmed rather than reach out for the help we need. Others of us indulge our Inner Child by overspending and putting ourselves in financial jeopardy, buying things rather than paying attention to the pain that is covered over by the spending.

When we do not take care of our health and safety, it is because our Adult believes our Child is not worth it, just as our parents may have believed about us or themselves. And the more we ignore our own health and safety, the more we reinforce our own sense of worthlessness and unlovability. As we engage in the Inner Bonding process and gradually discover the roots of our false beliefs about ourselves, as well as discover our own preciousness, we will naturally want to treat ourselves more lovingly. We will know we deserve it.

Lance

The Situation

Lance sought me out for help because he felt he was dying inside. Twenty-six years old, medium height, slender, fair, and good looking, he felt he had nothing to look forward to, and he was destroying himself with alcohol and marijuana. He had dropped out of college in his third year of pre-med, and was working as a clerk in a factory.

> I spend every night alone getting drunk or stoned. There must be more to life than this. I feel old. I don't go out with women because I'm too afraid of rejection. I don't have any friends. I've had a ton of therapy. I know my mom emotionally and physically abused me. My parents split up before I was born. I was a problem child and was always getting into trouble. I did okay in school, and after high school I wanted to go to an art school. But my mom put me down for my art my whole life and told me I had to be a doctor. I hated college, and here I am doing nothing with my life.
>
> My mom still puts me down and I always feel guilty when I'm around her. I see my dad once in a while, but he's pretty fucked up himself. He's been an alcoholic and is now going to AA. I guess maybe he's trying to straighten out. I guess I'm like him even though I never lived with him. If I didn't drink and smoke grass, I don't know what I'd do with my time. Nothing interests me anymore, not even art. I just feel dead and empty inside. Sometimes I think about killing myself.

Lance was functioning in the world as an abandoned Child with no Adult to take care of him. He was a little boy in a grown-up body, lost, frightened, alone, and doing the best he could to get by. But his Adult did seek help, which was the first step in getting well.

The Exploration

Lance learned the Inner Bonding process in our first session, and I asked him to commit to reading *Healing Your Aloneness* and dialoguing for fifteen minutes in the morning and fifteen minutes at night. I suggested he start attending AA meetings. He needed to move out of his isolation and receive support from others who understood his pain. He agreed.

He got half-way through the book by the second session and had done some dialoguing, but was having a hard time with it. His Child wouldn't talk to him. He just wanted to drink. He had attended one AA meeting and hadn't liked it. He "couldn't get into the God stuff." I suggested he see God as his own Higher Self, something that existed within rather than without, and he seemed to accept that. I asked him to ask his Inner Child why he wouldn't talk to him.

LANCE: *(Looking at the bear, his voice flat and uninterested, saying the words by rote rather than asking a real question)* Why won't you talk to me?

MARGIE: Lance, I don't think I would want to talk to you if you were so disinterested in me. There must be a good reason why you seem so disinterested in your Child. Do you have any idea what that reason might be? Who treated you like that?

LANCE: My mom. The only time she noticed me was when she was mad at me. She was never interested in me at all. Neither was my dad, on the rare occasions that I saw him.

MARGIE: Do you believe your Child is worthy of your interest?

LANCE: I don't know. He just seems like a stupid, empty kid.

MARGIE: Lance, let's try this. Close your eyes and visualize yourself when you were a little boy. See what you looked like and what kind of person you were. Pretend you have a little boy, your own child, who is exactly like you were when you were little. How would you describe that little boy?

LANCE: Well, he's a cute kid.

MARGIE: What else?

LANCE: He's kind of shy. He loves to play basketball, and he loves to draw. He can spend hours by himself drawing and playing basketball.

MARGIE: Is he mean? Does he hurt other kids or is he nice?

LANCE: Oh, he's very nice. He never likes to hurt anyone. He especially never likes to hurt Mom, but he always seems to hurt her anyway. She doesn't like him.

MARGIE: Would you like him if he was your little boy?

LANCE: Yeah, I would. He's a good kid.

MARGIE: But does he believe your mother didn't like him because he isn't likable?

LANCE: Yeah.

MARGIE: Try asking him again why he won't talk to you.

LANCE: *(Looking at the bear intently, speaking with some real interest in his voice)* Why don't you want to talk to me?

CHILD LANCE: I do.

ADULT LANCE: Then why didn't you talk to me all week?

CHILD LANCE: Because you didn't really want to talk to me the way you do right now. I don't want to talk to you when you're like Mom. I hate Mom, and I hate you when you're like Mom.

LANCE: God, that was weird! I didn't believe I had a kid in me until that voice just came out of me! I was sure he just wasn't there. This is feeling really strange . . . God, I can't believe I'm like my mom.

MARGIE: How could it be any other way? She was your model for an Adult. You learned how to treat yourself from how your mom and dad treated you and themselves. . . . How did you want your mom to treat you when you were little? Pretend she is sitting in that chair and tell her how you wish she had treated you.

LANCE: I'll try, but I don't think I'm good at this stuff. . . . Um, uh, Mom, why couldn't you have been nice to me like other kids' moms were? I just wanted you to like me. I wish you had liked my art. I wish you had liked taking me places or watching TV with me. I wish you had smiled at me once in a while. You were always so angry and uptight. I just wish you treated me as well as you treated your cats.

MARGIE: How did she treat her cats?

LANCE: She would hug and cuddle them and pet them and never yell at them, even when they did something wrong. They could do no wrong. She always loved them more than me.

MARGIE: It sounds like your Inner Child would like you to treat him the way your mother treated her cats. How would you feel about trying that? Do you think he deserves to be treated as well as your mother's cats?

LANCE: Yes, he does. He really does. He's a good kid. I'm going to try that.

It's hard to know what it means to be a loving Adult to your Inner Child when you don't know what it looks like. Lance was helped by remembering the image of how his mother treated her cats. He started dialoguing with his Child, using the same interested loving energy that his mother used with her cats. Within a few months I could see the life beginning to come back into him.

Lance had stopped drinking and getting stoned and was attending AA meetings regularly. In the following sessions we explored his codependence with his mother, always trying to please, always seeking her approval, even to the point of giving up his own dreams of art school to do what she wanted. No matter what he did, he never got her approval. He finally recognized he never would, but that he could give it to himself.

The Loving Behavior

Lance realized that he would never be happy with a job just to earn a living. He wanted to be an artist; and from what I saw of his work, he had a lot of talent. He decided to take some night classes in art at a junior college.

He was terrified before attending his first class. His old rejection fears surfaced but he went anyway, and it proved to be a turning point in his life. The teacher was very supportive, and Lance decided to finish college with an art major and get a teaching credential so he could teach art. He went through night school, and the last I heard he was about to graduate and was dating a girl he had met at school.

In a phone conversation he told me that he still attended AA and CoDA meetings on the weekends because he liked them. He was also playing basketball again, which he said his Child loves. He said he still dialogued out loud a few minutes each day, just to check in, but that he felt he was in contact with his Child throughout much of the day and that he is delighted and grateful for his Child's artistic talent. Finally, he said, he felt free of needing his mother's approval. Their relationship actually improved. Also, he felt closer to his father than he ever had.

I felt grateful for his mother's cats and Lance's determination to love his Child. Without that, he could have been dead by now.

Childhood Trauma and Abuse

Issues of personal health and safety are often related to childhood trauma and abuse. The more we were abused, the worse we feel about ourselves and the harder it is to take good care of ourselves.

Daren

The Situation

Daren first sought help with me because of his struggles with alcohol and cocaine and his resulting financial distress. Daren, dark, stocky, with piercing blue eyes, was in his late twenties. He owned his own construction business, which was falling apart because he was overextending himself financially to pay for his cocaine habit. He was hitting bottom and was ready to do something about it.

In the first session Daren claimed that although his father left home when he was little, he had a happy childhood because his mother was so loving with him. I sensed that Daren was in great denial about his childhood, and that the substance abuse was one of the ways he was able to deny the deep, underlying pain that showed in his eyes. He smiled and laughed a lot, but all I felt from him was great sadness and grief.

Daren agreed to attend thirty AA meetings in thirty days, a necessary commitment to begin his recovery process. Daren could not access his Adult for any significant period of time while he was drinking and using drugs, but he had enough functioning Adult to make the decision to move into recovery. He also decided to attend some Narcotics Anonymous meetings.

The Exploration

Within a few weeks of beginning his Twelve-Step programs, Daren was able to begin his Inner Bonding work, and he became as committed to his dialogue process as to his Twelve-Step work. Within a few months his childhood memories began to emerge, and with the memories came the pain that he had worked so hard to suppress with the substance abuse.

His father left his mother when Daren, the middle of three children, was three years old. He rarely saw his father after that. His mother had to work nonstop to support the children, since the father sent no money. While his mother worked, Daren was left with his younger sister much of the time, alone, frightened, and hungry, while his older sister was in school. Sometimes his mother left them with neighbors who sexually abused both Daren and his little sister. Later, his mother married a violently abusive man who terrorized the children.

As Daren's clear memories emerged, he went into months of deep grief from the terror, pain, and aloneness he had felt so much as a little boy. Eventually Daren was able to release the rage he felt at his mother for not protecting him from his stepfather and from the neighbors. He saw why he had established the belief that controlled much of his life: "I don't matter. I don't count." He attended a few Survivors of Incest Anonymous (SIA) meetings.

Daren was a sweet and caring man. In order not to turn his rage onto others, he turned it onto himself. He started to drink when he was eleven, and by fifteen was a drug addict. Because he believed that he didn't matter, he could abuse his body without even realizing he was abusing himself.

In his relationships with women and friends, Daren was always the caretaker, again coming from the belief, "I don't matter." He felt used in all his relationships, because he constantly put himself aside in deference to others' wants and needs. He realized after about six months of Inner Bonding work that he needed to go into abstinence regarding relationships, just as he had done with drugs and alcohol; because until he was more deeply bonded with his Inner Child, he would continue to be involved in codependent relationships. He added CoDA meetings to his list of Twelve-Step meetings.

Daren struggled hard to develop a loving Adult regarding his business problems. He was a hard worker, but his handling of money seemed always to come from his abandoned Inner Child.

DAREN: I can't seem to get a handle on what this block is about money. I'm always overdrawing on my account and then checks bounce and I'm embarrassed. I don't like it, yet I keep doing it over and over again.

MARGIE: You must have a good reason for doing it.

DAREN: There's something about money itself that really bothers me. I want it, but when I have it, I can't stand keeping it. It makes me nervous when I do have extra money and I always find some way to blow it.

MARGIE: Daren, ask your little boy what his feelings are about money.

DAREN: *(Picking up a bear)* Little Daren, what do you feel about money?

CHILD DAREN: It scares me.

ADULT DAREN: Why?

CHILD DAREN: It makes me feel bad things. I get all scared inside about money. Bad things happen.

ADULT DAREN: What bad things?

CHILD DAREN: You know. The bad things with the people next door.

ADULT DAREN: Oh my God! Now I remember! They would give me money after they abused me so I wouldn't tell! And they told me if I ever told anyone they would kill my older sister! I believed them! I was so scared of them. *(He starts to sob, his whole body shaking with the memory. He hugs the bear and sobs deeply for about five minutes.)*

God, no wonder I hate money. No wonder it scares me. It's always made me anxious and I've never known why.

Memories and awarenesses like this do not happen suddenly. They occur after months of dedicated Inner Bonding work, when the Inner Child feels that he or she can trust the Inner Adult to be there for the unbearable pain. I've seen it happen over and over again, yet each time I feel a sense of awe when memories like this come up, memories to which the person had no access before doing their Inner Bonding work. I always feel privileged to be let in so deeply with another person and to be allowed to participate in their healing process.

The Loving Behavior

Daren continued to attend his Twelve-Step meetings, cutting down to three times a week. He no longer felt any desire to drink or take drugs. He continued to dialogue daily and to give his Inner Child time to grieve. And he spoke to his Child every day about money, letting him know that it was not the money that hurt him. Gradually his relationship to money shifted, and he was able to handle it from his Adult.

A year after starting his Inner Bonding work, Daren began a relationship with a woman. He was now ready to face his codependency issues within a relationship. As he found out, we can deal with many issues when we are alone, but our deepest issues get touched off in relationships. His learning is an ongoing process, as it is for all of us.

Paul

The Situation

Paul came for help because his third marriage was breaking up and his consulting business was falling apart. Paul was a small but powerfully built man in his late forties. In the first session he told me that he had spent time in jail due to his violence, which would erupt unexpectedly and he would be out of control. He was very much afraid of his violence, but he had no idea where it came from.

His violent aspect was in sharp contrast to his personality the rest of the time—soft, caring, sensitive, and creative. He felt like there was a demon in him that would eventually destroy him, wrecking his relationships and his work.

The Exploration

Paul's mother was a very mean woman who screamed at Paul and his younger brother and hit them daily. All his life he had hated his mother and adored his father, a hardworking, successful accountant. At the beginning of our work together, Paul only had wonderful things to say about his father.

Slowly, through working diligently with his Inner Child, Paul began to remember other, contradictory things about his father, such as his sudden violence, especially toward his younger brother. Paul's brother, large and outgoing in contrast to Paul's quietness, seemed to infuriate Paul's father.

But these memories did nothing to help Paul's own violence, which continued to erupt periodically. There had to be something more.

One evening, after having sex with a new lover, Paul found himself crying. He picked up his bear, asked his Inner Child why he was crying, and his Child said, "Daddy took my body away from me." Paul got scared with this information and shut down.

He came in for the next session upset and confused. I had him visualize that situation after sex and talk to his Child about what he meant.

> PAUL: *(Looking at his bear, anger coming up)* I don't want to talk to him. I want to beat him up.
>
> MARGIE: Why?
>
> PAUL: I don't know. He's a bad boy. *(Pause, anger subsiding)* Okay, I'll talk to him. Paul, what did you mean when you said, "Daddy took my your body away from you"?
>
> CHILD PAUL: I'm afraid to tell you. You're gonna get mad.
>
> ADULT PAUL: I really want to know. I won't get mad at you.
>
> CHILD PAUL: Daddy did bad things to me and made me do bad things to him.

Paul was stunned at the beginnings of memory of his father's sexual abuse. It took many more months for these memories to surface clearly, while Paul struggled with his love for his father, as well as his deep rage. I assured him that he could continue to love his father even if his father had abused him, but that Paul needed to know the truth in order to heal his Child.

As the memories emerged and Paul worked through his rage at being so violated and betrayed by the man he loved so much, his violence slowly diminished. One day Paul came in and told me he was no longer afraid of his violence. It no longer felt out of control.

The Loving Behavior

It was Paul's dedication to Inner Bonding that finally gave his Child a safe arena to speak his truth. Because Paul had been terrified of this truth and the pain that went with it, he had spent most of his life completely cut off from his Child, who would then erupt violently at unexpected times. Paul's inner work was slow; it took a long time to reach these memories, but it was his willingness to stay in contact with his Child through daily dialogue that finally created the safety to remember.

Paul found that once he remembered and grieved these memories, taking better care of his Child in all ways began to come naturally. He began to exercise regularly, eat well, and he moved into a relationship with a woman who was open and caring, unlike the other women he had chosen. All of his relationships improved, including his relationships at work. Because he no longer hated his Child for what had happened to him, he could give him the love he needed.

Loving Your Inner Child When You Are Alone

It is very important to know that we can not only take care of ourselves financially and survive alone, but that we can be happy and fulfilled alone. Whether we end up alone because of death, separation, divorce, or because we cannot find a mate, we need to know that we cannot just survive but thrive.

Many people move into and stay in dysfunctional or abusive relationships because they are afraid of being alone. Many people end up pushing away the ones they love by trying to control them because of the fear of being alone. One of the very important explorations in dialoguing with your Inner Child is to find out what gives him or her joy alone and then take action to bring it about. Whether it's something your Child wants to do, learn about, or create, your Adult needs to make sure it happens.

Over and over I have seen that others seem to treat us as we treat ourselves. Often I hear people complain about not being supported by a mate, a friend, a boss, or a parent, and as we explore their inner relationship, it becomes apparent that their Adult is not supporting their Child. People also complain that others do not respect their boundaries, that they feel violated by other's behavior toward them. As we look inward, it becomes apparent that the Adult is not setting boundaries to protect the Inner Child.

Our external relationships are mirrors for our internal relationship. Others will love us and support us when we learn to love and support ourselves.

Epilogue

It seems sad to me that we have to work so hard to understand and discover what love and loving behavior looks and feels like. If we had been brought up in families where loving behavior was the way of life, it would be natural to us. If our parents and their parents had been loving to themselves and to us, then there would be no confusion concerning love. But because that is not the case, we have to start somewhere to break the codependent cycle that causes such pain in our lives.

Inner Bonding is a place to start. I hope the examples I've presented here, along with *Healing Your Aloneness*, have given you enough of a base to begin your own Inner Bonding work. Discovering the loving behavior is an ongoing process, one that I will be working on my whole life as life presents to me its difficulties and challenges.

I would very much like to hear from you about your experiences in discovering the loving behavior in particular situations in your life. I'd like to hear about what has worked for you and what has not worked. I'd like to know about your situation, your explorations, and what you've tried regarding loving behavior.

Those of you who want to take the time to do this, can write to me at the following address:

Margaret Paul
Inner Bonding Therapy
2531 Sawtelle Blvd #42
Los Angeles, CA 90064

Happy dialoguing! Please give that little girl or boy in you a hug from me.

Notes

Introduction

1. Erika J. Chopich, Ph.D. and Margaret Paul, Ph.D. *Healing Your Aloneness: Finding Love and Wholeness Through Your Inner Child* (San Francisco: Harper San Francisco, 1990).

1. Finding the Life We Lost in Living: Understanding Inner Bonding

1. Jeremiah Abrams, *Reclaiming the Inner Child* (Los Angeles: Tarcher, 1990).
2. Dr. Erika Chopich and I defined these terms in greater detail in *Healing Your Aloneness: Finding Love and Wholeness Through Your Inner Child* (San Francisco: Harper San Francisco, 1990).
3. Carl Jung, in Abrams, *Reclaiming Our Inner Child*, 27.

2. Taking the Road Less Traveled: The Inner Bonding Process

1. For a fuller explanation of intent and the ways we protect, refer to Jordan and Margaret Paul, *Do I Have to Give Up Me to Be Loved By You?* (Minneapolis: CompCare Publishers, 1983).
2. This third step of Inner Bonding was first developed by Dr. Erika Chopich. You can gain a deeper understanding of this core step by reading Erika J. Chopich, Ph.D., and Margaret Paul, Ph.D., *Healing Your Aloneness* (San Francisco: Harper San Francisco, 1990).

3. Creating the Inner Bond: Using the Five Steps in Your Own Life

1. Many of the questions in the following sections are from Erika J. Chopich, Ph.D., and Margaret Paul, Ph.D., *Healing Your Aloneness* (San Francisco: Harper San Francisco, 1990).
2. Ellen Bass and Laura Davis, *The Courage to Heal* (New York: Harper & Row, 1988).

4. Who Is Crying in the Night?
The Abandoned Child and the Intent to Protect

1. Erika Chopich, Ph.D., Coauthor, *Healing Your Aloneness: Finding Love and Wholeness Through Your Inner Child* (San Francisco: Harper San Francisco, 1990).

5. Heading for Home:
Parenting, Reparenting, and Staying Bonded

1. Stanislav Grof, M.D. and Hal Zina Bennett, *The Holotropic Mind: The Three Levels of Human Consciousness and How They Shape Our Lives* (San Francisco: HarperCollins, 1992), pp. 108–9.

2. Pia Mellody, in *Facing Codependence* (San Francisco: Harper & Row, 1989), says that anything less than nurturing is abusive.

9. Becoming Role Models for the Future:
Loving Your Inner Child with Your Children

1. Pauline Ness, *Toughlove* (Nashville: Abingdon Press, 1982).